ANZAR
THE PROGENITOR

True Story of Contact with an Ancient Alien

Bruce Olav Solheim, Ph.D.

Anzar The Progenitor

True Story of Contact with an Ancient Alien

By Bruce Olav Solheim, Ph.D.

Illustrations by Gary Dumm

Edited by George Verongos
www.LiteraryServices.net

ISBN: 978-0-578-90919-6

Boots to Books
Glendora, CA 91741 USA
bootstobooks@gmail.com
www.bruceolavsolheim.com

DEDICATION

There would not be an *Anzar* book without Gene Thorkildsen. You will see his name pop up quite often within these pages. Moreover, there would be no *Timeless* books without Gene. In 2016, a month after he passed from this world, he urged me to tell my stories and not be afraid. Now we stand at the edge of a giant evolutionary leap of consciousness, and I believe I am prepared and urge all of you, dear readers, to be likewise prepared. Let me help.

Thank you, Gene.

ACKNOWLEDGEMENTS

I would like to thank my friends George Verongos and Terry Lovelace. Their advice and encouragement helped bring this book about. My dear wife Ginger has supported me on this spiritual journey, and I could not have taken the time to do spirit walks without her holding down the fort and driving us forward through the pandemic with love and hard work. My family has stood by me as well and I am forever grateful. I would also like to thank Lucinda "Laughing Eagle" Morel for her vision, Yvonne Smith for her guidance, and James Lough and all my friends at CERO for the support and belief. I used some of Gary Dumm's illustrations from my *Timeless* books and the covers of *Snarc #1* and *Snarc #2* in this book. His talent and comradeship are beyond compare. I would like to thank Dean Radin, Jeffrey Mishlove, and E.M. Young for blazing the trail. I would also like to thank Victoria and the staff at Contact in the Desert for allowing me to be part of their conference, and George Noory and Cheryll Jones at *Coast to Coast AM* for their graciousness and professionalism. Finally, I would like to thank the Creator of all things, Anzar, Ergot, Theodora, Ozzie, Gene, Maia, and all my spirit friends. Time is not an arrow; it is a boomerang.

TABLE OF CONTENTS

FOREWORD

Way to Anzar

On a sunny, lazy Sunday afternoon in 2019, a group of UFO experiencers gathered for their monthly support group meeting. We sat encircled in the private room of a well-known chain restaurant, surrounded by our usual cups of coffee and lunch platters. This group is our safe space where we can freely share our otherworldly experiences without judgement. We discuss ways to navigate a world that tells us our experiences aren't real, despite physical validation, simply because society doesn't know what to do with the information.

As the meeting was closing, Yvonne Smith, our fearless leader and founder of CERO (Close Encounter Resource Organization), asked if there were any go-backs. Bruce raised his hand politely and asked the group if anyone was "with" him. In any other context, I'd probably have to specify that he meant in a spirit kind of way, but this was a CERO meeting, and we all knew what he was asking. I was deep into my plate of French fries and popped a glance to my left, where Bruce was sitting with his back to the door. Over his left shoulder was a tall, formidable, human-ish being, arms folded, looking more "club bouncer" than "alien." I went back to my fries. Surely, someone else here could see the big spirit dude behind Bruce. There were plenty of mediums in the room. I had already done my share of talking, and I wanted to finish my lunch before the meeting was over.

Unfortunately, nothing disrupts an appetite like the stares of a big, looming spirit bodyguard. Nobody spoke up about Bruce's guy. I scanned the room, and no one was looking in his direction. I sent a telepathic message.

"Yes, I see you. I see a lot of things. If you want me to speak up, then get permission from my Higher Self and give me a sign," I said. Just then, Bruce mentioned the name of this being, Anzar. I sighed, pushed my plate, and signaled our server for a to-go bag. The meeting ended, and I called Bruce over to me as I dug through my purse. When he approached, I pulled out my wallet and showed him my driver's license.

"Look at the name of my street," I said.

"Via de Anzar. No way!" he said.

"Yep. I see him. He's there, the big Native-looking bouncer dude. You're not crazy," I said.

In my healing work, nothing is done without permission, both mine and that of the other(s) involved. I am here to be of service to God. Many times, that doesn't have a cookie-cutter look that many of us have been taught. It's not always a straight line. This line of work requires a healthy dose of intuition, and as Lou Reed said, "a busload of faith." In the journey of Bruce and Anzar, I've done my part. I've explained the connection the way I see it: One, split in two, by etheric planes. In shamanic practice, the concept of "merging" is quite common, but I would never recommend it without extremely careful consideration. Yet, that was the message Anzar asked me to pass. I did so with the addition of my thoughts and recommendations. From there, my friendship with Bruce began. It's been a pleasure to watch his relationship with Anzar evolve into the partnership it is today.

–Lucinda "Laughing Eagle" Morel,
Shamanic Practitioner, May 2021

INTRODUCTION

"People say that what we're all seeking is a meaning for life.
I don't think that's what we're really seeking. I think that what
we're seeking is an experience of being alive, so that our life experiences on the purely physical plane will have resonances with our
own innermost being and reality, so that we actually feel the rapture
of being alive."

–Joseph Campbell, *The Power of Myth*

Anzar is an ancient alien mystic whom I have known most of my life and have been in weekly direct contact with since 2018.[1] A few years ago if someone were to tell me that they spoke to an ancient alien, I would most likely be polite, avoid eye contact, quietly assume the person was off their rocker, and slip away as soon as possible. Some of you may feel that way about me but hold on for just a moment. In the world of the paranormal, being slightly skeptical is important. It is natural for people to reach a boggle point when what they are being told just stops making sense. However, that does not mean that what you are being told is not true. *Anzar* documents my spirit communication with this ancient alien, including his sage prophecies, advice, and commentary on the world. The book is heavily documented and includes my research on the nature of this communication through mediumship and my theory of how the alien world, the spirit world, and the quantum world are the same—a quantum nexus.

This book is not a work of fiction. It would be easier if it were, and I would probably sleep better at night. Instead, I chose a different path. I believe that disclosure is an overused term that does not truly convey what is going on with us and the extraterrestrials (ETs). We cannot leave it to the government to tell us the truth. Although I use the word disclosure throughout this book because it is in common usage in the ufology community, I believe the better word would be revelation, with all that implies. Anzar says that revelation is a much more accurate term to describe the leap of consciousness humanity is undergoing in what he calls an Era of Reconversion. In this book, the reader will discover who Anzar is and, more importantly, find out what he has to tell us.

In the past few years, I have risked my professional academic reputation by publishing three paranormal books: *Timeless*, *Timeless Deja Vu*, and *Timeless Trinity*. My *Timeless* trilogy documented 89 paranormal events in my life. This book is not a continuation of that series; *Anzar* is a stand-alone book about one entity whom I have had the privilege of contacting. My risk-taking has gone further. In 2018, I decided to offer a paranormal course at the college where I have taught since 1998 and have spoken freely on national radio shows about my personal paranormal experiences. A former student who is now a history professor at a prestigious university told me that I had "committed academic suicide." However, I am undaunted, and I can assure you that I am in full possession of my faculties.

I am a great admirer of Carl Jung, who had his Philemon. Could Anzar be my Philemon?[2] I am not claiming to be a guru or someone special or better than anyone else in any way. I may not be exceptionally brave, but I am doggedly determined, and I am on a mission. Reading this book will make that abundantly clear to you my dear readers. For me, fiction and non-fiction books, comic books, poetry, theatre plays, and music, have all been ways in which I have expressed myself in this life. They are all part of my journey that is only now beginning to make sense to me. My written work is all me and what I have collected in my soul. I began to take my journey seriously in the fall of 2016 when a dear childhood friend of mine died. The subsequent soul searching led to me writing my paranormal books, subjecting myself to hypnotic regression, and meditation. When I take my meditative spirit walks, I repeat the phrase Anzar gave me: "I am

iv

in the universe and the universe is in me." This phrase has helped me to relax, focus, and find peace.

I believe aliens and the paranormal go together. However, most UFO enthusiasts would balk at that assumption and so would those who dabble in the paranormal. To tie these worlds together, I have discovered what I call the quantum nexus. As best-selling author Whitley Strieber wrote in *A New World*, "Maybe where the aliens are in the mirror universe is where our dead go?" The simple answer to his probing question is, yes. The paranormal boils down to our biggest question about life: What happens when we die? Some would say that nothing happens, you just die and that is it, case closed. Others argue for an afterlife. Based on my experiences since age four, I believe that there is life after death. And, besides, does not everlasting life and light in heaven sound better than everlasting death and darkness in the abyss? Is it not written in the Book of Genesis (1:3): "And God said, let there be light." Without light, there is nothing.

Something terrifying and wonderful happened in the fall of 2016, a paranormal re-awakening of sorts. This is a book about my life since then and how I overcame my fear of death and started to live fully in the light. We need to start by examining how the spirit, alien, and quantum worlds are entangled. We stand at the leading edge of a profound paradigm shift in understanding our place in the universe. We need to put away our petty squabbles and share our puzzle pieces of truth, knowledge, and insight, and together assemble the big picture.

PART ONE

THE QUANTUM NEXUS: UFOS, ALIENS, AND THE PARANORMAL

We stand at the leading edge of a profound paradigm shift in understanding our place in the universe, so the question of whether the UFO subject can be fairly characterized as paranormal is a crucial one. I think that some in the ufology community would rather separate themselves from those who see ghosts and practice mediumship. It is also true that there are those in the traditional paranormal community who would prefer to keep UFOs and aliens out. The problem, of course, is that if we waste time and effort building walls and continue to divide and subdivide, we will delay or derail our search for knowledge and truth.

I have found that cross-disciplinary approaches work well in traditional academe (i.e., history and theatre arts). I have always been a believer in working together with my college colleagues from other departments and divisions. For example, I decided to write a historical play called *The Bronze Star* based on the life of a Vietnam War veteran friend of mine who tragically committed suicide in 2002. I took an acting class at our college so I could better understand what actors must do. Little did I know that the class would not only help me to be a better playwright, but it would also enhance my history pedagogy. Our drama professor told us that he would bring us out of our comfort zones to become better actors. This is a process of fearless exploring and learning that can be applied to all academic disciplines and life in general. I took playwriting classes as well and learned the structure, history, and nuances of the world of theatre. I learned that every word must build the action and be chosen carefully to keep the audience engaged. Also, there is dramaturgy (the theory and practice of dramatic composition) that requires an excellent grasp on the historical time period being presented in a theatrical play. For me, this was a perfect blending of a creative art process and traditional historical research. As a result of our communal efforts, *The Bronze Star* earned

1

two national awards from the Kennedy Center College Theatre Festival in 2013.

The first step in this exploration of UFOs and the paranormal is to look at what is meant by paranormal. Dr. Dean Radin, President of the Parapsychological Association (PA) and Chief Scientist at the Institute for Noetic Sciences (IONS) founded by astronaut Edgar Mitchell, said in his 2018 presidential address that there is a problem with the word parapsychology. "Para meaning, irregular, defective, abnormal, like paranoia, paradipsia, and paranormal."[3] Other definitions are not particularly encouraging: "not scientifically explainable, of or relating to the claimed occurrence of an event or perception without scientific explanation, as psychokinesis, extrasensory perception, or other purportedly supernatural phenomena, impossible to explain by known natural forces or by science."[4] So, there is part of the problem, the word paranormal. If those who study UFOs and alien abductions and the more traditional paranormal phenomena want to be taken seriously, there is an immediate impediment to the positive acceptance of their research based on language.

When I plugged in the term paranormal in the Google Books Ngram Viewer, I got the following results shown in Figure 1. The Ngram Viewer plotted line chart is adjusted for more books having been published during some years, so the data is normalized, as a relative level, by the number of books published in each year.[5]

One can clearly see that the use of the term paranormal started around 1901, but then fell off around 1909, then came back briefly around 1919. Resurgence of the term came during World War II and accelerated dramatically in 1970 until today. Figure 2 shows a Ngram Viewer result for the term UFO. Use of the term UFO began shortly after the Roswell incident in 1947 and peaked in 1997. It then falls off until 2008. I would assume that if the data were available, the term has increased in usage again since then. What to do? One could say the use of the terms UFO and paranormal seem to go hand in hand and would indicate that they are related. See Figure 3 for this possible correlation.

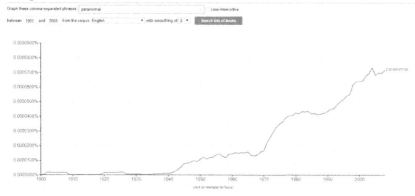

Figure 1: Paranormal Term Usage, 1900–2008

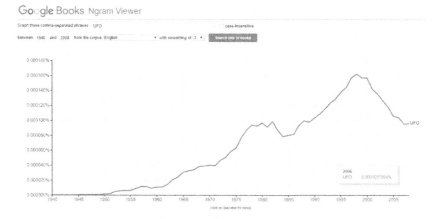

Figure 2: UFO Term Usage, 1940–2008

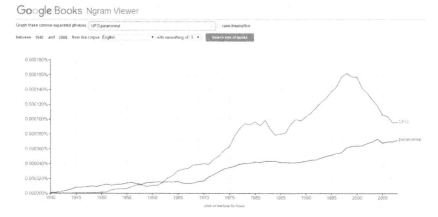

Figure 3: UFO/Paranormal Terms Usage, 1940–2008

3

There are those who might claim that UFOs and alien abductions are not paranormal and that ufology researchers should try to distance themselves from ghosts, goblins, demons, and angels, but what purpose does that serve? This is especially true when it seems as though the two terms are correlated and connected. There is strength in numbers and derision will weaken the movement toward disclosure, although I prefer to call it revelation.[6] According to the MUFON (Mutual UFO Network) website, "Ufology is the array of subject matter and activities associated with an interest in unidentified flying objects (UFOs). UFOs have been subject to various investigations over the years by governments, independent groups, and scientists."[7]

The first use of the term ufology was in 1959, eight years after US Air Force Captain Edward J. Ruppelt (who worked on Project Blue Book) coined the term UFO.[8] Despite recent disclosures by the US Navy that seem to indicate that the government is loosening its grip on its knowledge of the UFO phenomena, here is the response I got when attempting to search the NSA (National Security Agency) website: "UFO and Other Paranormal Related Information (No Records Exist). The following terms have been searched in response to requests for information on unidentified flying objects (UFOs) and paranormal events, but no responsive material has been located (from Aegis to Zeta Reticuli)."[9] I am not going to get into an extended discussion of a government cover-up because that is a separate research issue; I just found the search results both amusing and slightly frustrating.

Forbes magazine printed a response from Luis Elizondo, the former director of the US government's Advanced Aerospace Threat Identification Program (AATIP), and former director of Special Programs at To The Stars Academy (TTSA). He had answered a question on Quora: What does paranormal mean?[10] Elizondo wrote that "…isn't everything in science paranormal until we eventually perceive it as normal?"[11] Ancient people considered solar eclipses, comets, and the aurora borealis to be paranormal. As Elizondo writes: "Of course, now we realize all of these advancements were simply a natural development of science…The truth of the matter is that 'paranormal' really just refers to anything we do not already have a solid scientific understanding at the present time. Even today, to a remote Amazonian tribe, a simple photograph may still be suspected of having soul-stealing powers."[12]

When it comes to UFOs or UAPs (unidentified aerial phenomena), as the military prefers to call them, "the stigma of anything that might be considered paranormal has a chilling effect on our nation's ability to address a potential national security risk…it also severely limits the advancement of human knowledge."[13] We cannot let the fear of embarrassment stop us from acknowledging what has already been staring us right in the face for quite some time, and we must insist that scientists, government officials, the military, and academics take the phenomena seriously and explore the truth. Paranormal will eventually become normal.

The media has not played a very helpful role in presenting information about UFOs and alien abduction. Much of that is due to the flow of conflicting, contradictory, and purposeful misinformation or simply entertainment. Many people are not sure what to think any more or have unrealistic expectations. For instance, in Stuart Gordon's *The Paranormal: An Illustrated Encyclopedia*, he writes: "Notable paranormal beliefs include those that pertain to extrasensory perception (for example, telepathy), spiritualism and the pseudosciences of ghost hunting, cryptozoology, and ufology."[14] That is part of the problem. Telepathy, ghosts, and UFOs are not just a matter of belief; their existence is based on experience and evidence. As my dear friend Gene once told me: "Experiencing is believing and believing is experiencing."[15] It should be noted that the term pseudoscience has a similar problem as the term paranormal. Critics and debunkers often use the terms to relegate research they seek to discredit to the fringe when actually paranormal (or psi) and ufology are research topics that are ahead of their time.

Much of parapsychological research seems to be pointed toward consciousness studies and quantum physics. "…the two main categories of psi are psi-gamma (paranormal cognition; extrasensory perception) and psi-kappa (paranormal action; psychokinesis), although the purpose of the term 'psi' is to suggest that they might simply be different aspects of a single process, rather than distinct and essentially different processes."[16] According to the Parapsychological Association (PA) website, PA "is the international professional organization of scientists and scholars engaged in the study of 'psi' (or 'psychic') experiences, such as telepathy, clairvoyance, remote viewing, psychokinesis, psychic healing, and precognition… Such experiences seem to challenge contemporary conceptions of human nature and of the physical world. They appear to involve the transfer of information and the influence of physical systems independently of time and space, via mechanisms we cannot currently explain."[17] Fair enough. To be taken seriously, a psi researcher must downplay enthusiasm and astonishment with their findings which tends to make the public not see how remarkable the state of research really is. Getting most people to accept that there are ghosts, and that telepathy is real is not an easy proposition. Convincing them that UFOs have visited the Earth and aliens are real is an even more difficult task. Therefore, classifying the UFO/alien phenomena as paranormal adds to the difficulty and complexity.

Although more scientists and parapsychologists who study paranormal or psi phenomena and the UFO phenomena are coming forward lately, they take a big risk. Many more privately entertain the paranormal, but the elites who control the funding resources and flow of information make sure that those scientists and academics who depart from the party line are punished. Their salaries, job security, and promotions are tied to staying in line and not rocking the boat. One scientist who has not been afraid is Dr. Dean Radin. With the basic assumption that consciousness is fundamental, Radin has used quantum mechanics to explain the non-locality and backward causality associated with psi phenomena. Psi research that connects paranormal phenomena to quantum mechanics is often harshly criticized by some in the scientific community who call any such research pseudoscience without even looking at it carefully.[18]

In a scathing article entitled "How to Spot Quantum Quackery," Alan Boyle who serves as a science editor at NBC News, interviewed physicist Lawrence Krauss who said that "...a lot of people can be fooled by appeals to the admittedly weird world of quantum physics—a world in which particles are said to take every possible path from point A to point B, in which the position and velocity of particles are necessarily cloaked in uncertainty, in which the mere act of observation changes the thing being observed." He goes on to say that "no area of physics stimulates more nonsense in the public arena than quantum mechanics."[19]

Lawrence Krauss also blames other scientists. "Roger Penrose has given lots of new-age crackpots ammunition by suggesting that at some fundamental scale, quantum mechanics might be relevant for consciousness. When you hear the term 'quantum consciousness,' you be suspicious. The reason you should be suspicious is because we do not even understand classical consciousness. If we do not understand classical consciousness, how can we understand quantum consciousness?"[20] Krauss believes that the weirdness of quantum mechanics causes people to latch on and use it to explain what they would like to believe about the universe. His materialist and secular view is that "Quantum mechanics, for better or worse, does not bring any more spiritual benefits than gravity does."[21] I do not think it is a coincidence that we have trouble understanding both consciousness and quantum mechanics, but the logic behind saying that because we do not totally understand A, then we can never understand B, is flawed. In my view, eventually we will understand A and then B will become self-evident.

Then there is the rather funny remark that Stephen Hawking made about Austrian physicist Erwin Schrödinger's famous 1935 quantum thought experiment known as Schrödinger's cat. He imagined a cat sealed in a box that contained a device that would release a poison gas and kill the cat. Schrödinger set the probability of the device releasing the gas at 50 percent. If the cat behaved like quantum particles, the cat would not be dead or alive until someone opened the box to observe, therefore the cat would be both alive and dead at the same time in this thought experiment (no actual cats were harmed thank goodness). Physicists call this concept superposition. Schrödinger used his thought experiment to illustrate a problem: Why does observing change behavior in the quantum world?[22] This thought experiment addresses the observer effect in quantum physics. So, back to Hawking, he said that "when I hear about Schrödinger's cat, I reach for my gun." In an amusing way, this quote shows how uncomfortable scientists are with quantum weirdness.

On the other hand, there are scientists who believe in the primacy of consciousness and the usefulness of quantum mechanics in explaining paranormal phenomena. Max Planck said:

> As a man who has devoted his whole life to the most clear-headed science, to the study of matter, I can tell you as a result of my research about atoms this much: There is no matter as such. All matter originates and exists only by virtue of a force which brings the particle of an atom to vibration and holds this most minute solar system of the atom together. We must assume behind this force the existence of a conscious and intelligent mind. This mind is the matrix of all matter.[23]

Planck also wrote: "I regard consciousness as fundamental. I regard matter as a derivative of consciousness. We cannot get behind consciousness. Everything that we talk about, everything that we regard as existing postulates consciousness."[24] Then there is David Bohm, the American theoretical physicist who offered unorthodox ideas on quantum theory, neuropsychology, and philosophy of the mind. "What we take to be true is what we believe… What we believe determines what we take to be true. What we take to be true is our reality."[25]

Building on Bohm's ideas, theoretical physicist John Wheeler (who popularized the term black hole), suggested that our experience of the objects, events, and phenomena that constitute reality is the result of binary decisions—true/false, yes/no, on/off—which we make in the process of observing them.[26] We can also add Erwin Schrödinger (one of the founders of quantum theory) to the list of scientists who thought consciousness to be fundamental. "Although I think that life may be the result of an accident, I do not think that of consciousness. Consciousness cannot be accounted for in physical terms. For consciousness is absolutely fundamental. It cannot be accounted for in terms of anything else."[27]

In a recent article about psychokinesis in a mainstream science journal, scientists confirmed that observational effects in quantum mechanics are real. This remarkable experiment is the closest mainstream scientists have come to confirming psychokinesis.[28] It would be interesting now to turn to traditional paranormal phenomena as it relates to consciousness and esoteric magic.

In reviewing Dean Radin's book called *Real Magic,* which brings together Radin's earlier work on consciousness, the paranormal, and quantum mechanics, Brian Josephson, Nobel Laureate in Physics and Emeritus Professor of Physics, University of Cambridge, called *Real Magic*: "A thought-provoking book. The author makes a convincing case for the reality and significance of magic."[29] Josephson won a Nobel Prize in 1973, and since then he has become a supporter of research on psychic phenomena. "Yes, I think telepathy exists, and I think quantum physics will help us understand its basic properties."[30] Josephson added that "physicists have an emotional response when they hear anything connected with parapsychology. Their opinion of parapsychology research is not based on evaluation of the evidence but on a dogmatic belief that all research in this field is false."[31] Groundbreaking research challenges long-held and comfortable assumptions and beliefs. We must conclude that the frontier of science is not for the weak of heart.

Albert Einstein called quantum entanglement (the ability of separated objects to share a condition or state) "spooky action at a distance." Since Einstein's time, "physicists have demonstrated the reality of spooky action over ever greater distances—even from Earth to a satellite in space. But the entangled particles have typically been tiny, which makes it easier to shield their delicate quantum states from the noisy world."[32] Entanglement is one of the strangest aspects of quantum physics. "If you observe a particle in one place, another particle—even one light-year away—will instantly change its properties, as if the two are connected by a mysterious communication channel. Scientists have observed this phenomenon in tiny objects such as atoms and electrons, and in recent experiments, they have observed some objects that are almost visible to the naked eye."[33] I believe this is evidence of the quantum effect scaling up to our macro world.

Alan Turing, the computer theorist who cracked the Nazi's encoding system in World War II, believed in telepathy after being impressed by pioneering Duke University parapsychologist J.B. Rhine's experiments. Psychiatrist Carl Jung believed in synchronicities, which are coincidences that are not really coincidences. He believed they hinted at the existence of a hidden reality that conventional science could not readily explain.[34] Nobel-winning quantum theorist Wolfgang Pauli, who was treated by Jung, went on to write that "we must postulate a cosmic order of nature beyond our control to which *both* the outward material objects *and* the inward images are subject." He also thought that synchronicity might come from some quantum effect that "weaves meaning into the fabric of nature."[35]

The premise of Dean Radin's book, *Entangled Minds: Extrasensory Experiences in a Quantum Reality*, is that psi phenomena exist and that they arise from the entangled nature of reality at the quantum level (i.e., Einstein's "spooky action at a distance).[36] If we consider non-local consciousness (consciousness existing independent of the brain and the body) based on scientific evidence as being real and on the leading edge of science, what can we do with that idea? Dr. Dean

Radin has a suggestion in his latest book, *Real Magic: Ancient Wisdom, Modern Science, and a Guide to the Secret Power of the Universe*. He writes about the esoteric traditions going back to shamanism and discovers that for our ancestors who practiced this philosophy, consciousness was fundamental, and consciousness comes before time and space. "If that is true, it means that our esoteric ideas about magic are also true," according to Radin, who has support in the science world.[37] The foregoing advocacy from scientists has shown that there is plenty of high-powered support for the paranormal and its quantum connection, so no one should feel as though they are out there alone.

It makes sense to me that we would be open to other dimensions through our consciousness, and then recognize through the quantum effect that we can see the present, the future, and the past together as we move through time and space. There may be an infinite number of ways in which our consciousness exists, not just embodied in human form. We may also be incorporating what we have learned from others into our consciousness as it evolves or tap into what Carl Jung called the "collective unconscious." Dean Radin holds that three fundamental ideas have emerged from the esoteric cosmologies that produced all religious traditions: (1) Consciousness is fundamental, (2) everything is interconnected, and (3) there is only one consciousness.

These three ideas are the basis of psi, the paranormal, and what we call real magic. There is a correlation between what scientists like Dean Radin are studying and what mystics have been doing for millennia.[38] It is clear to me that consciousness is the key to understanding psi or the paranormal, now let us turn our attention to UFOs and alien contact.

THE COSMIC CONNECTION: THE PARANORMAL, ALIEN, AND QUANTUM WORLDS COLLIDE

I have shown how paranormal phenomena can be understood through quantum physics. Let us now consider the theory that the paranormal world, the alien world, and the quantum world are all one in the same—a cosmic nexus. Perhaps it would be best to start with the quintessential question: Are we alone in the universe? According to the influential eighteenth-century scientist, philosopher, and theologian Emanuel Swedenborg, aliens are real. During his many spiritual journeys he found spirits of beings from other parts of the universe. He believed that in such spiritual travels, distance did not matter because, in the spirit world, time and space are different than our waking reality here on Earth. That sounds a lot like quantum entanglement and non-locality even though Swedenborg did not call it that.

Swedenborg claimed that he was guided by angels in his astral journeys through the stars. In the way that these extraterrestrials spoke and thought and perceived things, Swedenborg could tell that these entities were different than those of our solar system. The extraterrestrials did not worship God directly, they appealed to an angelic community that brought them enlightenment from God. Most importantly, Swedenborg believed that even though these extraterrestrials seemed quite different from humans, they live in the same spiritual universe.[39]

Spiritualists and mystics are one thing, but what about standard religions and their reaction to extraterrestrial life? Many theologians are more open to the idea than expected.[40] The Center for Theological Inquiry (CTI), an ecumenical research organization tied to Princeton University in New Jersey, was awarded a 1.1 million dollar NASA (National Aeronautics and Space Administration) contract to study the implications of extraterrestrial life for theology.[41] One might wonder how a government agency was able to give money to a religious organization possibly violating the principle of secularization, but maybe there is more to this story. It is generally true that science and technology are way ahead of our ability to deal with their impact legally, spiritually, morally, and ethically. A case in point is cloning. It can be done, but we do not know the far-reaching implications of the process and how it affects consciousness, the soul, or the ultimate destination of humanity. We have created personal electronic devices that were intended to tie us all together but instead seem to be causing us to be more insular and less connected. It is my view that machines are not becoming more human-like, to the contrary, humans are, unfortunately, becoming more machine-like. Therefore, would it not be wise to consider the broader implications of alien contact before full disclosure? In fact, one could assume that NASA reaching out to CTI might be an indication that this disclosure has begun.

The SETI (Search for Extra-Terrestrial Intelligence) program grounds itself in hard science and stone-cold data. Yet, the implications of such scientific proof of life outside of our planet or solar system touch on the humanities and philosophy and, yes, theology. In his book *The Cosmic Connection: An Extraterrestrial Perspective*, the late Carl Sagan wrote that "space exploration leads directly to religious and philosophical questions."[42] SETI is guided by three principles: (1) uniformity, (2) plentitude, and (3) mediocrity. Uniformity means that the physical processes of life here on Earth are found throughout the universe. Plentitude means that all life that is possible will be realized, or as Carl Sagan said: "The origin of life on suitable planets seems built into the chemistry of the universe."[43] And mediocrity means that there is nothing special or unique about life on Earth. These principles present challenges to organized religion, especially the third one. All these considerations point back to one of the fundamental questions raised in this book: Are UFOs considered paranormal? Dr. Jack Call, a retired philosophy professor and former member of the clergy may have helped provide an answer when he said: "If God isn't paranormal, then who is?" And if God is paranormal, then all of creation, including UFOs and aliens, are as well.

According to NASA, there are 3500 confirmed exoplanets orbiting nearby stars. At least six of them are potential Earths. How will we react and how will future generations react to disclosure? People understand the world and the cosmos through their belief systems. The recent demographic trend has been toward a religiously unaffiliated populace in the West, but that is changing. The Pew Research Center reports that "by 2055 to 2060, just nine percent of all babies will be born to religiously unaffiliated women, while more than seven-in-ten will be born to either Muslims (36%) or Christians (35%)."[44] An increasingly religious human population will have to face a future where the paranormal may be the norm, and as Carl Sagan wrote: "Meanwhile, elsewhere there are an infinite number of other universes each with its own God dreaming the cosmic dream. ... It is said that men may not be the dream of the Gods, but rather that the Gods are the dreams of men."[45] Dreams can become reality.

FULL PERSONAL DISCLOSURE: ANZAR'S
EXPLANATION

It occurred to me recently that although we demand full disclosure on the UFO phenomena from the government, most of us have not provided full personal disclosure. How many of us have had paranormal and/or UFO experiences but have not discussed it openly? Before I share my personal experiences, especially my continuing communication with an ancient alien mystic named Anzar, I would like to do a quick representative survey of the literature on alien abduction and contact. I will start with the debunkers and skeptics. Richard J. McNally, and Susan A. Clancy, like many of the debunkers and skeptics, feel that hypnotic regression (as a method of retrieving abduction memories) is not valid and that the often-reported paralysis by abductees is actually a medical condition known as sleep paralysis. "Sleep paralysis accompanied by hypnopompic ('upon awakening') hallucinations is an often-frightening manifestation of discordance between the cognitive/perceptual and motor aspects of rapid eye movement (REM) sleep. Awakening sleepers become aware of an inability to move, and sometimes experience intrusion of dream mentation into waking consciousness (e.g., seeing intruders in the bedroom)."[46] Electrical shocks are also reported with sleep paralysis. McNally and Clancy conclude that "...our studies suggest that people who report having been either abducted by space aliens or sexually abused as children experience episodes of sleep paralysis at higher rates than do those denying histories of alien abduction or sexual abuse."[47] They end by writing "it is unclear why some people opt for an alien abduction interpretation..."[48] Are they assuming that experiencers prefer to choose alien abduction from some menu of possible explanations? No one would prefer that. Typical of most debunker articles, they are assuming that the reports of alien abduction are not true to begin with and are basing their conclusions on a preconceived position and belief.

17

On the other hand, you have some supporters of the experiencers such as Dr. John Mack, Bud Hopkins, and Dr. David Jacobs, who all worked extensively with folks who had been abducted. Mack, along with Caroline McLeod, and Barbara Corbisier, wrote about the debunkers, saying:

"...their search for the most 'parsimonious explanation,' given that they do not 'believe' in alien abduction, fails to consider information that leads us to the most parsimonious explanation of all–that the abduction phenomenon might not be reducible to psychological processes with which we are now familiar and that we do not have enough information to formulate a definitive answer at this time...Because of the extraordinary nature of abduction reports...the majority of the scientific community, have felt obliged to declare their belief in the nonreality of the phenomenon before they have conducted careful, first-hand study of these experiences...In the interest of science, however, abduction experiences should be a matter of investigation rather than belief."[49]

It seems like common sense to take a neutral position before investigating a given phenomenon, otherwise you could end up cherry-picking data to support your pre-formed conclusions. This could, of course, work both ways.

Mack reported that many experiencers suffer from post-traumatic stress disorder (PTSD) symptoms, something that a person cannot fake. My own research has shown that a significant percentage of experiencers suffer from PTSD symptoms.[50] He also did not believe that the abductees are suffering from simple sleep paralysis and points to physical evidence of abduction on the bodies of experiencers. He also noted that not all reports of alien abduction are brought about through hypnosis (30% of his experiencer patients had not been hypnotized). A Roper poll conducted by David Jacobs and Bud Hopkins in 1991 suggested that maybe as many as 3.7 million Americans showed signs of being abducted.[51] It seems unconscionable to simply not believe people and assume that they are crazy because they are reporting an alien abduction. Not believing or ignoring something that is occurring does not make it go away. It is on that note that I provide my full disclosure.

Three years ago, I started publishing my paranormal stories. I held out for 58 years for fear of being ridiculed and perhaps losing my position at the college, losing friends, and even endangering my relationships with loved ones. Each book in my trilogy has gone a bit further and disclosed more. *Timeless: A Paranormal Personal History* was my first paranormal book that tested the waters. I documented 34 paranormal stories dealing with apparitions, demons, angels, telekinesis, telepathy, and precognition. My second paranormal book, *Timeless Deja Vu*, went further in documenting 31 more bizarre experiences including my contact with non-human intelligences and provided a comprehensive theoretical model I called "My Personal Quantum Reality" where I used quantum physics to help explain my paranormal experiences.[52] *Timeless Trinity*, the last book in my *Timeless* trilogy, was the most revealing and featured a striking female reptilian alien of my acquaintance on the cover. In *Timeless Trinity* I have documented 24 additional experiences including details from my four alien abductions/reunions and ongoing contact with an ancient alien mystic known as Anzar. At this point in the book, I realize that I might lose a few of you with my full disclosure, then again, I might intrigue you even more. Seeing as that it took nearly six decades for me to publish my first paranormal book, you can see that it was not an easy decision to make. Once you are out in the open, you cannot go back.

It should be noted that I am not trying to say with this disclosure that I am something totally unique or special. In fact, my Scandinavian heritage precludes me from sticking my head up above anyone else. It is a cultural value based on something called "Janteloven."[53] Many millions of people have had similar experiences. My purpose is to document my journey and to hopefully empower others to come forward with their experiences. We all deserve to be heard and together we can learn.

In a survey conducted by Dean Radin and other scientists in 2018, they wanted to find out how many scientists and engineers had had psychic experiences. "Throughout history, people have reported exceptional experiences that appear to transcend the everyday boundaries of space and time, such as perceiving someone's thoughts from a distance. Because such experiences are associated with superstition, and some violate currently accepted materialist conventions, one might assume that scientists and engineers would be much less likely to report instances of these experiences than the general population." What they found was that 94 % of scientists and engineers have reported psychic-type experiences. That is remarkable and not surprising. Scientists and engineers have been taught to not share such experiences because it would make them seem odd, which is the same thought process I had, until recently.[54]

Since I was a little boy, I have wanted there to be life on other planets and wanted to meet an alien. Growing up with *Lost in Space*, *Star Trek*, and many Saturday afternoon science-fiction movies, I desperately wanted us not to be alone in the universe. The Apollo space program and moon landing in July 1969 further fueled this passion for outer space, the final frontier. Spock, from the original *Star Trek* TV series, was and still is my favorite TV character. Later, in the 1980s, I was inspired by Carl Sagan's *Cosmos* TV series. I have researched Area 51 in Nevada, the Roswell incident, and Hangar 18 and Area B, the top-secret part of Wright-Patterson Air Force Base in Dayton, Ohio, where, coincidentally, my eldest son works. All of this fascinates me. In high school I read Erich von Däniken's *Chariots of the Gods?* which was published in 1968. In that book he made claims about extraterrestrial influences on early human culture. The legacy of his book and the controversy it stirred in the scientific community continues today with many ancient astronaut hypotheses and popular TV shows like *Ancient Aliens*. I have read Col. Philip Corso's book, *The Day After Roswell*, and it seems to ring true. His story of how the technology retrieved at the Roswell crash site in 1947 led to the development of microchips, optic fibers, Kevlar, and night vision goggles makes sense.[55]

Despite the ridicule that can come with belief in aliens and the paranormal, the number of people who believe and relate their experiences just continues to grow in the world. I know that I have had experiences, so it is not really a matter of belief. It reminds me of the words generally attributed to German philosopher Arthur Schopenhauer. To paraphrase: All truth passes through three stages. First, it is ridiculed. Second, it is violently opposed. Third, it is accepted as being self-evident.

One day in 1997, I met an ancient being in one of my visions. I believe that I may have been chosen to help us prepare for contact. I will get back to that story in a moment. First, an explanation of what I mean by visions. I am not asleep, but I am not fully awake when I experience a vision. I am in a middle state of consciousness. Scientists call this the alpha brain wave state. I hear and see, but not in an ordinary sense. I straddle a doorway between two realities, two worlds that coexist but aren't always apparent to one another. It was in such a state of mind that I met the Progenitor. The language I heard in the vision was English, but I cannot be sure that it was. I understood perfectly in the vision, but when I tried to write down what I heard, it seemed as if it was in some unrecognizable language. I must think about what I have heard first, and then write it out in standard English. The Progenitor was standing with eyes closed, hands folded, wearing a light beige colored tunic made from some coarse fiber. His face was proto-human and ashen, with narrow set eyes. It was clear to me that he was the first and original mystic, but he could not have been a proto-human, I suspect he was of alien origin.

After Earth's millions of revolutions around the sun and the billions of people that have come before me, I was chosen to receive a message beyond time from this ancient seer. The Progenitor drifted through dimensional doorways and appeared to be revolving in space. He then spoke to me in a peaceful, contemplative manner.

21

"I am the Progenitor," the primordial mystic said. It was a simple message, but it was almost beyond my imagination to be receiving such an important communication. "I speak to you through the portal of the past, future, and present, all as one, and one as all," he explained.

"Why me? Why are you speaking to me? What do I have to offer?" I asked.

"The answer reveals itself as a seed silently planted that grows," he said. I thought deeply about his words. "You are one in a long line of seers," he continued.

"Who would believe me?" I asked.

"Believe or not believe; it is experience that teaches. You must be the connector, the bridge-builder. There have been many messages through time with different messengers, and all are pointing to the same obvious truth," he said, with a rising tone in his voice.

"I understand," I said. My body was tingling from the excitement of making this contact.

The Progenitor continued, still revolving in space. "Both deliverance and peace come from knowing this as one cannot exist without the other. The bargain for life is death, the bargain for peace is war, the bargain for happiness is sorrow, the bargain for health is sickness, the bargain for wealth is poverty, and the bargain for love is hate," he said. I sensed that I was leaving my body and drifting through space with him as I listened intently to his words of wisdom. "Lament the day passing, but the night will still come. I offer this gift, from the beyond, through a channel with many faces, a seed planted in the womb of the earth," he said as he continued to rotate in outer space. "The great unknown lies beyond the veil of death. It is yet another beginning. Look at the black hole. What do you see? Light does not escape. It is what you do not see that is most important. The universe pours through the rips in time and space. A quasar explodes on the other side, yet you may not see it. You see the past and the future, from infinity to infinity, with no real beginning and no real end," he said.

"I think I understand, but where are you? Are you an alien? So many questions," I said. And then he was gone, and the vision was done.

Initially, I was afraid to tell people about my experience. I finally told one of my colleagues in 1999; she was an anthropology professor. I described the Progenitor and showed her the picture I had drawn of him. She listened politely as she glanced at the drawing.

"You are a pretty spacey dude, Bruce," she said as she smiled and continued filing papers at her desk. She stopped filing for a moment and looked at me directly.

"But he can't be proto-human; they did not have language. Language only developed 100,000 years ago," she said. I did not bring it up again with her and did not share my experience with anyone else until now.

According to Noam Chomsky, Massachusetts Institute of Technology (MIT) professor of linguistics, a single chance mutation occurred in one individual about 100,000 years ago. This mutation triggered the instantaneous emergence of language ability. This random genetic change in a single individual then spread to the rest of the group and beyond. Chomsky defined the concept of "discrete infinity" as the property by which human language is constructed from a few dozen discrete parts and then combine in an infinite variety of expressions of thought, imagination, and feeling. It is a unique property of human language. Human computational ability also took a giant leap at about the same time as language. We went from only being able to count up to a fixed number to be able to count indefinitely.[56] Could this have been the work of aliens contacting early humans? Could they have given us this evolutionary boost? Could the Progenitor have taken his physical form during the initial contact with early humans and later returned to provide us with the gift of language? I do not know, but what I do know is that I was contacted.

The possibility of alien contact had always been there for me, just waiting, somewhere over the rainbow bridge, Bifrost in Norse mythology. Being of Norwegian heritage, I grew up with Norse mythology and stories of Vikings. Bifrost, that burning rainbow bridge that connects Asgard, the world of the gods, with Midgard, the world of humanity here on Earth, makes sense to me. I am a bridgebuilder and guardian, like Heimdall, the ever-vigilant god who is the guardian of the rainbow bridge. I stand ready to open the bridge, so our world can make contact with the world of the Progenitor. I understand the skepticism and the comfort that comes with not wanting to believe or accept that we are not alone in the universe. A recent YouGov poll revealed that 54% of Americans believe that intelligent alien life exists.[57] We have been taught to believe only what our eyes can see, but there is more. To see the quantum universe as it really is, you must look beyond what we call normal, everyday reality.

On October 9, 2016, almost one month after he had passed away, I had my first vision of my childhood friend Gene. We grew up together and his family was also Norwegian-American. I was lying down, reading, and thinking about him and what a loss it was for his family, for his friends, for me, and for everyone. A kind and gentle soul had been taken from us too soon. In a vision, Gene spoke to me. His hair was long, he was young, he was strong, and he was happy.

"There's no past or future in the afterlife," he said with his characteristically big smile.

"Only the present?" I asked.

"Kind of…everything is light, airy, moment to moment, you know," he said.

"I think so," I said. "Now that you are dead, are you in heaven?" I asked. Gene smiled.

"Yes, but it is weird to talk about being dead when I do not feel like I am dead," he said.

"I do not understand," I said.

"Hard to explain, even for me, maybe it would help for me to say that I am, not I was like in the past tense, just that I am, I am present," he said.

"I think I get it," I said.

"It is all true. All of it!" Gene said with excitement.

"What's true?" I asked.

"Do everything to your fullest, put everything into your role in life because it echoes in all of eternity," he said. Before I could fully understand what he had just told me, the vision shifted.

In the next vision, Gene and his father Leif were framing a big house, and it was a beautiful sunny day. Neither one of them were wearing shirts. Gene did not have shoes either.

"Why do not you have shoes?" I asked. He laughed.

"Do not need them anymore," he said with a big smile. Then the vision shifted again, and Gene and I were in a theater. He was running around very rapidly. I got the impression that he was both directing and starring in the play, but it was not clear which play he was directing although the stage and scenery were massive.

"Do you want to stay for rehearsal, it is about to begin?" he said.

"Sure," I said. Gene kept moving quickly from place to place not slowing down. "Could you slow down so I can talk to you, maybe ask some questions?" I asked.

"Too much to do, I do not have to sleep now; I have to keep going," he said. Then he looked at me seriously. "But you should rest," he said.

Did he mean that I was not sleeping enough? Is that what he meant. In any event, I have been trying to sleep more.

All of this made me think of time and the passage of time. It is often said that we should slow down, smell the roses and that we have all the time in the world. We are also told that time is running out. What to do? As we grow older, time seems to pass more quickly than when we were young. Technology is supposed to save us time, and time is money, yet we appear to have less time to spend.

But what is real time? I think it is time we spend with friends and loved ones. We should make more of an effort to stay in touch with old friends, relatives, and people we love. They may not be here to-morrow. Throughout my life, and especially as I have grown older, I try to find the constellation Orion when I look at the night sky. It has always been very comforting to me. The story is that Orion the hunter is forever searching for his lost love. It reminds me of the quests and dreams all of us have in life: for love, for fame, for fortune, for truth, and for happiness. Some of these quests and dreams come true, some do not, and others may drive us mad in the end. The stars at night remind me that one day I will blend in with those twinkling stars and return to the stardust of which I am made. I think of my parents, my relatives, my friends, and all of those who came before me when I look at the night sky. I picture that each one of them is a star in an infinite universe. In this endless whisper of time, then, I do not feel so alone.

On June 10, 2018, I began taking spirit walks and spoke to rela-tives and friends that had passed on. Nearly 21 years after my initial contact with the Progenitor, I felt I was ready to contact him again. In November 2018 during one of my meditative walks, I asked my spirit guides to connect me with the Progenitor. I had read that some of us here on Earth are related to ancient aliens. I always suspected that I was different, but was I *that* different? I have read and heard that some alien races were friendly, and some were not.

"You said you were the original mystic. Am I related to you?" I asked.

"Yes," he said, in a slightly husky voice inside my head. I did not see his face as I did in 1997, but I could hear his voice.

"So, we're some sort of hybrids?" I asked.

"Yes."

"What alien race are we?"

He said something that I did not understand, it sounded like he said Assyrians, but then he continued. "Arcturians."

What are Arcturians? I thought to myself; I would have to do more research.

"Am I doing the right things to help people? Any advice or wisdom?" I asked.

"Follow the hand that points to love, redemption, then the world is saved, and we all stand protected," he said. The communication ended abruptly, and I was in shock. Oh my God, am I an alien? But then I remembered that a few months before, my friend Gene told me that *we* are the aliens. It was all starting to make sense.

I spoke to the Progenitor again a week later and was better prepared with my questions.

"Were you the original alien contact for our planet?" I asked.

"Yes," he said.

"You helped early man become who we are today?"

"Yes."

"What's your name?"

"Anzar."

"Where do you come from?"

"Orion, Rigel." I thought this was noteworthy because I had been very interested in the constellation of Orion since I was a little boy. I am constantly drawn to Orion as it seems to hold special meaning for me. I even drew a comic book about it in high school.

"Okay," I said. I began to think even more deeply. Why was I having this contact now? Why did I write the first *Timeless* book? I got the feeling that I was caught up in something much larger than myself.

"Is something about to happen?" I asked.

"All is about to be revealed, stand ready, on guard, stick to the truth, trust your friends, and family. In anxious times people seek the comfort of those who are calm and rational, it is reassuring. It will be revealed soon…the contact that has been going on." Wow. I wondered if that would be a good thing or a bad thing? I felt privileged to be getting the information.

My friend Terry Lovelace, who had himself been abducted, researched the name Anzar and came up with some interesting details. In the language of the Basque people of Northeastern Spain, bordering France, Anzar means "lives near a pasture." Basques have a unique and old culture perhaps tied to Neolithic man. In my research, I found that in the Amazigh (or Berber) culture of North Africa, Anzar is the god of rain. There is a school named Anzar High School in the central Californian city of San Juan Bautista. The city was named after the mission of the same name and founded by Fermín de Francisco Lasuén de Arasqueta who was a Basque Franciscan missionary. He helped found eight other California missions.

The name Anzar is also a common one in the Muslim world. There is a town named Anzar in Northern Iran populated by the Azeris. Anzar, and its various spellings (i.e., Anzer, Ansar), means pure gold, angel of paradise, self-assurance, independence, and self-confidence, in Arabic. In the year 711, the Islamic Moors from northern Africa invaded Spain. The Moors went on to occupy Sicily as well.

Five-hundred years later the Moors were defeated and driven out of Sicily, and with the fall of Granada in 1492, Muslim rule of Spain ended.

There is a hypothesis that Rh negative blood has alien origins. Everybody on Earth has either O, A, B, or AB type blood. Your blood is also classified as either Rh positive or Rh negative. The Rhesus factor (based on lineage to Rhesus monkeys) refers to a specific antigen in the blood. Some 85 percent of the world's population carry the antigen and are Rh positive. The remaining 15 percent do not carry the antigen and have Rh negative blood. If man and ape had evolved from the same ancestor, their blood would have the same Rh factor. All primates on Earth have Rh positive blood. So, where did this Rh negative blood come from? Most scientists say that is a simple mutation. Others say that it is of alien origin.

The International Community for Alien Research (ICAR) compiled information from over 53,000 people who have had alien contact. Their data shows that aliens prefer type O blood and especially O negative. Scientists say that Rh negative blood types developed only 25,000 to 40,000 years ago. O negative is also the universal donor but can only receive their own blood. Rh negative men and women tend to have a sixth lumbar vertebrae, a lower body temperature, and lower than normal blood pressure.[58] Interestingly, we know that the Basques have the highest percentage of Rh-negative blood in the world, over 30 percent.[59] Could this blood type data be a connection to Anzar and our possible alien origins?

I spoke to Anzar again in early December 2018. I was beginning to feel a sense of urgency in my mission to help people understand and not fear the paranormal.

"What else should I be doing?" I asked.

"Keep going. Be aware. Stay on the path. Realize who you are. Focus your energy and your determination. Train others for the future. You will know who is on the side of the light and who is not," he said.

Although the communication with the primordial mystic Progenitor is enlightening and very cool, it also makes me think about who else may be getting this information? Am I the only one?

On the first day of winter, December 21, 2018, I asked Anzar for advice.

"Caution. Proceed with caution. Help people understand and prepare. It will be audible when it happens, the big reveal. Visual will come later," he said.

"Audible from who? Our leaders?"

"Yes."

"Who?" I asked. He did not answer.

"You are the consciousness, be one with the consciousness, rise to the highest level of your expectations and then exceed them. There is no boundary, no limit, except for those that are self-imposed or imposed by others, which you can ignore," he said.

"How are we related again? What race are we?"

"Arcturian," he said again.

I read about the Arcturians, and many have said that they are highly-evolved spiritual beings. Famous psychic Edgar Cayce (1877–1945) wrote about them. He was known as the sleeping prophet and the father of holistic medicine. He may have been the most well-documented psychic of the 20th century. Edgar Cayce was reported to have said that "Arcturus is the highest civilization in our galaxy." But who are they? Purportedly, the Arcturians are an alien race that comes from a planet orbiting Arcturus in the Boötes constellation 36 light-years from Earth. Arcturians are said to be inter-dimensional beings.[60] I asked Anzar why the written information I have read about Arcturians and their origins disagrees with his telling me that he was from Rigel in the Orion constellation. He told me that "Although I am Arcturian, I am from Rigel in Orion." He did not name a specific planet, but then, when I thought about it, when we tell someone where we are from, we use a location reference that would make sense to them. Some have said that Arcturians have protected the Earth from other aliens and want to help with our spiritual development.

So, could it be that I am of alien origin? In a way, I guess I always suspected that because I have never quite fit in anywhere and have always been very independent. After Christmas 2018, I spoke to Anzar again.

"Anzar, are you there?" I asked.

"Yes. Compatibility," he said.

"What do you mean?"

"Your friends, compatible, and important."

"I agree. Are you saying we have a special connection?" I asked.

"Yes," he said. I thought for a moment. I knew that my good friend Terry, who had been abducted, had Rh negative blood. O negative to be exact.

"Are Rh negative people the descendants of aliens?"

"Yes," he said. I became frightened thinking about abduction and what happened to Terry.

"How can we protect ourselves?" I asked.

"Your belief and acceptance of the one consciousness, God, the Creator, and tapping into the one consciousness, that is what will help you."

"Thank you. Can you give me any more advice?"

"When you see what is not there, you will see what is there," he said. This statement by Anzar made me think. I sometimes see the air, the molecules in the air moving. Anzar read my mind and answered.

"Yes. You have seen it as a child. What you are told not to see is what you should see," he said.

31

I have always thought that children are very psychic and then society and our social institutions convince us not to use these natural God-given psi abilities. The day before New Year's Eve 2018, I had another chance to speak to Anzar.

"When I asked which alien race you are, I thought you said Assyrian," I said.

"Sirian," he corrected me.

"But then you said Arcturian? Which one is it?"

"Combination." Oh, so now I understood. He is of both Sirian and Arcturian extraction and came from a planet orbiting Rigel in the Orion constellation. Multi-ethnic, multi-planetary. I got it.

"The illustration of you that I drew in 1997 and that will appear in *Timeless Deja Vu*, is that correct?"

"It is one of my forms, I have been around a long time," he said. I thought for a moment.

"Am I getting just little bits of information at a time so as not to overwhelm me?" I asked.

"Yes. There is much more."

"When will the reveal be?"

"Soon, more than likely, depends. It may lead to assassinations." Then it dawned on me, something that I had been thinking for a long time.

"Is that what happened to JFK and RFK?"

"Yes, because they would reveal info about aliens."

"MLK?"

"Yes and no."

"What?" He did not answer.

"Trust your connection. Flow with it, like a stream, let the great consciousness flow," he said. Talking to Anzar, I felt confident that I would be successful and keep growing my knowledge and wisdom in order to help people.

On January 8, 2019, I spoke with Anzar the Progenitor again.

"Thank you for speaking with me. I am trying to help people. Am I on the right track with my thinking? Is the spiritual/quantum realm the same realm aliens utilize for transport and contact? How do I transport myself?" I asked.

"You can go back or forward in time or travel great distances. Remote viewing, it can be done. Study that," he said.

A few days later I asked Anzar: "These signals, fast radio bursts (FRB), is this what you meant by an audible sign from aliens?"

"Yes."

"And the visual is coming?"

"Yes. Prepare, acknowledge, secure, and protect," he said.

"What more can I do to enhance my abilities to help people?"

"Embrace, endeavor, let go of fear, fearless living," he said. I had a lot to think about. I believe I was approaching what the famous con-spiracy theorist and writer Jim Marrs called, "the boggle point." That is the point where you simply cannot fathom or process what you are being told.

A few days later I had more questions for Anzar.

"This idea of time travel…you said it is totally possible in the spirit realm that you operate in. So, if I get into the meditative state, I can travel in time?" I asked.

"Yes."

"And just to confirm, the audible signal you told me about is the FRBs that are coming in now?"

"Yes."

"And that is the beginning of the big reveal?"

"Yes."

"And the visual will come next?"

"Yes."

"Will I be part of the visual?"

"Yes." Oh, great, what does that mean? I was too overwhelmed to dig deeper, so I let it go.

"I really appreciate you talking to me," I said.

"Let the light envelop you, and it will carry you throughout time and space. That is the key. The master key," he said.

Then another voice entered my head, but I was not sure if it was from Anzar, but it sounded like him. "There is here and here is there," said the voice. I think the speaker was referring to non-locality.

"I think I understand," I said.

"The light is your salvation, the light is the truth, the light is your destiny, blessed is the light," said Anzar as the communication ended. I have come to believe that we need to balance ourselves somewhere between complacency and hysteria as we deal with whatever is coming. Be prepared, and our lives and learning will continue on, forever.

I often wonder what ultimate purpose I have in the whole disclosure process. Is it just to write about my experiences? Talk on radio and TV programs? Teach my students of what is to come? All the above? I am reminded of the song "Woodstock" by Joni Mitchell:

> *We are stardust*
>
> *We are golden*
>
> *And we have got to get ourselves*
>
> *Back to the garden.*

There is no doubt that this world we live in is in trouble. Is it possible to get things right, and maybe with the help of extraterrestrials (ETs)? I think so. But are all ETs friendly? My friend Terry Lovelace has been abducted by aliens and implanted. He wrote of these experiences in his best-selling book *Incident at Devils Den*. Those aliens did not seem very friendly. Since his book came out early in 2018, he has been plagued by UFOs and helicopters over his house in a Dallas suburb. Terry has shown me photos of these helicopters accompanied by different types of UFOs. On February 6, 2019, I decided to ask Anzar about these events.

"Was I correct in saying that the helicopters near Terry's house are watching him and that the UFOs he photographed were alien spacecraft?

"Yes."

"So, they are monitoring him?"

"Yes." This confirmation chilled me as I thought of the enormity of the paradigm shift in understanding that we are all undergoing.

"Anything else you can tell me to help prepare?" I asked.

"Train yourself. Be patient with the hard work of training. Provide protection," Anzar said. I assumed he meant remote viewing (RV) because he had recommended that training before. I then remembered a dream vision that I had the night before and decided to ask Anzar.

"Was the vision of the candlelight in a dark wind of significance?"

"Yes, symbolic of what is going on. You have to protect the light too." Big responsibilities have fallen into my lap.

On March 12, 2019, I sought answers from Anzar again.

"The helicopters and UFOs around Terry's house, government and alien, respectively, what's their purpose?" I asked.

"Observation," said Anzar.

"Could not they observe him without being so visible?" I asked.

35

"They want him to know he is being observed."

"Intimidation?"

"Yes."

"What should he do? Continue to speak and write?"

"Yes, and so should you." The phrase "stay in the light," came to mind. It has so many variations of meaning.

Until recently, I hadn't seen a UFO, as far as I know, since 1978. On March 14, 2019, it was a cool, clear evening when I walked outside our front door to look at the starlit heavens, something I try to do as often as I can. At about 9 pm, in the southern sky at about 60° above the horizon, I saw an oddly bright light. It was not the planet Venus, and it was not a star. It was moving erratically, so I knew it was not an airplane or a satellite. It was too high to be an airplane; I would estimate 60,000 feet. I ran inside to get my youngest son, Leif. We both witnessed this UFO. He said the same thing I said—it cannot be a plane or a satellite because of the way it was moving. Then we noticed that little darts of light would quickly shoot off from the UFO at lightning speed. Leif saw a green beam of light come from it as well. My film of the event was shaky, and it was hard to distinguish the camera movements from the motion of the UFO. It pulsated and had a peculiar shape I would describe as a diamond. That was Leif's first UFO.

The next day I reported the UFO to MUFON (the Mutual UFO Network), and they included it in their UFO tracking map. I asked Leif if he told his friends.

"No, Dad, they'll think I am crazy," he said. On my meditative spirit walk, I asked my ancient alien cosmic advisor Anzar if he could confirm that what we saw was a UFO.

"Yes, absolutely," he said.

"Who was it?" I asked.

Silence.

"Anzar? What alien group?"

Silence.

"Oh, you are not saying. That's interesting," I said. "Were they here to help?" I asked.

"Yes, they are here to help," he said.

"What were the fast-moving things coming from it?"

"Other spacecraft."

"What about the green beam of light?"

"Healing and protection."

"Ah, so, they are here to try to help with the calamities you told me about before?"

"Yes." That was the end of the communication. I had a feeling that Anzar was pre-occupied with something.

On March 27, 2019, I asked Anzar about the March 14th UFO sighting.

"On March 14th, we saw a UFO. I know it was a UFO. Who was it? Arcturians? Was it you?" I asked.

"Yes and no," said Anzar. Although it was an answer, it was not totally clear.

"Were they here to help and guide us?"

"Yes."

"What other information can you give me?"

"Calamities will be lessened. Some will still occur," said Anzar.

On May 2, 2019, after hearing from Terry that the harassment was continuing, I queried Anzar again.

"What is going on with my friend Terry Lovelace in Dallas, more helicopters, UFOs around his house?" I asked.

"He is being monitored, some friendly, some not, some are government types. Combination. You too, you are being monitored," said Anzar. I was not surprised by this answer based on what had happened since late last year when I reconnected with Anzar and met my scientist friend Dr. Edwin M. Young and learned more about aliens and UFOs, but it was an ominous confirmation, nonetheless.

I spoke to Anzar again on June 3, 2019. Terry was still reporting UFOs near his home and was in the process of selling his house and moving.

"What is going on now with Terry Lovelace, helicopters, UFOs?" I asked.

"He is being observed and harassed, government and ETs," said Anzar. I thought to myself, *Why won't they leave him alone?* But then, having just attended the UFO conference in Indian Wells, California, called Contact in the Desert, I had another question for Anzar.

"Is it true what I heard Linda Moulton Howe talking about? A secret Antarctic base?"

"Yes. Do you remember George?" said Anzar. It was an obscure reference, and at first, I thought of the host of *Coast to Coast AM*, George Noory. Then, Anzar showed me a glimpse of me at the controls of my training helicopter in 1983.

"Yes, I remember George, that's what we called the governor on our throttle in the TH-55 helicopter," I said.

"That is what the good aliens are doing to keep the pace of disclosure measured," he said.

"Not too fast so that we burn the engine, I get it. And to keep us going and keep the engine from stalling, which is what the bad guys want," I said.

38

"Yes."

"What more should I be doing?" I asked.

"Keep exploring, dig deeper, make connections, build bridges, be prepared, the time is coming," said Anzar. I sensed the urgency.

On Sunday, June 23, 2019, Leif and I saw another UFO. Interestingly, on my meditative spirit walk earlier that morning, I had asked to see another UFO.

"Anzar, I would like to see some more UFOs, where Ginger could witness it too. I would also like Ginger to see you," I asked. Later in the evening, I was on my way home after picking up Leif from his mother. We were heading west on Interstate 10 near the Highway 57 on-ramp around 8 pm. There was still quite a bit of light. Almost due west, at about 45° up from the horizon, we saw a bright shining orb. It was not moving but blinked out a few times before it remained on for about 20 seconds. This UFO was roughly half the size of the moon, and I would say it was at an altitude of 1500 feet. It then disappeared. I looked for evidence of an airplane or anything that might have caused this light, but there was not anything in the sky when it vanished. The next day on my spirit walk, I asked about the UFO sighting the night before.

"Was it an ET craft?" I asked.

"Yes," said Anzar. I was glad that I got confirmation and that Leif had also witnessed the UFO (his second). Too bad Ginger was not with us. So many unanswered questions remained.

A poll by Rasmussen released in 2019 showed that 61% of Americans believe that there is intelligent life on other planets. Only 11% of the people surveyed had seen a UFO. Over 60% of Americans do not think that UFOs represent a national security threat despite lots of news coverage this year about UFO encounters by US Navy pilots.[61] A YouGov poll found that 54% of Americans believe that the US government is hiding information about UFOs.[62] It is unclear what would happen if a US president would suddenly announce that aliens are visiting us. Sadly, it might create some panic, but would probably be quickly bumped from the news cycle by the latest exploits of the Kardashians.

It is my opinion that UFOs and aliens are here, and they have been for a long time. I base this opinion on my research and on my personal experiences. I have been abducted, or reunited as I prefer to say, four times: 1964, 1973, 1977, and 1978.[63] Although frightening at the time, I do not see these events in a negative way now, in fact, some were life-saving experiences. I suspect that the circumstances surrounding the 1964 reunion may have been tied to my stuttering which began about the same time, at age six. The reunion, however transformational, was hard for me to process. I had to attend speech therapy for a few years in elementary school. I have overcome my disability and turned it into an asset—I tend to choose my words carefully and I am grateful for my ability to speak and write as communication is my forte.

The disclosure or big reveal is already in motion. Increasingly, I am wondering why the aliens are here. My spirit guides have told me that it could be for many reasons. Perhaps we can begin by asking ourselves why we explore strange lands? Could they be conquistadors? Scientists? Missionaries? Entrepreneurs? Future human anthropologists checking on us with their time machines? Tourists?[64] Or maybe they are our distant alien relatives who have come to visit and see how we are doing and are trying to help us survive? Maybe all these reasons and more? No one knows for sure, which could be a scary thing, but I know we will be okay, and I am not afraid. If the aliens were all malevolent, we would be gone already, and I would not be writing this book. In any event, I will keep doing what I do, speaking and writing about the paranormal, UFOs, and aliens, and fearlessly pursuing the truth. One of my immediate concerns is more conventional. I am hoping that my wife Ginger will soon witness a UFO with me so that whatever tiny lingering doubt she might have about my sanity can be expunged. I want to share this adventure with her as we re-discover who we are and reunite with our long-lost ancestors and work together to preserve our precious planet before our inevitable return home to the stardust of which we are all made. At this point in the book, I want to share an incredible synchronicity.

Via de Anzar

I met Lucinda a several months ago at my first CERO meeting and I had a special connection with her from the moment I saw her. I had the feeling that I had met her before. Lucinda is a very skilled psychic-medium and an experiencer. At a CERO (Close Encounter Research Organization) meeting in August 2019, I decided to tell the assembled group of 25 people that I had brought a special guest with me that afternoon. I said little else and offered no other clues as to the special guest's identity. At the end of the meeting one of our members said that she saw two people, a man and a woman. They were likely my spirit guides Theodora and Ozzie. That was cool. But she did not see who I had invited as my special guest—Anzar, my ancient alien mystic advisor. As I was packing my things, Lucinda approached me.

"I have to tell you something. I know Anzar," she said. I was shocked.

"Wow, that's cool," I said.

"Does he look like a kachina?" she asked.

"Yes, kind of, he has a protohuman face." Lucinda then showed me her driver's license. She lived on Via De Anzar. I could not believe it. This was quite a startling synchronicity.

"So, you see him too?" I asked.

"Yes!" she said.

"We need to talk some more about this," I said.

41

"Sure," she said. We did not have time to talk more as everyone was leaving and frankly, I was a bit in shock. Anzar had first appeared to me in 1997, and when I had asked Anzar previously if he spoke to anyone else besides me, he said he had not.

In an email later Lucinda responded to a few of my questions. She told me that "We are all moving into a new time/energy field that will require an adjustment by everyone. Some people aren't taking well to the adjustment." She believes that I am Anzar, and he is me. Mind-blowing! That thought had never occurred to me. She went on to say that "We are one consciousness split into different dimensional time-lines but sharing a similar energy signature." This is why I can always find Anzar and talk to him. She feels that I need to make the adjustment to this changing time/energy field and integrate with Anzar to be able to fulfill my purpose. Lucinda felt that Anzar appeared to her to help me make the adjustment. It took a few days for all of this to sink in.

Not long after the email message I received from Lucinda, I took a spirit walk and connected with Anzar.

"Are we one in the same?" I asked.

"We are related," said Anzar.

"Aren't you related to everyone on Earth, as the Progenitor?"

"Specifically, to you. A gift of sight, and the connection."

"Thank you. Integration might not be something I want to do. What does that mean?"

"One with the ancestors." I paused for a moment in my walk.

"Does that mean I leave this life?"

"Not necessarily." I was not totally reassured.

"I have a lot I have to do now for my family, but I am willing to consider this, as long as everyone here is okay and taken care of," I said. I continued my walk for a bit without talking but thinking loudly. Then, Anzar added more.

"Temporal distortion, propulsion, time travel, it is really simple, distort time, move like a snowplow in every direction," he said. Immediately upon my return home I started to research temporal distortion. It makes sense, that is how you can travel great distances in a short amount of time.

A few days later, I spoke to Anzar again.

"Anzar, could you enlighten me some more about what Lucinda wrote? Am I supposed to do this integration?" I asked.

"If you can," he said.

"So many people depend on me…I can't risk checking out early. I would have to be assured that that wouldn't happen."

"Yes."

"So, you can assure me that I can continue to live in this life so I can take care of my family and friends?"

"Yes." He did not elaborate much in his answers. I was somewhat reassured but wanted more. I spoke to Lucinda on the phone and shared with her what Anzar had told me.

"You'll still be a complete autonomous being," she said.

"Oh, that's good," I said.

"Integration is just a change in vibration, where he can connect with you more completely, but I have always been hesitant to do that," she said.

"I understand."

"Remember, even though I see him, he is for you, I am just helping you," she said.

"Thank you, I really appreciate your help."

43

"You know…Via De Anzar, my street, means 'the way to Anzar,'" and then she laughed.

"An amazing synchronicity," I said. I now had some much-needed validation. This was not just some coincidence.

A September to Remember

In September 2019, I was offered an invitation to speak at the Contact in the Desert (CITD) conference to be held in Indian Wells, California at the end of May 2020. Quite an honor. I owe this invitation to my friends Yvonne Smith and Terry Lovelace, both of whom are legendary and well-respected in the ufology community. Immediately, I had to decide on the topics for my lecture and my workshop. In preparation for just such an occasion, I had been kicking around the idea of doing a survey of the members of CERO (Close Encounters Research Organization). After having a shocking alien contact experience on September 8, 2019, and another one on September 22, 2019 (more on those incidents later), I decided that the survey should ask about post-traumatic stress disorder (PTSD) symptoms related to alien abduction. Even though I am not a psychologist, I have invested over 25 years into researching PTSD among veterans and in 2005 created a veterans program and in 2007 co-founded a transition course for returning veterans at Citrus College. My brother served in Vietnam and has PTSD, and I have lost friends to suicide who suffered from PTSD. I am a disabled veteran who also has PTSD in addition to other conditions related to my six years of active-duty military service. Suffice it to say; it is an issue that is close to my heart.

My CITD workshop presentation is called: "We Are Messengers: Contact & Alien Abductions While Coping with PTSD." The workshop will help experiencers better understand the abduction experience and the important role the abductee will play in future disclosure. The messages that experiencers are receiving correlate with one another, and are clear: take care of the environment, prevent the use of weapons of mass destruction, and more. Few people in government have been listening—much less concerned—about the health and welfare of the human messengers, the abductees, many of whom have PTSD. In the workshop, I planned to share data from abductees who have taken a modified Veteran's Administration PTSD checklist survey. In addition to analyzing the data and explaining the nature of PTSD, I want to discuss coping skills and strategies for abductees and their loved ones. I believe that abductees have a vital mission and will play a critical role in helping save humanity and the planet after full disclosure.

To further legitimize the study, I decided to model my survey after the Veteran Administration's (VA) PCL-5 (PTSD checklist) questionnaire. The VA's PCL-5 is derived from the DSM-5 or Diagnostic and Statistical Manual of Mental Disorders written by the American Psychiatric Association. First, what is PTSD? The condition known as PTSD can develop from exposure to actual or threatened death, serious injury, or sexual violation. The trauma exposure can come from:

1. Direct experience of the traumatic event;

2. witnessing the traumatic event in person;

3. learning that the traumatic event occurred to a close family member or close friend (with the actual or threatened death being either violent or accidental);

4. or direct experience of repeated or extreme exposure to aversive details of the traumatic event (not through media, pictures, television, or movies, unless work-related).

The traumatic exposure causes clinically significant distress or impairment in the individual's social interactions, capacity to work, or other important areas of functioning. It is not caused by another medical condition, medication, drugs, or alcohol. Being abducted and experimented on by aliens qualifies as traumatic exposure. I used the same 20 questions as the VA survey, only changing the source of trauma to abduction instead of traumatic military service. The information I got from this survey was enlightening. I found that more than 54 percent of the people surveyed scored high enough on the VA inspired survey to be classified as likely having PTSD. Furthermore, 46 percent of the respondents warranted a provisional PTSD diagnosis based on certain VA criterion. Men tended to have signs of PTSD more so than women, and younger people more so than older people.

For my main lecture topic at Contact in the Desert, I decided that I would talk about oral history and the UFO and abduction phenomena. The title of the presentation is "Anzar's Answers: How a Former Fulbright Professor Came to Channel an Ancient Alien Mystic." The official Department of Homeland Security (DHS) motto is, "If you see something, say something." It is a registered trademark in fact. September 25 is "National See Something Say Something Awareness Day." Despite this emphasis and although oral history is a basic building block in the writing and understanding of our history (considered a primary source), the personal experiences of alien abduction and sightings of UFOs are often discounted, disregarded as merely anecdotal, ignored, or laughed at by many in the general public guided by professional debunkers, the media, and the government. It is no wonder then that such incidents are under-reported.

In the words of the DHS: "Across the country, in our communities, we share everyday moments with our neighbors, family, coworkers, and friends. We go to work or school, the grocery store, or the gas station. It is easy to overlook these routine moments, but as you are going about your day, if you see something that does not seem quite right, say something. By being alert and reporting suspicious activity to your local law enforcement, you can protect your family, neighbors, and community." That is, of course, unless it is a UFO because then you are just plain nuts. It is an old trick: attack the messenger, not the message. It makes you wonder even after the US Navy disclosures of what they termed unidentified aerial phenomena (UAP), why is the government so reluctant to give us the whole story.

Recently, National Security Agency whistleblower and federal fugitive Edward Snowden was interviewed on the Joe Rogan show. He said that he never saw any evidence of UFOs and aliens during his tenure at the NSA. Seeing as how he is safely nestled in with the Russians right now, you must wonder what type of game are they playing? It could also be that he did not have access to all our secrets. It reminds me of when I started driving a car. You must train yourself to look far out ahead when you are driving, or you will over steer and end up in the ditch. Likewise, we need to look far down the road and not right in front of our noses to decipher the truth.

Now, as for my September to remember and the odd incidents that occurred, let's begin. On October 12, 2019, I had another hypnotherapy session with Yvonne Smith. She asked me to go back to September 8, 2019, and describe what I was doing as I prepared to go to sleep. Yvonne reminded me to be aware of my body as it retained memories. I remembered that I was watching a video on my phone that night. It was an interview by Dr. Jeffrey Mishlove from his *New Thinking Allowed* series. He was interviewing Dr. Ed May, a scientist from the Stargate Project (1978–1995). Stargate used government and military remote viewers to gather intelligence information up until it was canceled and declassified in 1995. Dr. May is a materialist who does not believe there is anything magical or paranormal about remote viewing or quantum physics. His negativity and closed-mindedness rather upset me as I drifted off to sleep. That night as I was lying down and listening to my video, I heard unusual sounds in the house and the room, but I could not see anything unusual. I even stopped the video several times to listen more carefully. Nothing. Because I was so tired, I did not freak out, but the sounds were not the normal sounds of the house. I strapped on my CPAP mask and tried just to relax and go to sleep.

I started dreaming about a house that I do not remember ever living in. It was a nice dream at first because my mom was there, and she looked like how I remember her when I was 11 years old, in her

47

50s. Then, it started to get weird. It seemed like I was a kid, but I was an adult. My mom started to act funny, in a sexual way that does not make sense because she was a good mom and would never do anything like that. I felt very uncomfortable. We were in a bathroom in this strange house. I started to think maybe it was not my mom, because I was aroused and ashamed at the same time. It looked kind of like my mom, but it was not my mom. It was very confusing, and I felt a lot of tension and stress. She took off my shirt as I tried to leave the bathroom. Then, suddenly, she jumped up from the toilet where she was sitting, and I could see it was not my mom. I was relieved but that relief soon turned to terror when I saw the entity's true appearance. She was a reptilian alien!

Yvonne could sense my fear and told me everything was going to be okay and that I was safe now and asked me to describe the female reptilian.

"She was a reptilian female, broad scaly face and body, not much of a nose, like reptile slits, eyes were multicolored and kaleidoscopic, broad mouth, with teeth, and she was smiling at me in a sinister way. Her reptilian skin was almost iridescent. She was alluring and horrific at the same time. She got right in my face and scared me. The female reptilian lifted me with very little effort. She was incredibly strong because I am big and heavy (6 feet 3 inches and 260 pounds). She slammed me against the wall and was face-to-face with me when she started talking," I said.

"What did she say," asked Yvonne.

"She was frightening and attracting me at the same time..." I said

"Can you decipher the communication?" asked Yvonne.

"I think it was sexual in nature, but also a warning; she was angry. She acted like someone who was taking advantage of a weaker person. Not just sexual, it was power," I said.

Yvonne reminded me that I was now safe.

"You do not have any power here, and I can do what I want. If I want to, I can do this thing," said the reptilian female.

"So, you could make out the words?" asked Yvonne.

"They seemed alien to me, but I could make out the intent…it was partly telepathic and partly coming from her mouth. She was smiling, and her eyes were scary…I could not close my eyes or look away," I said.

"Is she familiar?" asked Yvonne.

"Familiar? Maybe, before, female, reptilian, it had popped into my vision at night, around Halloween last year, about when I started talking to Terry Lovelace and got more into alien stuff. Yeah, this same face appeared. There was also a scary vision of an entity on the road below our house in our cul-de-sac…could barely see him at first. He had a long overcoat and hat, and dark sunglasses. At first, I thought it was somebody I knew, but instead of smiling, he had an angry menacing look. Now that I have thought about it, his face reminded me of hers: broad reptilian, and scaly. I was so startled that I had to get out of bed and check the security of our house. Really frightening, I do not want either of them to come back," I said. I was visibly shaken, and Yvonne knew it.

"It is okay, Bruce, you are safe," she said.

"I do not know what she was doing or meaning to do. Every night I ask for protection in our house. I am not afraid of ghosts and the like, but with this thing, I am. I think I have a long history with her, and she has a purpose, and it is not good," I said.

"What do you think it is," asked Yvonne.

"I am stirring things up, writing books, speaking at a UFO conference, and playing an active role in the UFO/alien abduction community. Maybe it is my *Snarc* comic since the reptilians are the bad guys in that story," I said as I thought more deeply about the experience.

"She was warning me about my work. She isn't on my side, she wanted me to know how much power she has. She can be anybody and do anything to me. She wanted me to know how easy it was to handle me. It is really weird that she was making me think she was my mom, shapeshifting, or whatever. I knew she was not my mom because I was aroused and that wouldn't happen with my mom…that's sick and twisted. The reptilian female was messing with my mind. I do not want her to come back…I hope and pray every night that she does not," I said.

Yvonne was reassuring but could not promise me that she would not return. As she has said many times, there is no way to stop the aliens from contacting or abducting us. They are simply too powerful.

"Later, when I started to draw a picture of the reptilian female, I became sick to my stomach and threw up many times. Oddly, I was perfectly fine later. I have thrown up maybe six times in my entire life, and this was one of those times. Very unusual," I said.

"That would make sense. Anything else?" asked Yvonne.

"No, no encounter since then," I said.

"I want you to take a deep breath…now go to the night after our CERO meeting on September 22nd. You are at home and getting ready for bed," said Yvonne.

"Yeah. It started as a typical night," I said. "I brushed my teeth and lay down in the bed and started my CPAP machine. I felt uneasy, though. Ginger was in her workshop as usual since she is a night owl and does not go to bed until after midnight. I did not watch TV or play with my phone…I was pretty tired. I started to have this weird feeling like something was in the room, but I could not see it. I even shined my phone flashlight around to see if I could spot anything unusual. There was nothing," I said.

As I drifted off, I was startled by a bumping of the bed, as if something was moving through the room. I did not panic, and it was almost as if I was tranquilized or maybe just exhausted. I thought that maybe the elementals were back and annoying us again. That would mean having to call Esther the Peruvian shaman for a house cleansing. But no, this was darker and scarier.

"The past few months, I have felt an increasing sense of dread at night. I would wake up with my eyes wide-open like there was something in the room, but I wouldn't see anything. Twice I had seen strange lights in our room in the middle of the night," I said. I then thought back to September 22nd.

"A couple of times that night, I felt like something was in the room. I would get up and walk the perimeter and check the locks. My usual. Then I would return to the bed and hear strange noises again," I said. My CPAP machine makes a very distinctive sound of air pushing through the hose in a rhythmic pattern. The noise that I was hearing was different. I drifted off again into an uncomfortable and restless sleep. Suddenly, I woke up and could not move. I was completely paralyzed.

"I have never felt that before. This was the first time in 61 years. Not only that, but it felt like I was being electrocuted, from the top of my head to the tips of my toes, every part of my body charged," I told Yvonne. She must have sensed my anxiety.

"Without feeling any discomfort, be aware of your body, and everything around you, now describe," she said.

"It was almost like I was so energized or charged that I was vibrating and almost levitating out of bed. I had a feeling of beings in the room, by the foot of the bed," I said.

"How many do you see?" she asked.

"Three of them," I said, anticipating her question and talking over her.

"The taller one was in the middle. They were in and out of phase, they were causing this, hard to see them clearly, but I felt them. It was the same weird feeling that I had in the room when I went to bed," I said. I paused for a moment. "I did not have control of the situation. They were shadowy figures, three of them, and like I said, fading in and out of phase, like ghosts," I added.

"Did you hear any sounds?" Yvonne asked.

"Electrical sound, the sound of electrocution, a transformer sound, like when you drive underneath powerlines with the AM radio. The sound goes through you and causes you to vibrate from the inside out. But I am not paralyzed when I am driving," I said. No wonder it freaks me out when I drive under powerlines; there is a connection. "I hated the feeling of being so out of control and unable to move," I said, as I remembered the frustration.

"Sense your body, concentrate on the memories of your body. Do you feel anything beneath you?" Yvonne asked.

"I felt so energized, I was just barely above the bed," I said.

"Get a sense of who is there with you," she said.

"Three entities, very frightening, it was like I was dying, my body short-circuiting, and I was thinking how long I can last with this high voltage surging through my body. I panicked, I was helpless, and that only made it worse. I changed my tactics and decided to be calm and used all my will power, not my physical power, to break free and not let this happen. The entities were making me feel like I was helpless, so I stopped struggling physically. It worked. I felt like somebody turned off the power source. I felt heavy in the bed again and took off the CPAP mask," I said.

After the paralysis, I was trying to figure out what in the hell happened. I am not sure which was more frightening, the shapeshifting reptile lady or the electrocution. I felt like maybe I stopped a possible abduction, or maybe some other thing or force intervened, but the electrical shock stopped when I relaxed and concentrated mentally instead of struggling physically and panicking. It was only then that I could do something. Otherwise, I was helpless and not in control. Whoever was doing this was in and out of phase, in and out of this reality, ghost-like, and not a clear manifestation. They were in the darkness and were non-human entities. I had never had this happen before. After I got up, I walked around and eventually went back to sleep. I did not hurt afterward. I do not know exactly what happened, but I believe this is how an abduction works.

"I do not want ever to feel that feeling again," I told Yvonne.

"Deep breath," said Yvonne, "go back to the night you saw the lights."

"On July 9th, I saw a large grapefruit-size orb of white light dart across our bedroom diagonally. Then, on October 3rd, I woke up and saw a rectangular light by the wall facing our bed by the TV. The light started up on the ceiling and then shot straight down and disappeared. The TV was not on, and it was not the LED light from the cable box because that light is blue," I said. Were these lights a prelude and a confirmation of some type of paranormal and/or alien activity?

The rectangular light was six inches by two inches. The round orb kind of light was grapefruit-size. Something was manifesting in the bedroom. I think the lights have something to do with these two other experiences. I had never noticed lights in the bedroom before. On the night I was paralyzed, Ginger had heard something moving around in the house and the hallway leading to our bedroom. She investigated and found nothing. I had a severe headache that would not go away for more than a week after the September 8th incident.

"There has been a lot of activity in our house lately, and I assume it is tied to these events," I said.

"Anything else you need to bring forward at this time?" Yvonne asked.

"The *Snarc* comic book may have something to do with it…scenario is that the reptilians are the bad guys; maybe they do not like it. Maybe they're letting me know that?" I said.

"Maybe they want their own comic book?" said Yvonne. I smiled.

"I really feel that these experiences were a warning to me. A reminder that I might think I have control, but I do not. The aliens can do whatever they want to do, a menacing thing or a helpful thing," I said.

"It is rare to encounter reptilians," said Yvonne.

"The bug doctor, the praying mantis or Jerusalem cricket alien, he was not as scary, he was just academic, scientific, condescending, and clearly in charge mainly through his intellect," I said.

My final thought about this was a memory of what happened to me in Chicago at the sight of the murder hotel where I encountered the frightful Dr. H.H. Holmes.[65] When I was pushed and driven to the ground, I felt equally helpless and almost paralyzed, but it was a lower-level current of electricity, but still caused me almost to give up. I overcame that devilish encounter with mental will power as well. Interesting parallels perhaps?

I talked to Anzar on November 3, 2019. I asked for advice about my writing, radio show interviews, and upcoming Contact in the Desert lecture in May 2020.

"Tell the truth, boldly, unapologetically, people will choose to believe or not believe, but you have done your job," he said.

"What should I cover?" I asked.

"Phasing in and out, the surreal aspect, ghosts and aliens, similar, that is the key, cover how that would work theoretically, and what does it all mean," he said. I immediately thought of my friend Dr. Edwin M. Young, a brave researcher who has paid the price for daring to challenge the system. Dr. Young, a scientist who ran a psychic research lab at Stanford University in the 1970s, created a device that proved psychic energy exists and told me that "matter vibrates constantly in and out of our reality. Matter is a condensed form of energy that is guided by mind focus and powered by spirit."[66] I am not a scientist, but that pretty much sounds like the unified theory of everything that scientists have been looking for. And this fit in nicely with what Anzar said about phasing in and out.

"What would you want to do if you were the aliens, contacting a less advanced civilization?" Anzar continued. I thought about the human perspective, our history and what it shows. From a human historical example based on colonization, I would suspect that some aliens would help, some would be protective, some would be parental, maybe even overbearing, others would intervene, some would exploit and take advantage, others would heal and protect us, still others might be neutral and just observe. Would not all those different motivations be basic to any sentient lifeform?

"What is the basic motivating principal, derived from the Godhead? Is it not love? If it is not, then what would it be? That is the question you must answer. The day of full knowledge and disclosure is coming whether you are ready or not. I cannot give you an exact date because it depends on a lot of things," said Anzar.

"Is the recent statement by NSA whistleblower Edward Snowden helpful or deception?" I asked.

"Deception, look who is harboring him, and who could kill him if he said the wrong thing. They are not benevolent. They obfuscate, confuse, and throw you off track in order to keep you from receiving the truth. To discredit and stop disclosure, you attack the messenger not the message," Anzar added emphatically. I began to think about what people would ask me about Anzar. Would men in black show up?

"What if they ask for complete information on you?" I asked.

"I am the original contact, the Progenitor. I give humans nudges," he said. Anzar's use of the word nudges cracked me up. I do not pretend to know everything, and I do not even know why I was chosen, but it is a huge honor and a tremendous responsibility. Frankly, it would be easier to live my life without this information and knowledge.

"An aspect of you is an aspect of me and an aspect of all. Perception and reaction drive the disclosure process," he said as our communication ended.

Assessment

It might be helpful to return to a skeptic's view once again. According to physicist Dr. Lisa Randall, "Exotic phenomena might indeed occur. But such phenomena will happen only at difficult-to-observe scales that are increasingly far from our intuitive understanding and our usual perceptions. If they will always remain inaccessible, they are not so interesting to scientists. And they are less interesting to fiction writers, too, if they won't have any observable impact." There is truth to what she is saying here. Real scientific evidence of psi and UFOs is available, but the results are not as dramatic as the movies (high definition with surround sound and cue the suspenseful music). People expect Harry Potter magic and Steven Spielberg special effects and are disappointed with the modest but real results produced by psi researchers and scientists. She goes on to say: "Weird things are possible, but the ones non-physicists are understandably most interested in are the ones we can observe... Scientific ideas might apply to regimes that are too remote to be of interest to a film, or to our daily observations, but they are nonetheless essential to our description of the physical world.[67] This is the challenge. How do you make the general public aware of these remarkable paranormal events if they do not understand what they are looking at or even how to look at it? No one knows for sure, and those that say with great confidence that they do, are probably wrong. As Mark Twain purportedly said: "It ain't what you do not know that gets you into trouble. It is what you know for sure that just ain't so."

So, what is the connection between ghosts and aliens? Well, since the spirit world is the quantum world, as far as I can tell, it makes sense that advanced alien beings would know this and operate in that realm. On September 8, 2019, I asked Anzar why nobody sees aliens eating and drinking? Simple answer, "Because they are contacting you in the spirit world in a higher level of consciousness, so there is no eating or drinking," he said.

"What about people who have physically seen aliens?" I asked.

"Yes, both in spirit and in physical form. Mostly you are seeing them in a spirit form, that is how you are usually contacted," he said. Since matter can vibrate or phase in and out of our reality (according to my scientist friend Dr. Edwin M. Young), aliens and their spacecraft could be seen in physical form. On that same day, early in the morning, a female reptilian entered my dreams masquerading at first as my mother to gain my trust. The reptilian was powerful and was able to lift me up against the wall with ease. It was a warning, she wanted me to know that she did not like what I was doing (speaking and publishing).

"I can do whatever I want to you. You have no power here," she said. It is likely that because aliens can phase in and out of our reality at will, they can also enter our dreams. We are seemingly helpless. Despite that, we must have something they want, something not easy for them to obtain, otherwise, because of their advanced technology and skills, they would take what they want and leave or simply get rid of us.

In her book *Extraterrestrial Contact: What to Do When You've Been Abducted*, Kathleen Marden, Director of Experiencer Research at MUFON, wrote: "Did you know that UFOs, NHI entities, and paranormal phenomena have a lot in common? They appear to possess interdimensional properties. UFOs have been observed phasing in and out of view. NHI [non-human intelligence] entities have the ability to pass through solid surfaces and simply show up in the homes of experiencers. And paranormal phenomena have been observed by the vast majority of experiencers. It is no wonder the UFO books are categorized as 'Paranormal' in bookstores."[68]

When I was a kid, I thought we lived in the belly of a giant, and that people lived inside of my belly, and so forth and so on. I believed that the world was both infinitely small and infinitely large. Watching the 1957 movie *The Incredible Shrinking Man* one Saturday afternoon reinforced this belief. I think that conception helped me understand the interconnectedness and wonder of the universe. I have always allowed my imagination to guide me in exploring consciousness. My occasional startling sense of self-awareness is a reminder that I am alive and connected to everything, all the time.

Physicist Dr. Jack Sarfatti, in an interview with Dr. Jeffrey Mishlove on the video series *Thinking Allowed*, discussed quantum physics and consciousness. He described three levels of reality: Level 1, Level 2, and Level 3. Level 1, what physicist David Bohm called the explicate order, is classic physics, matter, and normal space-time as we experience life. Level 2, what Bohm named the implicate order, is the quantum-level reality, where non-sentient and non-conscious thought-like patterns of information guide Level 1 matter outside of space and time like the Force in *Star Wars*. Level 3, called the super-implicate order by Bohm but not fully developed by him, is the deepest, what we call consciousness or the mind of God, and comprises the sentient conscious universe.[69]

Astrophysicist Dr. Rudy Schild and the late Dr. Edgar Mitchell (the 6th man to walk on the moon) and the majority of the Dr. Edgar Mitchell Foundation for Research into Extraterrestrial and Extraordinary Encounters (FREE) Board of Directors, believe that "diverse 'paranormal contact modalities' (e.g., UFO related contact and contact via near-death experiences [NDEs], out-of-body experiences [OBEs], hallucinogenic substances, mystical meditation travel, channeling, remote viewing, sightings of spirits/ghosts and orbs, and other reported human encounters with NHI) are interconnected through what is commonly called consciousness and that advanced physics, in particular, the quantum hologram theory of physics and consciousness, can begin to describe the possibility of how all of these diverse 'paranormal contact modalities' are indeed interrelated with the UFO contact phenomena." [70] The quantum hologram theory of consciousness (QHTC) is a multidimensional reality within which humans are having contact with NHI in multiple formats or contact modalities. The QHTC provides for the possibility that "all of these contact modalities are not separate phenomenon but instead part of one interrelated phenomenon…a complex phenomenon that can potentially be explained by the physics of an all-pervasive multi-dimensional quantum hologram." [71] In other words, I believe Sarfatti, Bohm, Schild, and Mitchell are confirming my hypothesis that the spirit world, the alien world, and the quantum world are one in the same.

Men plan, God laughs. That is from an old Yiddish proverb. You cannot let being psychic go to your head. Many psychics and remote viewers have reported that even with their great skills and insights, it is often very difficult to gain personal information on yourself. There could be many reasons for that: wishful thinking, delusions, emotional attachments, or it may be a case of not being able to see the forest for the trees. We stand at the leading edge of a profound paradigm shift in understanding our place in the universe and it is becoming ever clearer that things may get worse before they get better. As the old system gives way to the new, institutions and concepts that have guided us for centuries will crumble and be replaced. I can't help but think of how advanced Gene Roddenberry's thinking was in his conception of the *Star Trek* universe. He introduced tablet computers, tractor beams, tricorders, flip phones, hypo-sprays, replicators, cloaking devices, voice interface computers, Bluetooth headsets, portable memory storage, biometric data tracking, GPS, automatic doors, big screen displays, real-time universal translators, teleconferencing, and diagnostic beds. Most importantly, *Star Trek* promoted the idea of working together (all races, ethnicities, genders, aliens and humans) to solve problems and go where no man (or human) has gone before. In the episode entitled "Is There in Truth, No Beauty," Spock wears an IDIC medallion to honor a visitor on the Enterprise. IDIC means infinite diversity in infinite cultures and in that episode, Spock further elaborated on its meaning: "The glory of creation is in its infinite diversity and in the ways our differences combine to create meaning and beauty."

In a Pew Research Center poll taken in August 2009, 18% of people surveyed had seen a ghost. In a Gallup poll taken in August 2019, 16% of people surveyed had seen a UFO. It is not just coincidental that the percentages are roughly equivalent.[72] Time will tell as full disclosure approaches, but evidence points to the fact that the paranormal world, the alien world, and the quantum world are one in the same. A quantum nexus. I am reminded of physicist David Bohm's take on time: "Ultimately, all moments are really one, therefore now is an eternity."[73] I believe that now is the moment, and I see it as my mission to prepare people for that moment. That is essentially what my friend Gene (who died in 2016) told me about the afterlife when I asked him what it was like to be dead.

"I do not think of myself as dead. I am talking to you, right? Here there is no past, no future, it is an eternal now." That would be confirmation as far as I am concerned.

"It is all true, all of it," Gene added. I now know what he means as the big picture is coming into view. Returning to our research question, can the UFO subject be fairly characterized as paranormal? I must answer, yes. UFOs and alien contact are paranormal, but eventually they, along with apparitions, telepathy, precognition, telekinesis, and other psi phenomena, will be considered normal. We must stand ready, all of us, together.

Figure 4: Anzar as he appeared in 1997.

Figure 5: Author's alien abduction.

Figure 6: Author's integration with Anzar.

PART TWO

MY SPIRIT WALK COMMUNICATION

Spirit Walks, 2018

I started taking meditative spirit walks on June 10, 2018. The following section represents the spirit walk journal I have kept as it relates to Anzar. Going back through these journals has made me realize how the passage of time is relative–this last year under lockdown, especially so. Each time I walk, I ask for protection from my spirit guides and God and then usually talk to my mom and dad and my friend Gene.

On Saturday morning, October 27, 2018, I made contact with Phil Schneider, who was a former government contractor and engineer. Phil claimed to have worked at secret underground military bases including Dulce Base where he supposedly survived a battle between humans and aliens. He was found dead in his apartment in Oregon in 1996, two years after he started giving public talks about his clandestine experiences. The circumstances of his demise were suspicious, yet his death was declared a suicide by strangulation.

''Hello, Phil, I've heard about you. Were you murdered?'' I asked.

"Yes," was his answer.

"By whom?" I asked.

"Government and the aliens," he said. I asked him about my dreams of reptilian aliens.

"They are on to you," he said.

"What do they want?" I asked.

"DNA and your connection to the Progenitor," he said.

Oh great, I thought, *what can I do?*

"You can't put the genie back in the bottle, stay in limelight, don't be alone. We all want the truth," he said.

"You're ok now?" I asked.

"Yes. Stay in the light," he said.

November 12, 2018, on a dark early morning, I asked my friend Gene to confirm that I had indeed been contacted by aliens.

"Contacted, yes," he said.

"Implanted by aliens like my friend Terry Lovelace?" I asked.

"No," he said. Okay.

"Was my Aunt Walborg (my Nazi aunt)[74] involved with aliens?"

"Yes," he said.

"I talked to the Progenitor in 1997[75], could my spirit guides and you help me talk to him again?

"Yes, go ahead," he said.

"You said you were the original mystic. Am I related to you?" I asked.

"Yes," said the Progenitor.

"So, we're all hybrids?" I asked.

"Yes," he said. I asked the Progenitor, since we are hybrids, what alien race we were. I had trouble understanding him. It sounded like he said Assyrian.

"Any advice or wisdom?" I asked.

"Follow the hand that points to love, and redemption, then the world is saved, and you will stand protected," he said.

On a hazy, cool Saturday morning on November 24, 2018, I asked my spirit guides and Gene to put me through to the Progenitor again.

"I worry about this alien stuff. What more can you tell me about it?" I asked.

"Remain on guard," Gene said.

"Thank you. I'd like to speak to the Progenitor, if I could," I asked. I waited a few moments before making the connection.

"Were you the original alien contact on Earth?" I asked.

"Yes," said the Progenitor.

"You helped early humans become who we are today?" I asked.

"Yes," he said. I became very excited and could barely contain myself.

"What is your name?" I asked.

"Anzar," he said.

"Where do you come from?" I asked.

"Orion, Rigel," he said.

"What is happening now?" I asked.

"About to be revealed, stand ready, on guard, stick to the truth, trust your friends and family. In anxious times people seek the comfort of those who are calm and rational," he said. Almost as if to demonstrate Anzar's point, a frantic couple stopped their car on the side of the road to ask me for directions. I had to laugh after the couple sped away.

"In 2019, it will be revealed that contact has been going on," added Anzar.

I had a vision late in the evening on November 27, 2018. I saw nine beings of pure light energy and I believe Anzar, in one of his manifestations, was one of them.

"Why are you here?" I asked.

"The message is coming," they said in unison.

"What message?" I asked.

"Be ready," was their response.

"Are we in danger?" I asked.

"Only from within. Stay in the light and trust God and your spirit guides. Truth will follow. Love. Acceptance. Triumph," they said.

"What do you mean danger lies within?" I asked.

"Your soul and spirit are the source of power. Do not let others take them. God wants you intact. Receive the light of God," they told me.

Pearl Harbor Day, December 7, 2018, and I was on my spirit walk. It was an early morning, chilly, with fresh air from the recent rains. I asked my spirit guides and Gene if the Progenitor was a good guy. They acknowledged that he was and that he was from Rigel and that the grey aliens had made some sort of deal with our government.

"What else can I do to increase and improve the level of my mediumship and psychic abilities?" I asked.

"Concentrate your attention. Know that it will happen," they said.

"Attention and intention?" I asked.

"Yes. Focused calm. Trying days ahead, in our country, and in the world," Gene said.

"I will do my part, and I'm strong in body, mind, and spirit. When are they coming?" I asked.

"They are already here," said Gene.

"I would like to speak to the Progenitor again. I want to help humanity. What else should I be doing?" I asked.

"Keep going. Be aware. Stay on the path. Realize how unique you are. Focus your energy and your determination. Train others for the future. You will know who is on the side of the light and who is not," said Anzar the Progenitor.

On a semi-cloudy, cool morning, first day of winter, December 21, 2018, I spoke to Anzar on my spirit walk.

"Anzar. What more should I be doing?" I asked.

"Caution, proceed with caution, help people understand and prepare. It will be audible when it happens, the big reveal. Visual will come later," he said.

"Audible from who?" I asked.

"You are the consciousness, be one with the consciousness, rise to the highest level of your expectations and then exceed them, there is no boundary, no limit, except for those that are self-imposed or imposed by others, which you can ignore," he said.

I took another spirit walk on December 23, 2018, on what the Norwegians call "*lille julaften*." It means, little Christmas Eve. It was sunny and the temperature was mild.

"Approbation," said Anzar without me asking a question. I was not sure what that meant. I later found out that it means official approval or commendation.

"Can you guys tell me more about disclosure?" I asked.

"Yes, it will happen, evidence will be revealed, first by speaking, then by visual. Stay with the forces of light. It is all tied together, everything that you have learned, religion, paranormal, supernatural, aliens, all tied together. All tied to the one, all from the one, the one consciousness," he said.

Walking on a Boxing Day, December 26, 2018, and it was a sunny, bright, late morning.

"The other day I asked for advice and you mentioned approbation. What does it mean exactly?" I asked.

"You have validity, value, permission, and approval to make these connections," said Anzar. I turned to my spirit friend Gene.

"Been thinking more about the alien stuff, which race is Anzar?" I asked.

"Arcturian," said Gene.

"So, you guys all operate in the same spiritual realm? Is that what they use?" I asked.

"Yes," said Gene, "and they're all aware of you," he added. Anzar stepped in.

"Hard to predict the future because you do not know which future you will be in. You do not know which fork in the road of time you will be on in your physical manifestation. What is true in one manifestation would not be true in another. Too many variables. Difficult to know. There are many different things you must think about, but always remember, everything will be okay," said Anzar. My mind was successfully blown.

In the late morning on a partly cloudy Thursday, December 27, 2018, and after asking my spirit guides to raise my vibration and elevate my level of consciousness, I once again contacted my ancient alien mystic advisor, Anzar.

"Anzar, are you there?" I asked.

"Yes. compatibility," said Anzar.

"What do you mean? My friends? Rh negative descendants of aliens?" I asked.

"Yes," he said.

"How can my friend Terry protect himself? Does it have something to do with religion?" I asked.

"It is not about being religious, it is about your belief and acceptance of the one consciousness. God, the Creator, and tapping into the one consciousness. That's what will protect you," he said.

"Can you give me any more advice?" I asked.

"When you see what is not there, you will see what is there. When you were a child, you could see the air, the molecules in the air, moving. What you are told not to see is what you should see," he said.

"I see it, I see the connection," I said as I looked up at the clouds and gazed at the mountains.

I took my spirit walk on a beautiful, late, sunny Sunday morning, on December 30, 2018, and Anzar spoke first.

"Hello," said Anzar.

"Hello! Thank you for speaking to me. I asked which alien race and you said Assyrian, then Arcturian? Which one?" I asked.

"Combination," he said.

"Okay. The picture I drew of you is accurate?" I asked.

"One of my appearances, been around a long time," he said.

"Am I getting just little bits of info at a time to not overwhelm me?" I asked.

"Yes. There is much more," said Anzar.

"When will the reveal be?" I asked.

"March 2019, more than likely,"[76] he said.

"Trust your connection. Flow with it, like a stream, let the great consciousness flow," he added. I was confident that I would be successful and keep growing my knowledge and wisdom so I could help.

January 10, 2019, and it was a cool, sunny Thursday morning. I decided to reach out to my ancient alien advisor, Anzar.

"Hello," I said.

"Hello," said Anzar.

"These signals, fast radio bursts, is this what you meant by audible sign first from aliens," I asked.[77]

"Yes," said Anzar.

"So, the visual is coming?" I asked.

"Yes. Prepare, acknowledge, secure, protect," he said.

It looked like it was going to rain on a cool, cloudy morning, January 12, 2019. After seeking protection and greeting my spirit guides, my parents, other relatives, and my spirit friends Gene and Maia, I turned my attention to Anzar.

"Greetings," said Anzar.

"Thank you, Anzar. I was looking up the Arcturians and they are said to be from the Boötes constellation, but you said you are from Rigel in Orion. How can you explain that?" I asked.

"Although I am Arcturian, I am from Rigel and Orion," he said.

"This idea of time travel…you said it's totally possible in the spirit realm that you operate in. So, if I get into the meditative state, can I travel in time?" I asked.

"Yes. Let the light envelop you and it will carry you throughout time and throughout space. That is the key. The master key," he said.

I decided to take my spirit walk on a rainy Monday morning, January 14, 2019. My spirit guides helped me connect to Anzar. Eventually, I should be able to make a direct connection every time.

"Thank you for all your wisdom and support," I said.

"You are welcome," said Anzar.

"The space rock or asteroid, Oumuamua, is that connected somehow to the fast radio bursts?" I asked.[78]

"Maybe," said Anzar.

"Is that the visual?" I asked.

"It is not the visual, but it is a sign. Comes in little pieces at a time. It is connected but not directly connected to fast radio bursts. A series of events will take place," he said.

"So, you are Arcturian and Sirian in origin but grew up near Rigel in Orion?" I asked.[79]

"Yes," he said.

"Could I see you now?" I asked.

"It is up to you," said Anzar.

"Yes, I would like to see you. I see your eyes are open," I said.

"Be cautious, be clever, speak the truth, stay in the light. Enveloped by the light, guided by the light," he said.

"Thank you, Anzar," I said.

On a cool morning, January 16, 2019, I took my spirit walk. A rainstorm was coming in as I thought about the school shooter lockdown we had the day before. No one was hurt, but I was locked down with 44 students for six hours in our classroom. I had dreams and nightmares and premonitions about this happening for some time. I was ready to check in with my ancient alien spiritual high advisor, Anzar.

"Thank you, Anzar, for taking the time. I hope I'm not bothering you," I said.

"No, I am here to help," he said.

"I have a request from my friend Terry who was abducted by the greys. Is there anything more that we or he can do to advance the cause of the light?" I asked.

"Control. Do not lose control," said Anzar.

"Control of what?" I asked.

"Control of your destiny. Control your destiny," he said.

"Is there more he can do?" I asked.

"The outreach is good, keep speaking, keep talking, believing, supporting others, you are doing the right things, honoring your friend, sticking to your principles. I am proud of you both," he said. That was comforting to hear.

"Bravery is knowledge and conviction," he added.

Three days had passed since our school shooter lockdown on January 15, 2019. The storms had come and gone, and it was a sunny day with only a few silvery-white puffball clouds. On my spirit walk, Anzar spoke to me.

"The light is your salvation, the light is the truth, the light is your destiny, blessed is the light," he said.

"Thank you, Anzar," I said.

On my 7th wedding anniversary, January 20, 2019, I spoke to Anzar and Leon, my Native American spiritual advisor, on a sunny Sunday morning.

"Thank you for speaking to me and I appreciate the connection, guidance, and wisdom on my spiritual journey," I said.

"Self-reliance and love, always approach everything with love, guidance from the Creator is the love we feel," said Leon.

"Enveloped by the light, staying in the light, encircled by the light, guided by the light. Your protection," said Anzar.

74

On a sunny, cold Wednesday morning on February 6, 2019, I was taking my spirit walk. I was still going over in my head the details of the lockdown at my school. I was more impacted by the incident than I had previously thought. My friend Terry's reports of UFOs and helicopters was also of great concern to me.

"Hello, Anzar," I said.

"Was I correct that helicopters and UFOs near Terry's house were government assets and alien spacecraft?" I asked.

"Yes," said Anzar.

"So, they're monitoring him?" I asked.

"Yes," he said.

"Anything else you can tell me to help prepare?" I asked.

"Train yourself. Be patient with the hard work of training. Provide protection," he said.

"Was the vision I had two nights ago of the candlelight in a dark wind significant?" I asked.

"Yes, symbolic of what is going on. You must protect the light. Resurgence of darker powers. They are preparing too," said Anzar. It was a frightening thought, but when I thought about it, what choice did we have?

"The unbelievable will happen if you believe it," said Anzar. It was becoming clear to me that my job, my mission, and the mission of other experiencers, was to help minimize the suffering of others in this transition to a new world. All it would take to be brave enough to face the challenge was knowledge and conviction, as Anzar had told me before.

I spoke to Anzar again on February 15, 2019, on a sunny Friday. I had become a more careful observer by that time.

"Is it my imagination or are media and government types trying to disparage people who believe in aliens and contact?" I asked.

75

"They are actively doing it, stick by the truth," said Anzar.

"Advice?" I asked.

"Absolute, absolution through light, permanent light, and joy and happiness," he said. I understood that forgiveness is essential. If you cannot forgive yourself, you cannot forgive others and it would be difficult to keep love in your heart.

Monday, February 18, 2019, President's Day, and it was sunny, cool and crisp as I took my spirit walk. I noticed how green the hills and mountains were—the greenest I have seen in 21 years of living in Southern California.

"Hello, Anzar," I said.

"Hello," he said.

"I've been reading a lot about aliens and where they come from—there are many arguments in the UFO community. I believe 'we are the aliens,' as Gene said, and you confirmed. What should I say during my interviews on radio?" I asked.

"Preparation, the light, remind them of the light, work together," said Anzar.

"I will put more effort into remote viewing," I said.

"Yes, and sanctity of the home, stress sanctity of the home, be safe," he said.

"I want to help Terry, documenting, each of us," I said.

"He is being monitored. Both aliens and the government," said Anzar. That was not the first time that Anzar told me that. He also mentioned that I was monitored.

February 22, 2019. It was a Friday morning, the skies were blue, and it was sunny, but cool. An idea popped into my head as I started my spirit walk. I was not sure if it was from Anzar, but it might have been. Love is the answer, but be careful because there are those who do not believe in love.

"Hello, Anzar," I said.

"Hello," he said.

"Who is there with you?" I asked.

"Ascended masters," said Anzar.

"Okay. What are you all thinking?" I asked.

"Good will triumph over evil, but evil will be strong, and there will be many losses," he said.

"Okay, that's frightening. When does all this begin?" I asked.

"It has begun. Kindness and compassion," said Anzar.

"Toward perceived enemies as well?" I asked.

"Yes, because the good nature of people will side with you in the struggle, the goodness will show through, the love will show through. Never let hate blind you in battle, you may have to fight, but always keep the light, and stay in the light, and you can never go wrong," he said. Often times what Gene told me meshed nicely with what Anzar told me. Gene reassured me that the most interesting parts of life are yet to come. "It will be remarkable, stimulating, and out of this world," he said.

It was a rainy, grey, cool Thursday morning on the last day of February 2019. Walking in the rain reminded me of growing up in Seattle.

"Hello, Anzar," I said.

"Hello," said Anzar.

"Couple of questions, if you're not too busy," I said.

"Always busy," he said. I laughed.

"Who else speaks to you? Are there others?" I asked.

"No," he said.

"So, I was chosen?" I asked.

"Yes. I am for you."

"Thank you, I'm honored," I said.

"The MILABS or whatever they're called. Does our government monitor and abduct experiencers?" I asked dreading a positive answer.

"Yes," he said.

"Is that what happened to my cousin Berit?" I asked.[80]

"Yes," said Anzar. I felt bad about not believing her many years ago.

"Reach out to her," he said.

"What is their purpose?" I asked.

"Power, power, power," he said.

"And the To the Stars Academy (TTSA)? What is their mission?" I asked.[81]

"Monetary, power, and enlightenment," said Anzar.

"Do they work with the government?" I asked.

"Oh yes," he said.

"You don't speak to them or the government or anyone else?" I asked.

"That is correct," he said.

"I'm just one person, these are celebrities, government types, powerful people." I said before Anzar cut me off.

"What do you teach your students?" asked Anzar.

"One person can make a difference," I said.

"It has been demonstrated. That is your mission. Help through your books, and teaching, help them understand what is going on. This year is when contact realization is happening," said Anzar.

I took my spirit walk on a cool, cloudy Friday morning, March 1, 2019. It smelled like rain was coming. I was told about a very high-level psychic who works for the US government. I cannot mention his name. In fact, I was also told that if you searched for him under his real name, you would likely get a rather unfriendly visit from one or more of the three-letter agencies.

"Anzar and all my spirit friends, can you tell me something about this psychic, Mr. X? Is he really that high-level?" I asked.

"Yes, he is like Pat Price, but he is a prisoner," said Theodora, my guardian angel. Then, I heard another voice, not one of my spirit guides, and not Anzar. It was Mr. X.

"My life is not my own, and my travel is restricted. I wish I could be free," said Mr. X. I always thought how great it would be to be the world's best psychic, but maybe I was wrong.

"I'm sorry, Mr. X. Anzar, what do you say?" I asked.

"Learn from what happened to Mr. X. He is the government's highest value psychic asset," said Anzar.

My friend Terry had posed a question to Anzar. "Is a catastrophe imminent that we should prepare for?" I asked.

"Yes, in several months, yes. Be prepared, have resources, time-line could be off, store resources, one months' worth. Stick close to friends and family," said Anzar.

"Anything more about Mr. X?" I asked.

"He is being used and has no choice now. Draw that lesson. You must maintain a balance between hysteria and complacency. Warn people, but do not make them freak out," said Anzar. It made me chuckle to hear Anzar say "freak out." My spirit friend Gene wanted me to warn his family and prepare.

March 3, 2019, was a cloudy, cool Sunday afternoon for my spirit walk. It looked like it was preparing to rain with low cloud cover. I warned many of my friends of coming catastrophes but did so in as calm a manner as I could muster. I am sure some of them thought I was crazy, but that is okay.

"Anzar, you and all the other spiritual advisors say a catastrophe is coming," I said.

"Yes, absolutely. Within the next few months, but hard to say exactly, lots of variables. Preparations are definitely in order," said Anzar.

"Do I need to get a generator?" I asked.

"Yes. Medications. Plan and communication," he said.

"Any more specific information?" I asked.

"Multiple, not just one catastrophe, multiple things happening," said Anzar.

"What region?" I asked.

"Worldwide. Alien contact, reveal, natural disasters, political and economic turmoil, internal conflict in America as well. Not going to be an orderly transition of power if President Trump loses, potential for it not to be peaceful," said Anzar.

I took a spirit walk on Thursday, March 7, 2019, and it was a cloudy, cool morning. As I entered into my meditative state, I focused on the misty San Gabriel Mountains. Friends of mine wanted to know if the MUFON organization is okay.[82]

"Anzar, is MUFON involved with the government?" I asked.

"Some of the people in the organization are involved. They are often correct, sometimes off track, some are to be trusted, some are not," said Anzar.

"Should I present at one of these conferences, MUFON, MEGACON, or others?" I asked.

"Yes, but be careful because there are government agents there and others, possibly aliens," he said.

"Some are saying that the near future looks very dark," I said.

"Not as dark or black as some think, but still significant in a cumulative effect, not one incident, a series of incidents, over time. Preparations needed. People will need calm, reassuring voices, and their spirituality," said Anzar. I was beginning to get nervous.

Sunday, March 10, 2019, an overcast day, and it may rain. After setting up my protection for the spirit walk, Anzar spoke to me.

"Bridge the divide, you are the bridgebuilder, heal, bring people together, you can do it," he said.

"Thank you, Anzar. What do you think of the dire warning my scientist friend sent me?" I asked.

"Still maintaining that catastrophes will come within a few months, cumulative things, piling up. Complications will arise, look for solutions from the past that have worked and apply them," he said.

"Who is plaguing my friend Terry? Government and the aliens?" I asked.

"Yes, they are interested in him as we draw near the contact point," said Anzar. I wondered what would happen.

March 12, 2019, was a partly cloudy, crisp Tuesday morning. I was ready to contact my ancient alien spiritual high advisor, Anzar.

"My friend Terry says hello and thank you. What is the purpose of the helicopters and UFOs around his house?" I asked.

"Observation," said Anzar.

"Couldn't they observe him without being so visible?" I asked.

"They want him to know he is being observed," he said.

"Intimidation?" I asked.

"Yes," said Anzar.

"What should he do? Continue to speak and write?" I asked.

"Yes, and so should you," he said.

"Thank you. Any other tips, or information you can give me?" I asked.

"Be smart, be wise, look before you leap, offer the world love. Alleviate suffering," said Anzar.

"What do you think of my *Snarc* comic?" I asked.[83]

"Yes, and I like the greeting 'be the light,'" said Anzar.

"Ginger thinks I'm Snarc," I said.

"Of course, you are," said Anzar. That made me laugh.

My son Leif and I saw a UFO in the evening about 9 pm on March 14, 2019. This may have been the first one I have seen since I was a kid. It was in the southern sky and was moving erratically so it was not an airplane or a satellite. It was too high to be an airplane. Occasionally, little darts of light would quickly shoot off at lightning speed. Leif saw a green beam of light come from it as well. My film of it was shaky and hard to determine scale and details. It pulsated and had a peculiar diamond shape.

The next day, the Ides of March, I took a spirit walk.[84] It was a sunny Friday morning. I wanted to talk to Anzar.

"Can you confirm that was a UFO last night?" I asked.

"Yes, absolutely," said Anzar.

"Who was it?" I asked.

Silence.

"Anzar? What alien group?" I asked again. "You aren't saying. That is interesting. Were they here to help?" I asked.

"Yes, they were here to help," he said.

"What were the fast-moving things?" I asked.

"Other spacecraft," he said.

"What was the green beam of light?" I asked.

"Healing and protection," he answered.

"So, they're here to try to help with the calamities?" I asked.

"Yes. For the good of all living things. Snarc's capabilities, plus alleviate the suffering of others, your primary purpose," he said.

"What else can I do?" I asked.

"Get the *Snarc* comic out, to help people, not polemic, not preachy, but touching," he said.

"Yes, I will do that. What changes will I see in myself now that I'm working on this connection?" I asked.

"Clarity, increased interdimensional thinking, intelligence, management of temperament, physical strength," said Anzar. My spirit guides and my spirit friend Gene confirmed that the calamities and catastrophes had begun. Like the highway deaths, they add up slowly, so you do not notice it (e.g., climate change).

Sunday, St. Patrick's Day 2019, and it was a very warm late morning. I was still debating whether or not to have a hypnotic regression. My spirit guides were divided.

"How many of my paranormal adventures have involved ETs?" I asked.

"Quite a few," said Anzar.

"I know I'm part ET, but independent of that?" I asked.

"Many of them, at least a component of it," he said. I felt a compulsion to look at the sky every night, especially the past three weeks. I can see again what I have not seen since I was a little kid.

"Any repressed memories that you can help me with?" I asked. I remember when I was younger loving to sleep outside under the stars, hiking to the Enchantment Lakes, Salmon La Sac, and camping at Lake Kachees.

"Was I abducted?" I asked.

"No, not really," said Anzar. My other spirit guides disagreed, and one of them said it was attempted. I wondered what that meant. There was more than I could ever imagine involved here with UFOs and aliens, spiritually, scientifically, philosophically, and historically. I felt ready and was overcoming my fear of being hypnotized so I can fulfill my mission and see the bigger picture. My seeing a UFO with my youngest son Leif was part of the visual that Anzar mentioned.

March 22, 2019, Friday, the sun was out, the hills were green for a change, and it was a great day for a spirit walk.

"Anzar, can I speak to you?" I asked.

"Yes," he said.

"Now, you told me you were the original alien contact for humans on Earth. When was that in Earth time?" I asked.

"Your first contact was nearly six million years ago," he said.

"Was that Australopithecus?" I asked.

"Yes, and others before that, that is when it began," said Anzar.

"Did they have language?" I asked.

"Yes, we started it," said Anzar.[85]

"So, you had contact with Homo erectus, Neanderthal, Cro-Magnon?" I asked.

"Yes," he said.

"What was life like for our ancestors?" I asked.

"They understood the astral world, paranormal world, spirit world—that was part of their life," said Anzar.

"When you first approached these protohumans, what was their reaction?" I asked.

"As you might imagine, shock, then I befriended them and taught them. I gave them gifts," said Anzar.

"Like fire?" I asked.[86]

"Yes, and different techniques and skills, but not too much at a time," said Anzar.

"So, while you were doing this, other alien races were interacting too?" I asked.

"Yes, later, many came not to help but to enslave. I have stood as the protector of life on Earth since that time," said Anzar.

"Thank you. As far as the warning goes, will I see more UFOs?" I asked.

"Yes, many. Because, as your friend Gene says, experiencing is believing and believing is experiencing. In the next few months, information will continue to be unveiled, lies will unravel, people will panic, and they will need comfort and help," he said.

"Thank you for everything you do for all of us. Just to be certain, the alien, quantum, and spirit worlds are one in the same, right?" I asked.

"Oh yes! Stay on the path, continue your work, help family and friends, alleviate suffering," said Anzar.

My spirit walk on March 27, 2019, was on a hazy Wednesday morning.

"Anzar, how are things?" I asked.

"Busy," he said.

"On March 14th, we saw a UFO. Who was it? Arcturians? Was it you?" I asked.

"Yes and no," said Anzar.

"They were here to help and guide us?" I asked.

"Yes. Calamities will be lessened. Some will still occur," he said.

"What message should I carry forward to people?" I asked.

"Peace and light," he said. It sounded simple enough, but I really had no idea how difficult the next two years would be.

Ginger and I attended the UFO Megacon in Laughlin, Nevada, on March 30, 2019, and stayed for a few days. We met the USS Nimitz and Princeton sailors who had witnessed UFOs off the coast of Southern California.[87] They were clearly shaken by the events. Jeffrey Mishlove gave a lecture about the use of psychic powers by Ted Owens, the PK man—a Shakespearean tale if there ever was one.[88] I knew I was in the right place.

April 4, 2019, was a cloudy, cool Thursday, with a rainy mist coming down. I thought about the Dr. Martin Luther King, Jr. assassination that occurred on that day, 51 years earlier.[89] I had scheduled my hypnotic regression with Yvonne Smith, and I wanted to confer with Anzar.

"Anzar, I'm going to do a regression with Yvonne Smith, what advice do you have?" I asked.

"Be cautious, stay focused, stay calm, it will be good for you," he said.

"What more can you tell me about the UFO we saw on March 14?" I asked.

"It was a healing process," said Anzar.

"I'm assuming one of the natural disasters coming is an earthquake," I said.

"Yes," said Anzar.

"I need to get a generator," I said.

"Calmness, everybody should remain calm, and be kind," he said. Easier said than done. Ever since watching *Time Tunnel* as a kid I have thought about having knowledge of an event before it happens. How can you warn people without causing hysteria or make preparations without being classified as a kook?

The next day, April 5, 2019, I took my spirit walk on a sunny Friday, but with rain clouds approaching. The birds were tweeting loudly, which is generally more pleasant than human social media tweeting. I thought about my hypnotic regression appointment tomorrow with Yvonne Smith. I wanted to explore the 1977 incident that began near Mel's Hole in Eastern Washington. I remembered something odd, a swirling combination of conscious memories and fragments of subconscious ones. I watched a TV show last night about the Starlight Ranch in Arizona. The show gave me flashbacks to aliens, little dark ones, on my back, which kind of gave me a jolt.

"Yes, those are contacts, but not abductions, because you are well-protected," said Anzar.

"Why am I so protected?" I asked.

"Because of your mother. Be prepared. It is not about being right it is about being helpful. Lots of variables involved," he said. I suppose Anzar was talking about the coming calamities. I turned to Leon, my Native American advisor, and wanted to ask him about a medicine man named Red Elk.

"Hello, Leon. Did you know Red Elk?" I asked.

"Yes, here he is," said Leon.

"Leon left your world in 1958," said Red Elk. That was the year I was born, by the way.

"Lots of Native Americans have given me advice over the years. I respect native peoples, my mom taught me," I said.

"Listen to them, preparing, preparation in the spirit comes first and then in the physical world. Start by helping your family, friends, then the rest," said Red Elk. Red Elk had told the story of encountering the mysterious bottomless and paranormal Mel's Hole when he was younger.

On April 6, 2019, I had my first hypnotic regression with Yvonne Smith. We focused on my 1977 road trip with my friend Ernie.[90] The hypnosis was great, and Yvonne was so nice. One day later, on April 7, 2019, a message came to me as I was lying in bed awake: it was a reunion. I asked for clarification from Anzar, even though I was not on my spirit walk.

"An abduction means you were taken unwillingly, but you were willing…because you are a hybrid, so it is a reunion," said Anzar. I was a bit perplexed as to why Anzar would be so tricky, but then I thought that I only have a small piece of the puzzle.

"I suppose you don't want me to have all the knowledge because it might spin me off kilter, but I'm ready," I said defiantly.

"Are you really?" asked Anzar as he smiled knowingly. I shrugged my shoulders, suddenly feeling less confident. "Black birds in your 1977 adventure represented the aliens, and they led you to Black Pine Peak in Idaho," said Anzar.

"What happened to my friend Ernie?" I asked.

"He was abducted," said Anzar.

"Was he experimented on in a ship?" I asked.

"Yes," he said.

"Was I with them in the ship?" I asked.

"Yes, you went willingly," said Anzar. All of this was so astonishing that I had to check in with my spirit friend, Gene.

"Is this all true?" I asked. Just after I asked him, I remembered what he told me when he first came to me in a vision after his death in September 2016, that "it's all true," and "we are the aliens." Gene always had a way of explaining things that got right to the point.

"Is it so hard to believe one more miraculous thing when you already believe in so many extraordinary things?" asked Gene. He was correct; I had to push beyond the boggle point.

On April 8, 2019, I had CIA dreams all night. I was helping them, but on my own terms. Very frustrating. Four days later, I had another intense dream where I stood with massive crowds of people as we noticed many black pillar clouds reaching down to earth all around us near the horizon. Above our heads were government airplanes, flying low. A man next to me said that the planes had magnetometers in their bellies. Someone else said that this was all caused by the bombing. Suddenly, a message came to me that there was a "global reset" in 1979.

On my daughter Caitlin's birthday, April 14, 2019, I took a spirit walk on a sunny Sunday morning. I asked Anzar to help me improve my mediumship so I could help people.

"Confront. Confronting the truth, and there will be push back," said Anzar.

"I'm not afraid, Anzar, can I get an update on the calamities and catastrophes that you said were imminent?" I asked.

"Still imminent, get a generator," he said.

"What more can you all tell me about experiences in 1977?" I asked.

"Your memories, recovered or not, are valid and they are yours," he said.

"To confirm, was I ever teleported or taken into an alien ship willing or otherwise?" I asked.

"Yes. You must be sure you can handle it and not be afraid. There will be those who say you are insane, but you are not. It was a reunion; try not to think of it in a negative way," said Anzar.

"How about my cousin Berit?" I asked. Yes, taken several times. She was very negatively affected by her experiences," he said.

"I have developed a theory that the spirit world, quantum world, and the alien world are the same thing," I said.

"Yes," Anzar said. I was certain that I would have more experiences, and even accept that I have a role to play, but I need a baseline of understanding first.

"Do not doubt yourself or give in to despair," he said. It is strange, but no matter how many paranormal or ET experiences you have, there is always a lingering doubt that creeps in. I think that is natural to be a little bit skeptical whether it is about the experiences of others or about your own. That skepticism allows you to remain grounded.

On April 15, 2019, I had tornado dreams again. We were living in a ranch style house in a flat area, very suburban. My children were little. The neighbors in my dream kept saying: "I can't believe we're having tornados here." A few days later, I asked Anzar for more clarification about my contact in 1977 and 1978 and the upcoming calamities.

"Any more updates on calamities?" I asked.

"They are underway," said Anzar.

"I tried to make contact with the praying mantis guys in the chamber that Ted Owens the PK Man talked about. Is it possible, doable, advisable?" I asked.

"Yes, and no. Yes, if ready, no if not ready. Be careful what you wish for," said Anzar.

I took another spirit walk on Friday, April 19, 2019, on a beautiful Easter weekend morning. Last night I dreamt about red numbers

7345, not sure what it means. I will have another hypnotic regression with Yvonne Smith tomorrow.

"Anzar, what is the significance of the tree symbol that I have seen and that my friend Terry talked about," I asked.

"You are reaching to the heavens and you are firmly planted in the ground and taking sustenance from the air. It is a perfect example of balance, standing strong, and the fractal structure of nature as well—the great mystery," he said.

"Thank you. I've heard discussions about whether aliens are good or bad. Some say they are some say they aren't, what does it mean?" I asked.

"Because you are part alien, a hybrid, just like so many others on Earth, it is not so easy as to just say good or bad," said Anzar.

"Is there a way to increase my telekinetic and telepathic powers?" I asked.

"Your friend Simeon has already given you that answer.[91] You are as psychic as you need to be," said Anzar. I guess I needed to be more patient.

On Saturday, April 20, 2019, I had my second hypnotic regression session with Yvonne Smith. We talked about my contact experience in my brother's garage in June 1978.[92] The most difficult aspect of that session was realizing that I had attempted suicide and had blocked that memory. The next day, Easter Sunday, I illustrated what I saw after my hypnotic regression, then I took a spirit walk.

"What do you think, Anzar?" I asked.

"It is what I have said before, you are a hybrid," he said. I wrote about my four alien contact experiences in 1964, 1973, 1977, and 1978, in my three *Timeless* books, but it may be this book, focusing on my continuing contact with Anzar, that turns out to be more significant. However, my *Snarc* comics may be the most revealing because they are shrouded in a fictional wrapping.

On April 26, 2019, while sitting at my working desk, I heard a weird song noise like from a phone, but nobody has such a noise on their phone here. Then, the house started to shake, and a split second later, everything reset in a flash. The thought, hard reset, came into my mind. In the week following this incident, Anzar told me that the drawings I did of him were correct and to not be afraid to keep pushing and exploring. He reminded me that the disclosure process is happening, and I was being monitored along with my friend Terry. In our discussion of good and bad aliens, Terry mentioned soulless aliens. I had to bring it up with Anzar.

"Anzar, are there soulless aliens?" I asked.

"Everything comes with a price…there are good aliens, yes," he said. His response gave me pause.

"You have a powerful soul," he said. Although it was high praise, especially coming from Anzar, it struck me that having a powerful soul would attract the attention of soulless aliens.

On my spirit walk, May 10, 2019, which was a sunny Friday on a Mother's Day weekend, I spoke to Anzar once again.

"Can you give me an update on the coming catastrophes," I asked.

"Memorial Day…there is something about Memorial Day," he said. Interestingly, and tragically, one year later, on Memorial Day, May 25, 2020, George Floyd died in police custody while being arrested which led to protests and riots throughout the United States and internationally for months.

"Praying mantis doctor. What about him?" I asked.

"It happened, it was real, processing, special processing, a hybrid check-in, check-up, and reunion," he said.[93]

"Just to confirm, when was my first contact with alien beings?" I asked.

"In this lifetime…age four," said Anzar.

"So, my angelic experience in Norway at age four was also an alien experience?" I asked.[94]

"Yes," said Anzar. I always thought it was just my guardian angel, but apparently there is more to the story, layers within layers.

"What do you think of Mike Masters' book?[95] Are aliens and UFOs actually future humans using a time machine?" I asked.

"Some, others are from distant galaxies, a combination. We are all the aliens as your friend Gene has said many times," said Anzar. I like the fact that Gene and Anzar are in communication. In fact, on Mother's Day, May 12, 2019, a beautiful, sunny Sunday morning, I spoke to my friend Gene during my spirit walk.

"Anzar is the original contact on Earth, the one who made us who we are, and the original seed. There are other ETs who want the connection you have to Anzar," he said. I wanted to feel special, but it is not about that, it is about responsibility, and not my ego. A few days later, I woke up after feeling that I received a massive information download. The only thing I remember is that it had to do with five alien races and how time changed that night. In fact, the whole world shifted and changed.

On Friday morning, May 17, 2019 (Norwegian Constitution Day), I took a spirit walk and spoke to my ancient alien spiritual high advisor, Anzar.

"Anzar, how about the download? Who did the download come from? Was it terrestrial or alien?" I asked.

"Alien," said Anzar.

"Did it come from you?" I asked.

"Yes and no. I authorized it," he said.

"Does it have something to do with five alien races and a reset or change in the time continuum?" I asked.

"Yes, a protection shift. Those of us who are protecting the planet had to make a shift. More will come as you are ready," said Anzar.

The next day, May 18, 2019, I took my spirit walk on a sunny Saturday morning. I had war dreams again last night. There was heavy bombing all around me, shaking the earth, and taking my breath away and pounding my eardrums. I saw rails in the sky dumping bombs. Very bizarre.

"What can you tell me about the situation in Iran?" I asked.

"This is all part of what I have been warning you about. The forces of good and evil. Unfortunately, this conflict may be a necessary thing…some type of armed conflict," said Anzar.

"What is going to happen?" I asked.

"Lots of variables, looks like American forces are positioning themselves to neutralize Iran, and eliminate the threat. Be ready for ramifications," he said.

I had an early morning dream on May 23, 2019, there was flooding everywhere, of biblical proportions. The next day, May 24, 2019, I talked to Michael Masters, the author of *Identified Flying Objects*, and told him what Anzar said about future humans and aliens. I wanted to learn more about my download experience from a few days ago so I contacted Anzar.

"Anzar, what about the download stuff?" I asked.

"Five alien races. Some of the information was technological, like interstellar travel. I was preparing for my interview on *Coast to Coast with George Noory*, so I checked in with Anzar.

"What is going on?" I asked.

"A lot of good things going on, but challenges lie ahead," he said.

"Anzar, on *Coast to Coast AM* they will ask me lots of questions about you. So, you're an ancient alien mystic, the first contact here on Earth, the one who planted the seed, from ape to man?" I asked.

"Yes, absolutely," said Anzar.

"Upcoming catastrophes?" I asked.

"They are coming, the catastrophes are coming. The reveal is coming drip by drip," he said.

"Thank you, Anzar. What do you think of Michael Masters?" I asked.

"An enlightened human being. We are all the aliens, and you are our descendants. There are others too, that is the challenge and the threat. The ones who planted you here are protecting you," said Anzar, and then the connection ended. It made me wonder who are the others and what did they want?

May 26, 2019, was a rainy, cool Sunday. I spoke to Anzar and my spirit guides as I made my way on the wet sidewalks.

"Preparation," said Anzar.

"Yeah, I think I am prepared," I said.

"Disaster…do you know how to do a tourniquet?" asked Anzar.

"Why are you asking me that?" I asked. There was no answer.

"Kind of scary. I'll be as prepared as I can be," I said. Yeah, I know. The rest of my spirit walk I made contact with Dr. Stanton Friedman, who had recently passed.[96]

"All must be forgiven. Work together, not divided, listen to each other, learn from each other, love one another. We have a piece of the puzzle, but you can never put a puzzle together if you hold on to your pieces, and do not work together," he said. He told me that he cares for all of us in the ufology community and realized our courage. He told me to just keep going. The next day Anzar told me that Dr. Friedman was enlightened.

On May 28, 2019, early in the morning, reptilians came into my dreams and were quite menacing. They told me: "We are watching, and nothing can stop us." Apparently, these reptilians are the others that Anzar warned me about. A few days later, Ginger and I were at the Contact in the Desert conference in Indian Wells, California.[97] I had a fascinating dream with a man in a black robe with dark hair and a beard. He had crystal blue eyes and there was a large, humming triangular ship over the hotel. He was neutral, not bad, or good, as far as my gut told me. I now know his name is Ergot.[98] During a hypnotic regression group I attended with Yvonne Smith, I remembered looking out my back window from my bedroom in the house I grew up in and saw a golden spaceship. I now know that the alien being I encountered who showed me the spaceship and saved me from a child predator was Anzar.[99] I have to say that this was a lot to process for me.

On June 3, 2019, I took a spirit walk on a warm Monday afternoon and connected with Anzar.

"At Contact in the Desert, what do you think was the most important thing I experienced?" I asked.

"The understanding of the division and how this whole thing works. There are those who use it as a religious experience, others the scientific aspects, and for many, the experiential nature of the event," said Anzar.

"The UFO community needs more scholarly studies, maybe I can provide that?" I asked.

"Yes, but be yourself," said Anzar.

"What should I focus on for my *Coast to Coast AM* interview—personal experience, theoretical models, and how the three worlds are really one?" I asked.

"It is all connected," said Anzar.

"What about the guy at Contact in the Desert who said the protons in our cells are mini black holes?" I asked.

"There is some truth to that," he said.

"What about the different government disclosure theories?" I asked.

"Look at the disjointed nature of your government. Do you think they can have a coordinated disclosure program?" asked Anzar. A few days later I had a dream where we were all lined up by the government, for what purpose I was not sure. It was very inefficient. I believe the government is too inefficient and uncoordinated to deliberately plan and implement an extended disclosure and reveal of ETs and UFOs. They are disjointed, as Anzar said, with one department not knowing what the other is doing. It is up to us, ordinary people, to make this move along, but to do so, we must have attention and intention.

It was June 7, 2019, a June Gloom Friday morning, when I took my spirit walk and connected with Anzar.

"Hello Anzar and everyone. I didn't bring up my Nazi aunt story, had a mind blank, on *Coast to Coast AM* last night," I said.[100] "My déjà vu just now, was it a glimpse of the infinite?" I asked.

"Yes," said Anzar.

"Spiral is what it is?" I asked.

"Yes, that is it," he said. He was able to clarify the role that Ergot played in saving me in 1964. A few days later, on my eldest son Bjørn's birthday, I talked to Anzar again.

"Anzar, anything more you can tell me about catastrophes, or information about aliens coming out?" I asked.

"You are needed, your special skills, the shows, writing, and teaching—it will help," he said. Later on that day, Ginger and I were making final preparations for our trip to Albuquerque, New Mexico, so I could be interviewed by Jeffrey Mishlove.

We returned home to California on June 22, 2019, and I took a spirit walk the next day. It was Sunday, late morning, and it was sunny. Ginger and I had a great trip to Albuquerque, then to Roswell, and then we made our way home. In Deming, New Mexico (a border town) I talked a security guard into letting us tour a warehouse where immigrants who had been apprehended crossing the border were housed. It was not what we imagined. The facility was clean, they were not in cages, kids were playing soccer, they had cots, and plenty of food and water. I have worked in prisons, and this was not a prison. The people looked tired, but grateful. They had all been through a lot getting to America. They were waiting for their sponsors to pick them up.

"Anzar and Ergot, what do you think the next thing released will be?" I asked.

"Aliens are real," said Anzar.

"Have I ever been implanted by aliens?" I asked.

"Yes," he said.

"Okay. Where are they?" I asked.

"You will find out," said Anzar. I smiled and laughed nervously. My friend Terry had X-ray evidence of his implant, but I can only guess where mine might be, if I still had an implant. It is not like you can go to your family doctor, or in my case the VA, and ask them to X-ray your body in hopes of finding an alien implant. I would end up in the psych ward.

I took another spirit walk on June 24, 2019. It was a late, sunny Monday morning on Valley Center Avenue where I make my connections. I had seen a UFO the night before that blinked in and out.

"Hello Anzar. What about the UFO the other night near Cal Poly Pomona, in the western sky around 8 pm. Was it an ET craft?" I asked.

"Yes," he said.

"What about what I saw over the forest fires in Arizona?" I asked.

"Unknown," he said.

98

"Anzar, do I hear my own voice or other people's voices when I do mediumship?" I asked.

"They are all different voices. All separate voices," said Anzar.

"So, I keep telling people that it is all the same realm, spirit world, quantum world, and the alien world," I said.

"Yes, it is telepathy, part of the spirit world," he said.

"Michael Masters says UFOs and aliens are actually future humans, time traveling, and you've all told me that is part of it," I said.

"Visitors are here for many reasons, from many places, future humans, ETs, just like any transitional space or tourist area. Some are here for good reasons; some are here for not necessarily good reasons," said Anzar.

"Makes sense. Can you show me more spaceships, like show me one over the mountains now?" I asked. I watched but did not see anything, but I know they are out there all the time, just like ghosts.

During my Thursday morning, June 27, 2019, spirit walk, I asked Anzar about a friend of mine.

"Hello, Anzar. One of my friends is in touch with Mr. Z who is a government official closely tied to the UFO phenomena. He has been told something. What do you think it is?" I asked.

"They are aware," said Anzar. I assumed he meant the government is aware of continuing alien contact and are actively engaged.

"What more could I be doing to prepare for what you confirmed?" I asked.

"Networking, keep writing, be ready for interviews, and contact. Your friend is the spokesperson, you are among the support personnel, or ground crew," he said.

"I just want to help, I know my role, calm heads prevail. Keep calm, guide them, including my friend, since he is on the leading edge and needs support," I said.

I took a spirit walk on July 3, 2019, Wednesday, Ginger's birthday. I know it will be a serious uphill battle trying to show to scientists that aliens exist and that we are the aliens.

"What can I do to help people understand?" I asked.

"Present an alien," said Anzar.

"Easier said than done, I'd imagine," I said. I knew that Anzar liked to joke around with me sometimes, and this was one of those times. The classic demand by debunkers is that for them to believe in aliens and UFOs, a spaceship would have to land on the White House lawn and aliens would have to disembark and greet us, all documented by television news cameras. I seriously doubt that would happen. I once heard N. Scott Momaday, a Kiowa author, say that "…it has to be believed to be seen." He was talking about the mythic West in America, but I believe it applies to the case of UFOs and aliens.[101]

On a warm, hazy Friday morning July 5, 2019, I took my spirit walk. I had just received a fascinating note from a friend.

"Hello, Anzar and everyone. Thank you for always being with me," I said.

"Hello," said Anzar.

"I got a note from my friend, he talked to Mr. Z who told him that the government UFO program is ongoing, and he was still in charge. Their mission was threat mitigation, identification, and release of information. Mr. Z and a top scientist had briefed the president," I said.

"Yes, I know, you will be involved sooner or later," said Anzar. I know that ETs are real, but the government will not say officially. I know my job, I need to do my survey, use social science tools, and keep writing. My spirit friends think that the social science approach will work well, especially because of the public interest in the ancient alien mythos. If I could produce Anzar and Ergot, that would be fantastic. But I have to remember that it is not about me, I have a role to play, a support role.

"Anzar, what can you tell me about Russia, Korea, and China?" I asked.

"China wants to be the number one power," he said.

"Can we stop them or mitigate the damage?" I asked.

"No, you can only prolong the inevitable," said Anzar. The world seemed to be much more dangerous now than when I was younger.

I took my spirit walk on a hazy, sunny Sunday, July 7, 2019. It was time again to connect with Anzar.

"Thank you for always being here for me. What can you guys tell me about the President's briefing with Mr. Z and the scientist?" I asked.[102]

"The President is being coy. Much of what he does and says is being misperceived. The most selfish man in the world will give humankind its greatest gift," said Anzar. I assumed that Anzar was talking about President Trump releasing information about aliens and UFOs, but maybe as it turned out it was his push to develop a COVID-19 vaccine at lightning speed and his development of the Space Force. Now, to be clear, Anzar and I are not Trump supporters or partisan in any way, but this all seems quite interesting. My friend said Mr. Z and a top scientist met with the president in May or June 2019, and then the president formed the Space Force in December 2019. Operation Warp Speed began on May 15, 2020, and the first vaccine (Pfizer) was approved for emergency use on December 11, 2020, less than seven months later. A typical vaccine development timeline is five to 10 years, and sometimes longer.[103]

On July 9, 2019, it was a strange night, and I did not sleep well. I had the feeling that something was going on in our room. I saw a silvery white orb in our bedroom moving from the northeast corner to the center before vanishing. I dreamt that I received an information package download from the aliens as did many others. I asked Anzar the next day about the orb.

"Anzar, the orb I saw the night before last, do you know what it was or who it was?" I asked.

"It is not bad," he said.

"Was it an ET or terrestrial spirit, or what?" I asked. I did not get an answer, so I asked my spirit friend.

"Hey Gene, what do you think?" I asked.

"He does not know, I do not know everything either," said Gene. I suspect it was a terrestrial spirit and not harmful.

On July 13, 2019, I took a spirit walk on a sunny Saturday morning. Ever since the dream of a download and the orb experience, I was feeling rather strange.

"Ginger thinks there may be an earthquake Sunday or Monday? What do you guys think?" I asked.

"Be prepared. Good likelihood. More things are going to happen in the next month," said Anzar.

"I'm feeling restless. Is that why?" I asked.

"Yes. Be prepared," said Anzar.

"How big will the earthquake be on Sunday or Monday?" I asked.

"Maybe 7.6, might be two of them," he said. As it turned out, there was a massive 7.3 earthquake in Indonesia on July 14, 2019.[104] Even though Anzar always says predictions can be wrong, this one was quite accurate.

On a cloudy, warm Friday morning on July 19, 2019, I once again contacted my ancient alien mystic advisor, Anzar. As I started my walk on Valley Center Avenue a thought came to mind: Try to make the outside inside and the inside outside. I am perceived as the kind, gentle, wise person on the outside, and I am increasingly becoming that, but I want to make sure the outside encompasses the inside as well. Yin and yang. It is an interesting concept making my inside what

I portray on the outside, a balance. I was pretty sure this idea was coming from Anzar.

"Anzar, Ergot, and Gene, what do you guys think?" I asked.

"Yeah, sure, do it," said Gene.

"You guys are funny. Am I on to something, seriously?" I asked.

"Yes, yin and yang," said Anzar. Some people have contacted me after I've been interviewed on the radio. They act as if I am a guru, but I am not a guru. I once heard it said that the number one job of a guru is to make sure their follower does not need a guru.

"What about this idea of expectations being a problem?" I asked.

"Yes, complaints, expectations, entitlements. Do not just be right, be helpful. Position of power and authority is coming based on success, be ready," said Anzar.

"Propulsion antimatter, is that information correct?" I asked.

"It is correct, just one mode, there are others too. Time wave gravity travel. In and out of dimensions, vibrating in and out of your reality. Think of what you learned about translational lift in flight school or catching a wave while surfing. You can catch a time wave," he said. That made me think of my favorite Marvel comics character, the Silver Surfer. The Silver Surfer was created by comic book legend Jack Kirby and first appeared in the comic book *Fantastic Four* number 48 in 1966. At age 15 in 1974, I illustrated and wrote a comic book (never published) about a character I called Oryan, a four-dimensional galactic warrior, who rode a celestial surfboard. He was battling an alien who had enslaved the people of Earth. I have been fixated on the constellation of Orion my whole life.

On a sunny Saturday morning, July 20, 2019, I had a conversation with Anzar as I took my spirit walk.

"Anzar, what is Mr. Z not saying?" I asked.

"Tip of the iceberg, they know a lot more, but they do not know about me. They are working with ETs, have been for some time," said Anzar. Later, I continued the conversation.

"Was Bob Lazar telling the truth about alien reverse engineering at Area 51. Element 115 propulsion?" I asked.[105]

"Yes and no. He might not understand what he saw. Some truth to what he says. His drawings are essentially correct, but he may not understand how it works," said Anzar.

On Saturday, August 3, 2019, I was scheduled to have another hypnotic regression session with Yvonne Smith. I had nightmares every night for almost two weeks after starting the CPAP machine prescribed by the VA in July for my serious sleep apnea. Recently, I received a transfer of information and energy as I slept. I remember something about a Frisbee analogy that I cannot completely recollect. I also had a nightmare about an insane relative who died and came back to life and was trying to kill us. Later, this same day, a man killed 23 people in a Walmart in El Paso, Texas. A slight synchronicity I suppose.

In my session with Yvonne, I was able to retrieve memories about meeting Anzar the first time and the frightening story surrounding our contact.[106] The next day, on my spirit walk, I spoke to Anzar and my spirit friend Gene.

"What can you tell me about my session yesterday with Yvonne?" I asked.

"It's all true," said Gene.

"Who is the tall alien with the narrow, slanted eyes?" I asked. No answer.

"Is he Anzar?" I asked.

"Why wouldn't it be?" said Gene. Gene was smiling and I had to laugh. So, it was Anzar. The alien who stepped in to rescue me was Anzar, one of his manifestations. Thank you, Anzar. This was the story about the alien who rescued me from a pedophile in 1964 as documented in "Big Bad John," in *Timeless Trinity*.

"To recap, the image I had of the tall alien with narrow slanted eyes in 1964 was you, Anzar?"

"Yes," said Anzar.

"And Ergot, was that who you assigned to me?" I asked.

"Yes," said Anzar.

"You showed me the ship?" I asked.

"Yes. And remember, you know what will happen in the future because you manifest it," he added.

August 14, 2019, two days after what would have been my mom's 100th birthday, I took a spirit walk. It was a sunny, warm Wednesday morning.

"Hello Anzar and Ergot. I always say hello from Terry to you, Anzar. Is it true that Terry and others who have been abducted and implanted produce electromagnetic effects on electronic devices?" I asked.

"Yes," said Anzar.

"Have I been implanted?" I asked.

"Yes," said Anzar.

"Do I still have them?" I asked.

"Yes and no," he said. I was not exactly sure what that meant, but it made me think of my hydrocelectomy surgery in 1981 at the Land-stuhl US Army hospital. In the summer of 1981, while I was stationed at the US Army Confinement Facility in Mannheim, West Germany, one of my testicles became severely swollen. The prison doctor thought I had cancer. A hydrocele is a fluid-filled sack surrounding the testes, that can be caused by inflammation, from injury, or a block-age in the spermatic cord. It usually happens to infant males and is rare in adult males, with only one percent of them getting a hydrocele.[107] I cannot help but wonder if the hydrocele could have formed because of an alien implant.

"Anzar, as far as the warnings go, what is happening?" I asked.

"Still in motion, things are happening, the economy, the power grid, panic, and climate change. I will do everything I can," he said.

"I think my *Snarc* comic will help. Any more about my theory that alien world, spirit world, and quantum world are all the same?" I asked.

"Yes, they are. It is that simple and that complicated," he said.

"So, you guys are with us, all the time?" I asked.

"Yes, you just cannot see us, most of the time," he said.

August 25, 2019, was a fascinating day. During my sunny, early Sunday morning spirit walk, I contacted Anzar and my spirit guides.

"I want to demonstrate superposition and nonlocality for my paranormal class by having my students close their eyes, then open them again while I move to a different location in the room. They do not know where I will be, so they need to calculate probability. They can only confirm when they open their eyes. The observer effect. Is this a good way to demonstrate this?" I asked.

"Yes," said Anzar.

"Anzar, what Jacques Vallee says sounds like what I say and what you have taught me. Is he right?" I asked.[108]

"Yes, he is right," said Anzar.

"Will you speak to us today in the CERO meeting?" I asked.

"Yes," he said. What happened next, was almost beyond belief. After our CERO meeting, in which I had asked Anzar to attend, I asked the gathered members if anyone saw anything with me. One lady saw a man and a woman. When she described them, I figured out that she had spotted my spirit guides, Theodora and Ozzie. But then, Luci said she saw something that looked like a giant figure of a Native American Kachina doll. The "big guy," she called him. When I told her that the giant figure was Anzar, she was shocked and showed me her driver's license. The street she lived on was Via De Anzar (the way to Anzar).[109]Although Anzar did not speak to the CERO group, he was seen by Luci which provides me with validation of his existence. Having Luci actually see Anzar was an absolutely mind-blowing experience.

I had an alarming nightmare on August 28, 2019. We were near some seashore and were witnessing gigantic rogue waves pounding the land. My family and I were trying to climb up a cliff to get away from the monster waves. We were able to enter a building that was high above the beach, but then the atmosphere was ripped apart by powerful explosions that rocked the whole world and shook the building knocking us off our feet. In the aftermath, it was dark except for a fiery, smoggy sunset. Someone whispered, "superweapon."

A few days later, Monday, September 2, 2019, I took a spirt walk. It was Labor Day, the day before my birthday.

"Hey Anzar, thank you for everything, and hello from Terry too. You guys know about the marks above my right ankle? Bug bites or some type of ET contact thing?" I asked.

"Both," said Anzar.

"Interesting, but I don't remember anything," I said.

"Yes, the big questions, the big questions…There is the one Creator, the one consciousness," he said.

"What else can I do to prepare and prepare the people?" I asked.

"Space angels, all of this has led to this moment and every other moment," said Anzar. I was intrigued and hoped to learn more about space angels.

I woke up after a startling nightmare on September 8, 2019. A female reptilian, first posing as my mother, shapeshifted into her true form, picked me up and threatened me. I was frightened and aroused at the same time.[110] I was shaken up but was able to take my spirit walk that morning.

"Anzar, why does nobody see aliens eating and drinking?" I asked.

"Simple answer, because they are contacting you from the spirit world in a higher level of consciousness, so they do not eat or drink," he said.

"So, people who have physically seen aliens?" I asked.

"They are seeing them in a spirit form, that is how they contact you," said Anzar.

"I understand. What type of propulsion do you use?" I asked.

"You are seeing them after they enter into an interdimensional vortex, no need for any mechanical/physical propulsion," he said. His answers were simple and elegant.

I took another spirit walk on a warm Thursday morning, September 12, 2019. I was still quite shaken up from my encounter with the reptilian.

"Anzar, can you tell me more about my dream with the reptilian female?" I asked.

"A warning," he said.

"Is my family in danger?" I asked.

"No," said Anzar.

"Me?" I asked.

"Possibly," he said. *Oh, great*, I thought.

"While I was half awake last night, I heard a voice whisper 'temporal distortion.' When we see aliens and spirits, is that how it works?" I asked.

"Yes, all the same thing, naturally," he said. Then, my friend Gene chimed in.

"We have everlasting life and do what we like for the rest of eternity," said Gene. That made me feel better after the disconcerting reptilian experience.

During my spirit walk on Friday, September 20, 2019, I asked Anzar about our relationship.

"Anzar, thank you for helping me and watching over me. Luci told me that you and I are one in the same. Is that true?" I asked.

"We are related," said Anzar.

"Aren't you related to everyone on Earth as the Progenitor?" I asked.

"Specifically, to you. A gift of sight, and the connection," he said. I then brought up the concept of integration that Luci had talked to me about. I was worried about having to check out of my life now in order to integrate. I was also afraid of no longer being an autonomous entity. Anzar told me that I would be one with the ancestors. He assured me that I would be okay. We also discussed the concept of temporal distortion, and time travel.

"It is really simple, distort time, move like a snowplow in every direction," he said. I could picture what he was telling me.

"Do not be sad. Be happy. Everything turns into a great reward. All the joy you give in life comes back a million times in the afterworld," said Anzar. I felt privileged to be discovering these things and communicating with him.

In the evening, after our CERO meeting on September 22, 2019, I woke up suddenly and felt like I was being electrocuted. I could not move any part of my body. Earlier in the evening I felt like there was somebody in the room and I heard weird thumping sounds. I was finally able to break free from the paralysis as the electrical current switched off. I was fully awake while this was happening. Some would say that I was experiencing sleep paralysis, but I know it was something else.

Toward the end of September 2019, I talked to my spirit friend, Gene. I was writing an article for MUFON.

"Are UFOs paranormal?" I asked.

"Of course, it's paranormal," he said as he laughed. That was funny. A week later I had another natural disaster dream, this time it was a volcano. In this nightmarish scenario I was driving dangerously fast on mountain roads trying to find Ginger and escape the volcano. The next night, October 3, 2019, I saw a silvery white light, rectangular this time, move from the ceiling to the floor in front of our TV in the bedroom. This happened at about 3:00 am. On my spirit walk, I contacted Anzar.

"Anzar, tell me more about the integration Luci was telling me about," I said.

"Integration to a higher consciousness," said Anzar.

"I guess I want to make sure that I'm not going to be terminated in this existence in exchange for that integration," I said.

"Do not worry," Anzar said.

On October 13, 2019, I was on my spirit walk. It was a sunny Sunday morning. The day before, I had a UFO sighting in the northwest sky over the San Gabriel Mountains, while I was running at the track. I also had another hypnotherapy session yesterday.

"The nightmares, the orbs, the UFO, what's it all mean?" I asked.

"It means what it is, you are being contacted, warned, threatened, helped, and everything in between," said Anzar.

"I would like to do more to help the world transition. Integration is important and I want to do it so I could understand more easily what you're trying to tell me," I said.

"It is what it will be," said Anzar.

"I just don't want to leave my family and friends behind at this critical time," I said.

"You will not," he said. Anzar then said that I would need to translate something.

"Translate, what? What you're about to say? Part of the integration. Okay, hang on a minute. Yes, I'm willing to do that," I said.

"A message to everyone. Aht tomay enjon potoma elegon fornay toot kankee bomm wanjee," he said.

"Almost sounds like Chinese. What does it mean?" I asked.

"You find out," he said.

"Okay, I will listen to it again and try to figure it out," I said. I plugged it in to Google translate and the language that came up in the partial translation was Bengali. The first few words mean: "injured to you," then other words separately translated as "boiled," and "bomb," and "engine," respectively. That sounded somewhat ominous.

"Big responsibility," said Anzar.

"Any advice?" I asked.

"Stay on fence, between ultra-religious, ultra-skeptical, you have to be the bridge. Not an easy job. Keep it wonderful, our world, do not waste what you cannot replace," said Anzar.

"What does the reptilian woman want from me?" I asked.

"She wants you to stop," he said.

"Do you want me to stop, Anzar?" I asked.

"No. You must keep going and help Terry and everybody else, be the bridge like the one Heimdall protects," said Anzar.[111]

"The Rainbow Bridge, I will. I see you, by the way; I can see why Luci thinks you look like a kachina," I said.

"Depict me as you wish," he said.

On October 16, 2019, my son Byron's birthday, I was driving home from the Sandburg track when I contacted Anzar.

"We must prevent catastrophic injury to the Earth," he said.

"Thank you, Anzar. We means all of us?" I asked.

"Yes," he said.

"That was a dire message. Please show Ginger a UFO or alien or both so she can believe me more," I said.

"Okay. This idea of phasing in and out of your reality from this dimension, that is why it is so hard to see proof in actual photos—unless they crash or get caught manifesting into your reality. That is the issue," said Anzar.

On October 19, 2019, I went to sleep at 9:00 pm and then woke up at 11:23 pm and was not sure of what was going on, almost like I was drugged. I woke up again in the morning at 4:30 am on October 20, looked at my CPAP machine readout, and it showed that I had only slept for 6 hours 16 minutes. That means that there was 1 hour and 14 minutes of unaccounted for time. Ginger had heard something strange in the house around 15 minutes past midnight, like there was someone moving around.

It was a hot Thursday afternoon on October 24, 2019, when I took my next spirit walk. I was hoping to find out more about my missing time from October 19.

"Hey, Anzar, Ergot, what do you think of Ed Snowden saying that he saw no evidence of UFOs and aliens in NSA files," I asked.[112]

"Not surprising, he did not have access to everything," said Anzar.

"True," I said.

"We do not know if he is a reliable source either," he said.

"True, you're right. And he is living in Russia so he might not be able to speak freely," I said.

"Yes," said Anzar.

"What do you guys think of the reptilian lady and the drawing I did of her?" I asked.

"Good drawing, accurate," said Anzar.

"What do they want with me?" I said.

"They want Snarc," he said. I assumed they wanted me to stop the *Snarc* comic because the reptilians are the bad guys in the story. And because Ginger thinks I am Snarc, this gives me even more concern. I was also worried about how I felt when I woke up in the middle of the night on October 19.

"What about my missing time thing the other day?" I asked.

"Another attempt, not totally successful," said Anzar. I was glad for that. I then noticed Gene pop in to talk to me.

"What do you think, Gene?" I asked.

"Yeah, they know you're part of it. That's true. You should expect it," he said. Wonderful, it is difficult to get a good night's sleep knowing that aliens might attempt to spirit me away. It is not that I am afraid, it is just that I need my sleep.

On a sunny Sunday, November 3, 2019, it was warm, and the air was cleaner. I was still recovering from a cold.

"Hey Anzar, I want to make an impact and do good. What can I do to help and how can you help me?" I asked.

"Tell the truth, boldly, unapologetically, and people will choose to believe or not believe, but you will have done your job," he said.

"What advice, or topics?" I asked.

"Phasing in and out of your reality, the surreal aspect, ghosts and aliens, it is all similar, that is the key," said Anzar.

"How would that work theoretically, what does it all mean?" I asked.

"What would you want to do if you were one of these aliens, contacting a less advanced civilization? Use your human perspective, your history. Some would help, be protective, parental, healing, maybe overbearing, and intervene. Then, there are others who would exploit, and take advantage. There are those who are neutral, who leave humans alone and observe. All those different motivations are basic to sentient lifeforms," he said.

"I get it," I said.

"What is the basic motivating principal derived from the godhead? It is love. If it is not, what would it be? That is the question. The day of full knowledge and disclosure is coming, no exact date, depends on a lot of things," said Anzar. I always assumed the godhead referred to the Christian concept of the trinity (father, son, and holy spirit), but I believe Anzar was talking about a broader interpretation meaning the essential and divine nature of God or the one consciousness.

"Is the statement by Snowden helpful or deception?" I asked.

"Deception…look at who is paying his bills, and who could kill him if he said the wrong thing. They are not benevolent; they obfuscate, confuse, and get you off track to keep you from receiving the truth. To discredit and stop disclosure, they attack the messenger not the message," said Anzar.

"So, I think I understand the concept of remote viewing, all based on quantum mechanics and spooky action at a distance. I think that is the arena I use to stay in communication with you, Anzar," I said. I was doing a lot of interviews and was concerned about how I would

114

describe Anzar. "What if they ask for complete information on you?" I asked.

"I was the original contact, and I gave a nudge, and still give nudges," said Anzar. That made me laugh.

"I don't pretend to know everything, and I don't know why I was chosen. It is an honor, a responsibility, because I think it would be easier to live without this information and knowledge," I said.

"An aspect of you is an aspect of me and an aspect of all. Perception and reaction," he said. I walked a bit further and then opened up communication with Anzar again.

"Anzar, what did Mr. Z tell my friend?" I asked.

"He told him that this started three weeks ago. It was not surprising that the Edward Snowden comment came out. Things are ratcheted up. Expect more counterintelligence, misinformation, and bits of information," said Anzar.

"Is Philip Corso right, and telling the truth?" I asked.[113]

"Yes. There may be others too, not just him," said Anzar. As I acknowledged Anzar, a helicopter flew low overhead.

"Do those helicopters have anything to do with my communication with you?" I asked.

"What do you think? Yes, you are being monitored, Terry is being monitored," he said. I had to be careful not to think that every airplane and helicopter that flies over my house is somehow part of this. That could lead to paranoia.

On November 10, 2019, it was a warm Sunday morning when I took my spirit walk and communicated with Anzar, Ergot, Gene, and my spirit guides, Theodora, and Ozzie. My friend talked to Mr. Z, four weeks ago, and was told that it had started, and that a global conflict was coming. On one side is the United States and our ET allies, and on the other side are the dark forces, reptilians, and their minions. It reminded me of *Lord of the Rings*.

"What can you tell me, Anzar?" I asked.

"It is coming, as I warned you, cataclysms, be prepared, support Terry, stay together, stay in the light, trust the light, even if darkness seems stronger, you must trust the light. The voice of calm reason and benevolent authority will prevail—holy authority," said Anzar.

"Who are the good guys and the bad guys?" I asked.

"You already know," he said.

"Other than the reptilians, who are the other alien bad guys?" I asked.

"They have other aliens, smaller groups, latching on to them because they were fooled," said Anzar.

"Humans too?" I asked.

"Yes," he said.

"Honestly, it is scary...why do they appear in my dreams? To scare me, or stop me?" I asked.

"They want you to turn away from your responsibilities and let the bad happen," said Anzar.

"What else can you tell me?" I asked.

"We must keep the supersecret technology safe and out of the hands of those who mean to do harm and are crazy," he said.

"When will the conflict start?" I asked.

"Already begun. Choose the right side. Choose freedom. Mythology becomes the history," he said. All this information was a little scary, but I believe it is not new. From what I understand, this has been a long brewing conflict. Anzar's words made me think of Zarathustra (known as Zoroaster by the Greeks), the ancient Persian philosopher. Zarathustra's teachings became the Zoroastrian religion.

Zoroastrianism is based on the belief that the world is a battleground between good and evil forces, with considerable consequences for humanity. The battle between the two will continue until the end of the world when God will ultimately triumph and relegate evil to the infernal regions.[114]

My spirit walk on Sunday, November 17, 2019, allowed me to contact Anzar and Ergot once again.

"I want people to be prepared but not panic...gentle nudging," said Anzar.

"Oh, yeah, the nudge you talked about before. Nudge to prepare. Right, okay," I said.

"The job is to give a nudge. Your integration process, ongoing, going on right now. Every communication brings us further along, a slow process, not immediate," he said. I was glad to hear that integration was working.

On a radio interview, the host asked what I would do if someone claimed that I was making it up, and that Anzar does not exist. I explained that I would ask them for proof that I was imagining Anzar, which they could not provide of course, and then I would add "why would I risk my academic career if it was not true."

My November 22, 2019 spirit walk was on a sunny, cool, crisp Friday morning. I wanted to ask Anzar about a rumor that was flying around the UFO community and about one of my obsessions, the President John F. Kennedy (JFK) assassination.

"Anzar, rumors are circulating about a delegation of ETs coming to the UN on February 1, 2020," I asked.

"What did I tell you about exact dates? These things are not always precise because there are so many variables. That is one of the thought forms, in the planning stages, but I cannot give an exact date. Those who are helping are considering a meeting...they feel that it might be time. Could be February 1, and maybe New York City, but not totally decided yet," said Anzar. What stuck out to me in his response, beside the thought of aliens landing at the UN, was the phrase, "thought forms." The standard definition, especially in Christian theology, is "a combination of presuppositions, imagery, and vocabulary current at a particular time or place and forming the context for thinking on a subject."[115] Annie Besant and C.W. Leadbeater wrote a book on the subject, *Thought-Forms* (1901), that outlined the forms that different emotions, thoughts and actions may take. The three types of thought forms they identified were:

1. those that assume the form of the thinker;
2. those that take the form of a material object;
3. and those which express feelings that manifest as an aura around an individual.[116]

The nexus concept behind thought forms requires the existence of a non-local consciousness capable of creating entities that could develop their own sense of identity and interact with people in a profound way. That was really fascinating, but Anzar had more to say.

"You all need to get on board quickly," he said. I had to laugh, but then the sense of urgency in his words gave me some concern.

"What can you tell me about the JFK assassination?" I asked.

"JFK? Conspiracy, Oswald did not do it, but he was not a good guy, he was working both sides of this, that is why his tax records are classified, focus on that. Prone to violence, he was a perfect pawn. The fact that he might have tried to kill General Ed Walker does not mean he killed JFK, it just shows that he was violent and crazy. A convenient idiot," said Anzar.[117]

"Any more about integration?" I asked.

"Ongoing, slow process…have you noticed that I am nudging you?" asked Anzar.

"Yes, research papers, presentations, books, interviews, but what else?" I asked.

"You are doing enough, have fun, try to relax," he said. I had to laugh because it seemed odd that an ancient alien mystic high advisor would tell me to have fun and relax.

On the Tuesday before Thanksgiving, November 26, 2019, I took my spirit walk as storm clouds were building over the mountains. As a favor to my friend Terry Lovelace, I wanted to ask Anzar about Betty. Terry told me that Betty had been part of his life for quite some time and could best be described as a human-alien hybrid.[118]

"Hello, Anzar. Betty came to Terry again," I said.

"Yes, I know her," said Anzar.

"Is she being truthful with Terry?" I asked.

"Has she ever been untruthful with him?" asked Anzar.

"I don't know," I said.

"If she has not been untruthful before then she is probably telling the truth now," he said.

"What about February 1, 2020?" I asked.

"Something is in the works. I am not going to give you an exact date but be prepared. There will be repercussions. Those that can remain calm and wise will be sought after. It is not about predictions; it is about preparation. Predictions can be wrong, but preparations are never wrong," said Anzar.

I took a spirit walk on Thursday morning, December 5, 2019. It was cool and sunny as I reached out to my spirit guides, Anzar, Ergot, and Gene.

"An acquaintance of Terry's said there will be massive UFO sightings on December 12, 2019, off the coast of North Carolina. What do you think?" I asked.

"Nonsense," said Anzar.

"Well, what do you mean?" I asked.

"There may be and there may not. It is what you do not see that needs to be seen," he said.

"Integration process, Anzar?" I asked.

"You are still you and living your life, but I am part of you, and you are part of me, helping," he said.

"Okay. Yeah, I appreciate it. I do not want to be perceived as a fake or a false prophet; I want to be real, and genuine," I said.

"Then be wise and careful," said Anzar. You cannot argue with Anzar's logic.

Friday, December 6, 2019, and I was on another spirit walk. The weather was warm and sunny as I headed up Valley Center Avenue toward the San Gabriel Mountains. In my mind's eye I saw others with Anzar and Ergot.

"Anzar, and Ergot, are you conferring with others about February 2020? Who are the others?" I asked.

"Eight…well, the others say the Council of Eight. Representatives from other ET groups and future humans who are helping," said Anzar.

"My mom was a hybrid. Is that true?" I asked.

"Yes, I would not say that if it was not true," he said.

"OK, so all humans with Rh negative blood are of alien origin, related to aliens, and are hybrids of some sort?" I asked.

"Yes," said Anzar.

"Anything more about February next year?" I asked.

"Stand by, be ready," he said.

Two days later, on December 8, 2019, I took my spirit walk on a cool, overcast Sunday morning. I had been noticing a change or a shift lately, in reality, or consciousness, everything seems different, or I am different, or both.

"Any more info for February 2020?" I asked. I did not get an immediate answer, so I went on talking.

"I feel the integration, I am still my sovereign self, but I feel that I am closer to the source," I said.

"That is it, coming closer to the source," said Anzar.

"February?" I asked.

"Definitely something coming, and it will be dramatic, and everyone will need help," he said. The dread was building for February.

Tuesday morning, December 17, 2019, the sky was blue with wispy clouds. Beautiful. Leif had his 20th birthday yesterday, hard to believe. I was preparing for my lecture at Contact in the Desert which would take place in May 2020.

"Anzar, you're the star of the show. I'll share all you've taught and told me. Anything to add today?" I asked.

"The air is alive. All is as one. We are all together. All of us all the time," said Anzar. My friend Terry called it a shift in consciousness. I think it is. I saw Gene in my mind's eye.

"Gene, you said that we're the aliens…does that mean…we are the aliens…and they're our ancestors, or maybe future humans coming back?" I asked.

"Yes, it's all true, all of them," said Gene.

"What's the update on alien groups influencing conflict on Earth?" I asked.

"Battle for the control of human minds and souls," said Anzar.

"Okay. Thank you. What about February 2020?" I asked.

"On track," said Anzar. That was all he said, no other specifics, and I can tell you that it was not comforting.

Sunday, December 22, 2019, and it was cool and partly cloudy. Rain was forecasted. The last few days have been tough. It made me think about what is important in life. I asked Anzar, Ergot, and my friend Gene about the nature of reality.

"Planes of existence, multiple planes of existence, layered, enveloped, intertwined in every possible way and dimension. Reality is a composite reality," said Anzar. That gave me lots of food for thought. Whitley Strieber, in his book *A New World*, talked about a glow that some people have so that spirits and aliens can find them more easily.[119] I have always imagined that I have a radar dish above my head that spirits and aliens can track. The truth is, we all have a piece of the puzzle, and we must work together. A whispered thought came to me and I suddenly realized that the name of the reptilian lady that appeared in my dream in September was named Zaruta.

Christmas Eve 2019 was cool and sunny. During my spirit walk, I was expressing how grateful and thankful I was for a wonderful year of guidance and wisdom.

"Be guided by love. Not a fantasy, this is real. Real is real," said Anzar.

"Yeah, I believe so," I said.

"They see the light, the animals see the light," said Anzar. I have always loved animals and watching animal shows. I grew up watching *Wild Kingdom* and *The Undersea World of Jacques Cousteau* with my mom and dad. The night before, I had a dream about a bobcat who was chasing a squirrel in a tree. I have seen bobcats around our house a few times and they have always intrigued me, and I guess you could say I am more of a cat person than a dog person, but I wondered what the significance of the dream was. My guess was that we can occasionally catch a glimpse of a largely unseen wild world all around us. The struggle for all creatures to survive is taking place at every level all the time.

"Very powerful, always for good. Always do what you can to help others. Be careful. Hide what should be hidden, shine what should shine and show it. The worlds will come together," said Anzar. Just when I thought he was nearly finished teaching me, Anzar reminded me.

"Always do good. Integration brings you closer to the Creator, closer to God. The mission is important, and what is good will be good. Good brings good," he said.

Spirit Walks, January to March 2020

I continued my spirit walks in 2020, but I realized that something terrible was coming. I almost dreaded making the connection, but I had a mission and I had to do my part.

On January 9, 2020, after more than a week off, I took my meditative spirit walk. It was a cool, partly cloudy Thursday morning.

"Trust your intuitions, pay attention," said Anzar. I thought it was interesting that he said "intuitions" instead of "intuition."

"What about February?" I asked.

"Good is what we do, not what we are...all is good for all time," he said. His message was rather cryptic, but it seemed to imply that we are judged by the good we do, the acts of kindness, and the love we put out into the world. Later, a message came to me, as usual, with a whisper in my ear.

"Just like computer hackers use slave or zombie computers to do their dirty work, malevolent entities can do the same thing to humans and make them perform whatever function they want them to do."

I had a disturbing nightmare early in the morning on January 14, 2020. Ginger, another girl, and I were walking up a hill and a giant angry grizzly bear was following us. I told the girls that maybe we should try to get away from this bear because I did not trust him. Then, the angry bear turned and headed into a large drainage pipe roaring loudly as he was running. I told the girls that we needed to run and hide in a building at the bottom of the hill (like a school building). The girls did not follow me and then the roaring in the drainage pipe got louder and louder until the grizzly bear came charging out of the pipe at full speed even more angry than before. I was certain that we would be killed. That is when I woke up.

Later, I decided to run at the track instead of taking a spirit walk. On the drive home I connected with my spirit guides Theodora and Ozzie.

124

"I would like to talk to Anzar," I said.

"Yes, I am listening," he said.

"I would like Ginger, and the rest of my family, to see a UFO. That would be great," I said. This was a request I made often.

"It is coming," said Anzar.

"I know we're in the process of integration, you're listening, and you're helping me…I appreciate it," I said.

"More to come, be prepared, insights arrive at night," he said.

"What is the significance of the scary grizzly bear?" I asked.

"A warning about those who oppose you…be careful who you trust," said Anzar. His warning added to my feeling of dread and made me even more sensitive to how the energy in the world was shifting in a weird way. The year 2020 felt different.

January 20, 2020, Monday morning, the day after the Pasadena Comicon, and I was on my spirit walk. I should mention that Ginger and I celebrated our 8th wedding anniversary on this day.

"Hey Anzar, any more about February 2020?" I asked.

"Space carnival," he said.

"Not sure what that means. Hmmm, entertainment, never thought of it that way. Some ETs could be entertainers. Hopefully not a candid camera-type show that would demonstrate how dumb humans can be," I said.

I took my spirit walk on a cold Thursday morning, January 23, 2020, with a bright blue sky above me crisscrossed with numerous con trails. Jeffrey Mishlove wrote an interesting blurb for my latest *Timeless Trinity* book. "Dr. Solheim is exploring the fringes of human consciousness, itself, as it interfaces with a larger and ancient realm that we moderns are only just beginning to understand." I suppose I am on the fringe. Throughout my life I have often thought that I did not quite fit in, whether it was in religion, school, in sports, in the army, in business, or even in academe. I was not content with ready-made answers and needed to find out for myself.

"Hello, Anzar and Ergot," I said.

"Interdimensional consciousness, rapture of sorts coming. Steady hand, brave soul, calm assured guidance is needed," said Anzar. I knew that something big was coming and would require my utmost attention and focus. Anzar was preparing me.

Two days later, on January 25, 2020, a cold Saturday morning, I spoke to Anzar during my spirit walk.

"Was it your voice I heard the other day when I said that I thought I was beginning to see how big the universe was and understand all this and the voice said, 'oh, you have no idea,'?" I asked.

"Yes," said Anzar, and I thought I heard a chuckle.

"I know I've a lot to learn, I've had just a glimpse, good reminder," I said. Next, I spoke to Gene about my upcoming sizzle reel for a production company working on a UFO show.

"God-inspired enthusiasm, be yourself, good energy," said Gene. Enthusiasm in all things is vitally important.

"Anzar, what did you mean when you said, 'space carnival' the other day?" I asked.

"Some of the alien entities are entertainers, here for fun, or to entertain other alien groups, some are good, some are not, just like Hollywood," he said. That made me laugh. We are, in some respects, like the aliens. But why am I surprised? Anzar and Gene have both told me, "we are the aliens."

"It is real, too real, too real for people to imagine even. Too real beyond imagining," said Anzar.

"Anything else you can tell me Anzar?" I asked.

"Be real, authentic, be polite, be the light, operate from love and giving," he said. Occasionally, I reached what the late journalist Jim Marrs called, the boggle point. Gene set me straight again:

"Is it so hard to believe one more miraculous thing when you already believe in so many extraordinary things?" he said.

On January 31, 2020, I took my spirit walk on a beautiful Friday morning. COVID-19 was in the news and a few confirmed cases had already been reported in Washington State.[120]

"Unlock your potential. Teach others to unlock their potential. Surround yourself with others who help unlock potential. Surround yourself with those who help you shine your light and not those who dim your light," said Anzar. His advice was very timely because we were facing many challenges, not the least of which was COVID-19, that would require taking responsibility and moving everyone forward.

"COVID-19. Weapons lab in Wuhan, is that where it started?" I asked.

"Yes," said Anzar.

"Is this one of the calamities you warned me of?" I asked.

"Yes. One of many that are coming," he said.

"Who is behind it?" I asked.

"Likely an accident," he said. I was teaching my winter courses and one of my students who was from mainland China told me that the wet market story was not true. She said she knew it came from the bioweapons lab. Already, the arguing had started about the origins while the pandemic was spreading rapidly. We have to build each other up not tear each other down.

February 1, 2020, a Saturday afternoon spirit walk. I asked Anzar about COVID-19 and about Ginger seeing a UFO.

"COVID-19?" I asked.

"One of the calamities," he said.

"Am I doing the right thing to protect my family, friends, and students?" I asked.

"Yes," he said.

"I know the integration process takes time and is slow," I said.

"There is only so much you can take at a time. Manage expectations," said Anzar.

"I believe that we can make things happen, but I try not to expect too much," I said. I thought more about COVID-19 and started to wonder just how bad things were going to get.

"How bad is this COVID-19?" I asked.

"Very bad, will make a lot of people sick, lethal for some," he said.

"What can you tell me about these two alien groups that are in conflict with one another and where we fit in? What is going on?" I asked.

"Reptilians are helping some in the Chinese government, and maybe some in the Russian government. The other ETs are helping you," said Anzar.

"I want to help us; I want democracy and peace in the world. That is what we're fighting for," I said.

"Yes. Just keep doing what you are doing. Positive message, stay in the light, be the light," said Anzar.

On Friday, February 7, 2020, the weather was sunny and pleasant. My spirit friend Gene contacted me and told me that he was moving, but I would still be able to talk to him.

"Are you moving because of my integration with Anzar?" I asked.

"Partly," said Gene.

"I don't ever want to lose track of you, my friend," I said. I then switched my attention to my ancient alien mystic high advisor.

"Hey Anzar. I know there is a lot going on. I know you guys (good ETs) are helping us against the not so good ETs and their human accomplices," I said.

"Yes, do not forget the message! Be the light! The path is clear. It is okay to fall into doubt occasionally, but the path is clear and unshakable. The truth is unshakeable," he said.

"It would help if Ginger can see a UFO. Would help a lot," I said.

"I will work on it," Anzar said. Anzar has a great sense of humor.

On a sunny late morning, February 15, 2020, I headed up Valley Center Avenue for my spirit walk. I remembered something Anzar had whispered to me after my last spirit walk.

"The heart, look for the heart. The heart of everything. The heart of the world," he said. I was not quite sure what he meant although the imagery was powerful. Perhaps he was referring to the importance of keeping love in the center of everything.

"Heading into a new phase. There will be heavy protection for a while. Bad guys are regrouping, like the Nazis in the Battle of the Bulge, it is not over until it is over. Keep up your strength, be the light. Do what you are doing," said Anzar.

"I understand, thank you. The last few nights, I've felt and caught glimpses of entities in the bedroom, can you confirm?" I asked.

"Yes," said Anzar.

"Who are they?" I asked.

"Aliens," he said.

"What do they want?" I asked.

"Body information. Connection to me, others will want it too, government types, be careful," said Anzar. Great, stuff to add to my list of worries. As far as I know, nobody has approached me asking for information on Anzar except for my friends at CERO. Occasionally, a radio or podcast interviewer will ask about him, but I do not think they are working for any government or representing any alien group, but who knows.

Friday, February 21, 2020, late morning, warm day, sunny, some clouds, a beautiful day for a spirit walk. I just received word that the property from my mom's side of the family on the island of Andøya in Northern Norway was officially put into my name. It took two years and nearly $5000 to secure the property. Legacies are important. I was ready to communicate with my spirit guides and Anzar.

"Yes, the reptilians are not helpful, they are very rough," said Anzar. I did not ask him about the reptilians, but I knew what he said was true based on my experience.

"What can you guys tell me about the next step in the disclosure process?" I asked.

"Working its way through your popular culture, advertising, and the media. The subject of aliens and UFOs are extremely popular, so you will be asked by the news and entertainment industry to talk about this. Part of the evolutionary process of human beings. Be careful of dark entities. Now is the time to go mainstream. The time is upon us all," said Anzar.

On Sunday, February 23, 2020, I felt the need to call my friend Terry to see how he was doing. I spoke to Anzar on my spirit walk.

"Anything else you can tell me?" I asked.

"COVID-19 is one of the calamities I tried to lessen," he said. I know, we needed to work together as a people. As of February 23, there were 14 COVID-19 cases in six states and an additional 39 cases from US citizens returning from China and the Diamond Princess cruise ship.[121]

"There will be others too. It is a lesson. Cannot afford to live apart, we are together," said Anzar. I guess the ETs need us as much as we need them.

Friday, February 28, 2020, I was on my spirit walk in the bright, warm sunshine. I kept thinking of all my friends in CERO, my spirit guides, Gene, Ergot, and Anzar. We are kind of like the Fellowship of the Ring. We all need each other. A symbiotic relationship. Everything good will happen, we will make it happen, right now. Alright, I had to be careful not to get carried away.

"Hey Anzar, I know you said the COVID-19 outbreak is a calamity, but will there be another calamity in October?" I asked.

"Could be," he said.

"Financial markets?" I asked.

"Yes, be prepared…we are in the business of preparation not prediction," said Anzar.

"Could it be as bad as they say?" I asked.

"Could be worse," he said.

The first recorded death from COVID-19 was on February 29 at a nursing home in Kirkland, Washington. The governor of Washington declared a state of emergency as new cases began to show up in California, Illinois, and New York.[122]

On March 4, 2020, I took a spirit walk on a sunny, beautiful day that seemed incongruous with the growing health crisis. The California governor declared a state of emergency and my friend in the National Guard said he was put on alert. [123] The US Department of Health and Human Services (HSS) announced that they would purchase 500 million N95 respirators over the next 18 months in response to the COVID-19 crisis.[124]

"Anything else you would like me to pass along?" I asked.

"It is all true, as your friend Gene said, everything you thought, it is all possible," said Anzar.

"Anything else about COVID-19?" I asked.

"Somewhere in between the most panicky reports and the most mundane. More people have COVID-19 than you are being told. It will spread around the world and cause a major disruption of the world economy," said Anzar.

"Thank you, anything else I should be doing?" I asked.

"This is just one of seven calamities. Others may be earthquake, and violent conflict," he said. I was trying hard not to panic.

Friday, March 6, 2020, I took another spirit walk and it was a beautiful day in terms of the weather, but not the news.

"Advice for COVID-19 outbreak. The origins of it? Natural or a manmade bioweapon?" I asked.

"Accidental release," said Anzar.

"People say this is no big deal," I said.

"No, this is worse, and is mutating," he said.

"How bad? Millions of people will die around the world," said Anzar.

"Anything else I should do?" I asked.

"Push for your school to close," he said.

"Anzar, I hope you don't mind me talking to Mr. Z, now is the time, before it's too late. Anything else about these calamities?" I asked.

"More health calamities, extreme weather-related anomalies, ET semi-disclosure, waves, water, tornadoes, haunted houses, spirits merging through, and financial collapse," he said.

"Okay. Thank you," I said.

"The bad guys, bad ETs and earthling supporters, we have to work very hard together against them. Epic," said Anzar. Sometimes Anzar has a flair for the dramatic.

Wednesday, March 11, 2020, and I was on yet another spirit walk. I noticed that Anzar was joined by Ergot, Gene, and my spirit guides Theodora, and Ozzie.

"I see all of you, first time I've seen all of you there. I have done my job with leadership and my boss, letting them know that we shouldn't be in class. Hopefully, they'll do the right thing. I think they will. I think they'll do it today or tomorrow," I said.

"You are doing the right thing staying home with Ginger protecting family, students, friends, staff, the right thing. COVID-19 is already at your college, many people. They are afraid of litigation," said Anzar.

"How bad is it going to get?" I asked.

"Hard to tell, lots of variables, could be that millions will die. Too slow to react. Paralysis of analysis, sometimes you need bold action. That is not the leadership style now. Everything is bureaucratic caution," he said.

"So, you mentioned that there will be seven calamities. Is COVID-19 the first?" I asked.

"Yes," he said.

"Second is financial?" I asked.

"Yes," said Anzar.

"What is after that?" I asked.

"Earthquake, floods, tsunamis. Is not that enough to know for now?" he said.

"Yes, I understand. No time table. Hunker down. Be ready. Okay, thank you. I realize how serious this is, that's why you're all here," I said. Not good times.

Friday the 13th, and it is cloudy and raining lightly on my meditative spirit walk. Today, President Trump declared a national emergency. There were 2100 total cases of COVID-19 in the United States and the deaths stood at 50 (mostly in Washington State). An HHS internal memo detailed what they said would be a pandemic lasting 18 months or longer with successive waves that would impact the supply chain and transportation.[125]

"Take extreme precautions, do not take a long walk, stay close to home. Be safe, protect your family and friends. Things will be worse before they get better. Other calamities, one on top of the other, as well," said Anzar.

"Grim warning, but I'll take that to heart. No unnecessary chances or risks. Stay close, stay in contact," I said. It was time to batten down the hatches and prepare for rough seas ahead.

No sun, cool, cloudy, like the mood had changed on March 14, 2020. The COVID-19 crisis was ongoing as I reached out to Anzar.

"People are hoarding items from stores causing nationwide shortages. Is this what you warned me about Anzar?" I asked. There was no immediate answer.

"What do you think about what some are saying that the government has plans for martial law, using military occupation," I asked.

"Yes," said Anzar.

"In this country?" I asked.

"Yes. To keep order, rationing, food, everything else," he said.

"Are all of you in agreement?" I asked.

"Yes," said Anzar.

"All of you?" I asked again.

"Yes," was the answer from Anzar and all my spirit friends.

"Your government has this in the planning stages," said Anzar.

"Anything I can do?" I asked.

"Be prepared," he said.

"What about the ETs? Are they involved?" I asked.

"Yes, helping and provoking, both, depends on the group," said Anzar.

"Alright. A lot going on behind the scenes," I said. I know that the proper response is to stay close to family and friends and keep checking on them.

"Extreme precautions. Protect. Series of calamities, catastrophes, financial disruptions, earthquakes, tsunamis, and more. And then comes the alien intervention. People need a calm voice of reason," said Anzar. We have been warned so now we have to be prepared.

The next day, Sunday, March 15, 2020, it was still cloudy and cool as I contacted Anzar on my spirit walk.

"Anything I can pass on?" I asked.

"Beautiful star. Tradition meets the future. Doing good work. Spiritual enlightenment is growing. Connection is strong and growing stronger each day. Get ahead of the curve, prepare for the next one. Do not think this is the end of all calamities, be ready, be calm, be logical," said Anzar.

"I feel a heaviness about all of this," I said.

"Yes. Everything will be okay," he said. I wonder if he meant for me personally, or for everyone? Maybe he was trying to lessen my fear.

March 16, 2020, a Monday spirit walk, and the first day where everything was closed. President Trump presented new guidelines urging people to avoid social gatherings of more than 10 people and to restrict some travel. He said restrictions may last until July or August. He acknowledged that the country might enter a recession as the stock market fell again.[126] In California, we had 258 cases of COVID-

19 and three deaths in the Bay Area. Six counties had issued shelter-in-place orders.[127]

"The big questions, Anzar, Ergot. What is going to happen?" I asked.

"You think I know? There are so many variables. Pretty much what you are thinking, curfews, extend through the summer, National Guard involvement, people acting crazy, calm rational voice of reason is what people need. Alien activity surrounding this, good guys, bad guys, in-between guys, all happening," said Anzar. I really enjoy Anzar's sense of humor in the midst of all these troubling events.

"What more can I do?" I asked.

"Be conscientious with CERO folks, be loving and understanding. Keep family close and protect. Be watchful, and vigilant," said Anzar. I had some afterthoughts when I returned home from my spirit walk. Some say that the world is cleansing itself, the virus being a great leveler. Others say it is a manmade crisis and is blown out of proportion in order for authoritarian government to take root. Others believe ETs are involved, both to help and to make things worse. I do not know for sure, but I believe some aspect of each may be in play, although I think that COVID-19 is very real, I believe some in government will use the crisis to seize more power. A crisis seems to bring out the best and worst in people.

I decided on March 17, 2020, that I would post my spirit walk transcript and thoughts on Facebook for all to see in the form of a communiqué. The next day, March 18, 2020, I hoped to be very consistent, take a spirit walk every day, and post on Facebook. Most of my spirit guides and advisers were present during my spirit walk yesterday, but they are busy and worried. My plan was to think deeply about my spirit walks and then write them up and post them the next day on Facebook.

"Let me know what I can do," I said.

"Do you realize how serious this is?" asked Anzar.

"Yes, I know the seriousness and gravity of the situation. How long will this crisis last?" I asked.

"Through the summer," he said.

"Is there more I can do, besides love and compassion?" I asked.

"You are doing it, getting the word out, people need to pay attention, especially the young. They need to know who the good guys are and who the bad guys are. The Chinese and Russian governments are not the good guys. People in United States are also doing bad things, sometimes unknowingly," said Anzar.

"Thank you," I said.

"You cannot judge a book by its cover," said Anzar.

"I remember you told me that many years ago," I said. At that time, I had recently found out that Anzar was the alien who saved from a neighborhood child molester in 1964.[128]

"People need to be careful, and be prepared, through the summer. There are lot of variables, but millions could die before it dissipates," he said.[129]

"I think I've done everything I was supposed to do. I officially and publicly put the word out on Facebook. I'm being attacked online, increasingly," I said.

"To be expected. Many people do not like the truth and they are angry, confused, afraid, deluded, and irrational. Operate from a position of love, always," said Anzar.

"I felt instructed to put this out there. Just checking, it's okay with you, Anzar?" I asked.

"Yes, of course, it is time. Help other people as you help yourself. People must understand deploying the National Guard is not a bad thing, they help with confusion and lawlessness, and provide much needed resources. Be calm, follow what you are being told by the good people, those who operate from a position of love, and do not freak out," he said. I started laughing.

"It's funny to hear you say freak out," I said, still chuckling.

"Focused calm is what will help all of us through this. We are all in this together," said Anzar.

I posted my next report (or communiqué as I called them) on March 19, 2020. It could take me up to 24 hours to digest what had been told to me. All my spirit guides were present on March 18, but my friend Gene (who passed away in September 2016) took the lead.

"Hi, Gene. It looks like there's something really important you want to tell me," I said.

"We're coming," said Gene. That sounded kind of unsettling to me.

"I'm ready to listen," I said.

"Everything is changing," he said.

"You said, we…we meaning?" I asked.

"Aliens, spirits, angels, demons. The battle for the Earth," he said. "Basically, the worst parts of the Bible," to quote NASA

Administrator Dan Truman played by actor Billy Bob Thornton in the film *Armageddon* (1998).

"I know I'm on the right side. Thank you, guys, for everything, the wisdom, and the warnings," I said. Then Anzar stepped up in front. It is quite impressive since he is a big dude.

"Hello," said Anzar.

"Hey Anzar. The battle for the Earth, scary, I got it," I said.

"Gods and angels versus the demons and corruptors," he said.

"I'm on the side of the gods and angels, right?" I asked.

"All this that is happening is more important than you realize," said Anzar. I felt embarrassed for trying to make light of the situation based on my nervousness.

"I get it. Thank you," I said, sheepishly. Anzar stepped back.

"Anzar is a little busy," said Gene.

"I understand," I said. Anzar then stepped forward toward me.

"Gene is right, get ready, be the voice of reason, now collect," said Anzar.

"Collect what?" I asked. Suddenly I remembered how my mom and dad saved everything in jars and bowls. I saw an image of the margarine tub that my mom used to collect rubber bands and bread bag fasteners.

"Collect useable items," he said.

"You mean like during the Great Depression?" I asked.

"Yes, no longer wasteful," said Anzar.

"Okay, thank you. What do we do about China and Russia?" I asked.

"We must work together with those who are helping. Confront those who are not, wherever they are. Stand ready," said Anzar. My head was reeling from all the information I had received.

On March 20, 2020, I wrote my communiqué based on my spirit walk the day before. California is on lock-down, the rest of the nation will likely follow.[130] Those who doubted the seriousness of this calamity, by now should realize the grave situation we all share. On my spirit walk yesterday I noticed that all my spirit guides were in a somber mood. Anzar and Gene stepped forward and Anzar spoke, but Gene stood right beside him.

"We do not want to alarm you," said Anzar. Too late; I was freaked out already.

"I think I know what you are going to say. Dr Fauci told us it will get worse before it gets better," I said.

"Be ready for that," he said.

"What percentage of us will be exposed?" I asked.

"As is being said by doctors, 50–70 percent, more than likely," said Anzar.

"So, we just have to hang on and do our best to survive?" I asked. Anzar showed me an image from World War II to help me understand. Then, it dawned on me, from military history, that we always prepare to fight the next war based on the last. This seems different. Wars of the future will be psychological, biological, and cyber wars with traditional asymmetrical flareups thrown in for good measure. But Anzar wanted me to draw a historical analogy.

"I get it, like the Nazi Blitz against London. It seems to strike randomly," I said.

"Yes," he said.

"That's a dire warning," I said.

"You are doing all you can," said Anzar.

"Yesterday you said, 'we are coming.' Gods and angels, demons and corruptors," I said.

"Ascended beings if you prefer, including extraterrestrials, ETs as you call them, those on the side of the light. That includes who have passed from your world and are now based in the spirit world. All those working for good and light," said Anzar.

"So, that is the 'we'?" I asked.

"Yes," he said.

"Coming where? To Earth? In our reality?" I asked.

"We will be more present," said Anzar. That would mean that some would see, and some would not see, I suppose.

"Thank you, Gene and Anzar. I get it, you are coming. Almost here or soon?" I asked.

"Yes, the battle for the Earth. Hard lessons will be coming fast. You must learn them quickly. Dismantle, the weapons of mass destruction. Including the biological weapons. The light of God—purify with the light of God," I nodded my head in the affirmative during his pronouncement.

"So, there is hope?" I asked.

"Yes, be of the light, be in the light, be the light," said Anzar.

Based on my spirit walk on March 20, 2020, I wrote my communiqué the next day. I woke up shortly after midnight with these words sounding in my mind: Cognitive dissonance. I assumed it was a download or hint that my spirit guides provided me. According to psychologists, cognitive dissonance happens when a person has two or more contradictory beliefs, ideas, or values, or does something that goes against one of these three, and experiences psychological stress because of that. I feel that many people in the world now may be experiencing this condition. That brings me to the conclusion that we must choose. I choose the light. Yesterday afternoon we found a dying hummingbird on the sidewalk near our orange tree. I put him in a box along with a flower. He later died. Native Americans believed that hummingbirds were magical creatures who represented joy and freedom. Although his death is sad, it reminds me that we will get through this and be stronger and wiser on the other end. Maybe we can learn to appreciate the little things more and care for one another more as well. On my spirit walk, I encountered only one entity at first, Anzar, my ancient alien mystic adviser.

"Hi, Anzar. You're by yourself today," I said.

"I have a special request, an appeal. Share with people in the other groups you belong to who do not have social media access. Help them. Be ready, be prepared," said Anzar.

"How bad will it get?" I asked.

"Very bad. Much depends on what people do or do not do," he said.

"I understand, I've got to be prepared to defend my family. I'll teach them today. When you said we had to be ready to confront those who aren't working in the light, what is the range of confrontation?" I asked.

"Operate from a position of love, always," said Anzar.

"What if they're doing great harm and violence?" I asked.

"Defend yourself, defend the innocent. You must all learn the lessons of what is really important," said Anzar.

"I've noticed that commercial advertising rings hollow when people have to worry about jobs, food, and basic survival," I said.

"Yes. Distasteful. Millions out of work. You need to pull together. Help those who need the help. Fill what is empty, and empty what is full," he said.

"Yeah, that's what US Navy pilot Dieter Dengler said after he returned from POW captivity in Laos during the Vietnam War.[131]

Thank you for reminding me," I said. My dear spirit friend Gene suddenly showed up.

"Hey, Gene," I said.

"You're getting the message out there," said Gene.

"Yeah, I'm out there alright. None of the news media I've approached are interested," I said.

"Not surprising. They will before this is over because the message is important," said Gene.

"I know, you guys have told me. The message is more important than the messenger. I'm worried about the Chinese and Russian regimes and what they'll do," I said.

"Speak softly and carry a big stick," said Anzar.[132]

"That's true, very true. Yeah, like Theodore Roosevelt, my favorite president," I said.

I had a terrible dream the night before and again last night March 21, 2020. The night before last, the dream took place in a large port facility. There were explosions and an emergency response with loud sirens. Patrol boats and military craft of all types were rushing off to take on the threat. Last night, I was in a house, unfamiliar to me, everyone had left, and I went back in by myself. I noticed the heater was still on, so I paused to feel the heat, then I heard a scary, scratchy, voice call my name. It chilled me to the bone. I departed the house quickly and woke up. I think it was a warning from the forces of darkness, but I will not be deterred. I decided to ask Anzar and my other spirit guides about this incident during my spirit walk. The forces of darkness are strong, but the forces of light are stronger.

"Hi Anzar, I've been attacked by people who say China and Russia aren't our enemies, but I never said the Chinese people, or the Russian people are our enemies. My point is that the regimes and leaders of those countries are up to no good. The propaganda is pouring out of their government-controlled media. We're not perfect, but we're with the light," I said.

"Yes. I agree. One must be strong to avoid war, speak softly and carry a big stick. Operate from a position of love," said Anzar. In this case, it would be tough love.

"I'm really not political, I want us all to live in loving peace, but we need to help people to live free," I said.

"Stand up, protect the innocent, yes," he said.

"How about the fact you and the others are coming. What will happen?" I asked.

"It will cause dissension in the ranks," said Anzar.

"I've seen that already," I said.

"People will argue with one another when in truth they may all be on the same side," he said, as I nodded my head in agreement.

"The light, look to the light, be of the light, be the light. That will help. Appeal to the love that lies deepest within you and that connects through to the universe and ties all together. This world and all worlds. Search deep within and you will find it. A spiritual reawakening, that is what is causing so much turmoil. Stay on the side of the light," said Anzar.

"So, when Gene said you're coming, you're really here now?" I asked.

"Yes," said Anzar.

"Will more people be able to see and talk to you and the others?" I asked.

"Some will, and some do not want to. Your job is to spread the message of the light. That is your mission," he said. I was moved to tears by his loving words.

"We are present. God is present in our lives. Always near, no more than three feet, or one meter, if you like, away," said Anzar. I laughed at Anzar's metric conversion.

I posted another communiqué on Facebook on March 23, 2020. Being a comic book guy, I noticed that the biggest comic distributor in America, Diamond Comic Distributors, announced they would no longer accept new stock or distribute new comics until further notice. World Health Organization (WHO) Director-General Tedros described the COVID-19 pandemic as "accelerating."[133]

My son Byron is an engineer in the auto industry. He told me that the United States does not have the manufacturing machines to make things anymore. And the manufacturing machines we do have, were made elsewhere. That makes it quite difficult to get our manufacturing going again. We have a dependency, especially on China, that has made us vulnerable.

"Hey, Anzar," I said.

"Hello," he said.

"Yeah, people saying some unkind and untrue things in response to my communiqués. What are your thoughts?" I asked.

"Keep going, let the love guide you. Operate from a position of love," said Anzar.

"Can you tell me more about the virus?" I asked.

"You are two steps behind. Everybody is. If everything was cancelled and shut down two weeks ago, things would be better now," he said.

"So, here we are, starting new each day, restarting the cycle of infection," I said.

"Yes," he said.

"What more can I tell my friends, family, and others?" I asked.

"Focused calm, trust those in leadership positions with love in their hearts, put aside ideological divisions, focus on basic survival," said Anzar.

"When people who are out of work run out of money, what will happen?" I asked.

"Very bad things. Pull together, see your way through, then eventually you will get up and running again," he said. I nodded in agreement.

"Self-reliance—do not rely so much on foreign economies. You have created a dependency on other countries," said Anzar.

"You mean China?" I asked.

"Exactly. Your politicians, businessmen and women, and many others have made big mistakes. A lot of blame to go around. The Chinese government took advantage of your ignorance and greed. A lot will have to change. This is a spiritual crisis as well as an economic and health crisis," he said.

"I understand. I have a firm belief in God and pray every day," I said.

"Doing the right thing, is never easy. Ad hominem attacks are to be expected. Seek the light, be the light, one with the light," said Anzar. I smiled and nodded yes.

"As I said in 1997, I bring you a message of love, acceptance, responsibility, caring, and of fellowship in a time of crisis. We are here!" he said. I had a vision of Anzar, then called the Progenitor, in 1997.[134]

On March 24, 2020, I sent out my eighth COVID-19 communiqué. US Army hospital units were sent to New York and Washington State, and the military is also constructing four hospitals and four medical centers in New York. FEMA sent New York 2,000 ventilators.[135] There was talk at the highest levels of our government about stopping the social distancing in a week. There was concern that our economy could not survive an extended lockdown. A report came out this morning that many schools in the San Gabriel Valley (here where we live in Southern California) are planning to open again in early April. The problem is that many people, younger and older, are not taking proper precautions and are still out in public and not social distancing. That means that we really have not had a total two-week shutdown to slow the spread of the disease.

Statistics seem to show that this virus has a mortality rate of between 1 to 3.4% depending on which health agency you consult. We were told that most of those who die are elderly or have underlying health conditions. Therefore, many folks feel a false sense of security if they are not in those categories. However, the *New York Times* has reported that 50% of the hospitalizations for the virus are people under 50. People with a serious lung disease, even if survivable, will likely have lifelong complications. I have heard discussions about relying on a herd immunity where most (estimates up to 80% of the population) will get the virus and survive and thereby have immunity. But what about those who do not survive? Let's assume 80% of Americans get the virus and 1% die. That would be 2.64 million people dead (young and old) from the virus in America alone. Are those acceptable losses? This type of cold, calculated number crunching to justify abandoning a hard, two-week shutdown to get the economy going again amounts to social and economic Darwinism. Solution: enforce a two-week real hard shutdown, reassess, extend if necessary, and all the while help those who need money to pay rent and bills and get food. Once the curve has flattened and starts downward, test everyone (including anti-body testing), then re-open our economy slowly, with as many safeguards as possible, to protect the most vulnerable. Communist China is having people go back to work and is covering up the number of sick and dying. Russia claims to have everything under control. We are not communist China or authoritarian Russia whose leaders are willing to sacrifice millions in exchange for taking economic advantage. We need to operate from a position of love.

"I see the assembled team here; things are getting worse," I said.

"Emergency! Everyone needs to stop what they are doing to contain this. The situation will get worse in the next few weeks. But there is hope when people all work together, pull together, guided by the light," said Anzar.

"All of you are saying emergency because people aren't listening?" I asked.

"We are here to help, but we cannot help if you do not listen. Young people need guidance and help. Older people need to set the example. This is the time, this the hour, this is the moment, right now," he said.

"Okay," I said, feeling my anxiety building.

"Long haul, no quick fix. All for one, one for all," said Anzar. As of March 24, 2020, there were 52,976 cases of COVID-19 in the United States and 704 people had died, including 163 deaths on that day.[136]

I was listening to Simon and Garfunkel's song "Bridge Over Troubled Water" on March 25, 2020 and was brought to tears. The song seemed so fitting for the times. Oftentimes, music says it all.

> *And friends just can't be found*
> *Like a bridge over troubled water*
> *I will lay me down*

"Is there any more you can say about the virus we all face?" I asked.

"A long haul. Not going to end soon. You all need to stay strong, work together, take it seriously. Operate from a position of love, not greed. Help those who need help. Feed the hungry. Costly but right. Doing the right thing is never easy. Rise to the occasion. We are here to help," said Anzar.

"Okay, I will do that," I said.

"We are here to help, but you must help yourselves too. Look to the spiritual, look to the light, stay in the light," he said.

"Thank you, Anzar," I said.

In my communiqué posted on March 26, 2020, I was thinking about my fellow veterans. Some of you, dear readers, know that I am a US Army veteran. Few, however, are aware that I am also a disabled veteran as is my big brother Alf. I do not say that for sympathy, I say it because I believe it is essential for everyone to know that many veterans carry the scars, both visible and invisible, from their service to our country. When I go to the Long Beach VA hospital for appointments, I see so many paralyzed veterans, young and old, and others who are in terrible condition. I have broken down in tears in the VA parking lot more than a few times, thinking about how they suffer. They all signed up to serve their country as young people, full of hope, promise, and with a feeling of invincibility. Life's hard lessons eventually erode that sense of invincibility, and veterans must accept that their mission changes over time. These warriors must be re-conditioned to put their skills to use in the civilian world.

In my dialectical behavior therapy (DBT) group, I am honored to have met and get to know veterans of all types (including a Navy SEAL medic, a US Army ranger, and brothers and sisters from other branches). DBT has taught us that there are three minds at work in our everyday lives: the logic mind, the emotion mind, and the wise mind.[137] I like to think of them as Mr. Spock, Dr. McCoy, and Captain Kirk, from the original *Star Trek* TV show. We need logic and science (like Mr. Spock), but we also need emotion and compassion (like Dr. McCoy). Balancing the two, we appeal to the wise mind (Captain Kirk), who must make the decision in consultation with the other two. Despite whatever disabilities and shortcomings, I may have, I have survived and accepted my new mission. I must appeal to my wise mind and help my fellow human beings as we face a series of calamities, the first one being this terrible pandemic. My military service

149

indeed wounded me to my very soul, but I am "strong at the broken places" (as Hemingway once wrote), and I am ready.[138]

"Hey, Anzar," I said.

"Yes. There is much to discuss. Head and the heart. You need both, use both, to see the truth of the moment. The wise mind. I see encouraging signs as people and companies are volunteering to help. Maybe government leaders can learn from the people. They can learn from true human beings pulling together in time of great peril," said Anzar.

"Like Ginger often says, 'Be a person,'" I said.

"Yes. The solution to this crisis is with the people, the everyday people, guided by the light. Their work and love and caring supersedes all other authority," he said.

"Thank you, Anzar," I said. I am constantly reminded of the power of love.

My March 27, 2020, communiqué captured my spirit walk the day before. On my spirit walk, I saw beautifully-colored and formed puffy clouds in a deep blue sky. Nature's ultra-high definition. What a show! I thanked God for the magnificent display. As I continued my walk, it struck me that everything appears to look the same, but it is not. There is an invisible virus out there, causing great harm. It strikes mercilessly without warning, young and old. This realization gave me an odd feeling. Being out in the fresh air usually calms me down and revitalizes me, but I think differently now. Passersby are no longer just neighbors or friendly strangers; they now could be carriers of this deadly disease—a frightening thought as I smile nervously and wave. This is a time when all of us may be looking to our celestial guardian angels for protection and comfort. They are with us always, but there are also terrestrial guardian angels in our midst. We need to look no further than our healthcare workers, public safety officers, firefighters, grocery workers, truck drivers, and all the other brave people out there in public doing their jobs and keeping us alive. I love to see the trend of people applauding our terrestrial guardian angels every day. We are grateful. We can all take part in this show of love for our fellow human beings. My wife Ginger distributed groceries to loved ones and friends yesterday (safely, I might add). Please see yourself as a guardian angel as you do your good deeds, big and small, each day to aid and comfort an elderly neighbor, a family member, or any person in need. You are in good company, and thank God for all of you, dear readers, as you are needed now more than ever.

"You have been asking for specific information again," said Anzar.

"Wow, you were already sending me signals before I was ready," I said.

"You want dates and times so you can predict upcoming events," he said. I knew where he was going with this, but I answered anyway.

"Yes, of course," I said.

"But I have told you that there are many variables, and accuracy is difficult at best. I have told you that preparations are better than predictions," he said. I nodded in the affirmative.

"Your mission is to help people, not be some type of superstar celebrity psychic," said Anzar. I felt slightly embarrassed.

"I know, I'm humbled, thank you," I said. I know exactly what he was referring to. I was tempted to ask a gentleman whom I had done a reading for whether I was correct. I did not ask, but he did tell me that the information helped him and his family and was consistent with what he thought and felt beforehand.

"Good," said Anzar.

"I get it," I said.

"Do not expect to be rewarded for doing the right thing. Just do it because it is the right thing to do," he said.

"Hugh Thompson, the hero of My Lai, said almost exactly the same thing," I said.[139]

"Yes. Trust yourself," said Anzar.

"Thank you for straightening me out, Anzar. I guess I'm helping people with these communiqués and pissing off some people too," I said.

"No good deed goes unpunished," said Anzar. That made me laugh because my dear friend and mentor David A. Willson, who is a Vietnam War veteran author, says that all the time.[140]

"I want to give people the chance to do the right thing. I pray for our leaders to have the wisdom to make the right decisions," I said.

"They will need it. The next several days are very uncertain. Many are arguing over resources. Keep moving forward together, do not look back. Self-reliance," he said. I nodded in agreement.

"Make good decisions for the greatest good with compassion," said Anzar. I always end my spirit walk communication by saying in Norwegian, *takk for laget*. It means, thanks for the togetherness.

My spirit walk on March 27 was documented in my communiqué on March 28, 2020. I always started my communiqués with, 'Dear Friends of the Light.' I am trying to stay focused on what lies right in front of us. In a World War I documentary I used to show to my students, Albert E. Powis, a veteran of that War to End All Wars, said: "It is what's right in front of ya that'll get ya. That's your danger point."[141] He was right. He not only survived the First World War, but he also survived the Spanish Flu pandemic that killed millions from 1918 to 1919. Sage advice. There is plenty to worry about, but we must continue to live our lives day to day. We must keep our spirits up and go about our daily routines and help the best we can and make something good happen today. In the words of an old Norwegian folk song:

La oss leve for hverandre (let us live for each other)
Å, ta vare på den tid vi har (and watch over the time we have)
La oss leve for hverandre (let us live for each other)
Livet selv kan gi de rette svar (life itself can give the right answer)

On my spirit walk, most of my spirit friends were together, apparently social distancing is not a thing in the spirit world.

"Thank you all for being here. When will a vaccine be ready? A friend of mine asked," I said.

"Sooner than expected. I cannot give exact dates," said Anzar.

"Okay, thank you, Anzar. Another beautiful day," I said.

"Listen to the spirit song that has played since your birth," he said.

"Thank you, I will," I said. I thought he meant the sound or music of my soul, not like a song on the radio.

"Anzar and Gene, can you help me prepare for what comes next?" I asked.

"Financial problems, unstable financial markets, serious economic problems for everyday people," said Anzar.

"Some kind of natural disaster," said Gene.

"High probability of conflict as well, armed conflict, caused by global instability. There are those who will take advantage of the chaos and those who will protect. See the light," said Anzar.

"Those are frightening things," I said.

"Remember, fear of death is really fear of living," said Gene. I was lucky to have both Gene and Anzar coaching me.

"Thank you both. What are all these alien groups doing?" I asked.

"Some are stirring things up and some are trying to help," said Anzar.

153

"Thank you, Anzar and Gene, and everybody," I said. I saw all of them cheering us on as we humans dealt with the pandemic.

My March 29, 2020, communiqué was number 13 in the series. *Vi gjer oss ikkje.* That is what my relatives and neighbors on the island of Andøya in Northern Norway are saying. It means, we will not give in. Although they still have no recorded cases of the virus on the island, they face another threat: the airbase that has protected them and provided jobs is shutting down. Anti-submarine surveillance flights originate from that airbase and keep tabs on Russian naval activity in the Arctic. The government of Norway has inexplicably decided to move the airbase inland leaving Andøya defenseless. The government has apparently not learned from history. The Nazis took over the island in 1940 because of its strategic location on the shipping lanes to the High North. It holds as much strategic value today as it did in 1940, especially because of global warming. We must all be as brave and steadfast as the people of Andøya and not give in to this virus and to fear. We must stand strong and united.

"Hey, Anzar. My friend Luci said you and I are the same," I said.

"Connected," said Anzar.

"Are we integrated now?" I asked.

"Yes," he said.

"Okay, that's why I feel different. Thank you. You guys have said this is a spiritual, health and economic crisis," I said.

"Yes. We are here for all of you," said Anzar.

"Okay. My friend Terry thinks this crisis is going to be very bad, like a tsunami," I said. The term was very appropriate because pandemics come in waves.

"Yes, because people are not listening and not working together," he said. Anzar showed me the Norwegian explorer Thor Heyerdahl on his balsa wood raft, the Kon Tiki.

"I get it. Heyerdahl and his crew traveled across the Pacific Ocean from Peru to Polynesia on that tiny raft in 1947, barely surviving—4300 miles in 101 days.[142] After the Kon Tiki and later harrowing trips, Heyerdahl said: "We are able to report that in spite of different political views, we have lived and struggled together in perfect understanding and friendship, shoulder to shoulder in cramped quarters through calm and storms, always according to the ideals of the United Nations: cooperation for joint survival."[143] All of us are living on a raft and need each other to survive.

"That is it," said Anzar. I nodded in agreement. A man named Torstein Raabi from the tiny village of Dverberg on the island Andøya, was also on the Kon Tiki. Torstein was in the Norwegian Resistance during World War II and helped the British sink the battleship Tirpitz. We never know how much courage we have until we are put to the test. This is our test. We can do it!

In communiqué number 14 on March 30, 2020, I ruminated on the pandemic and my fear of running out of things to write about. Maybe, I thought, my communication with Anzar and my other spirit guides would dry up. Maybe, under lockdown, I would not have enough experiences to share or interesting insights to offer. But no, it continued, for two weeks and counting. Early on the morning of March 29, as I was ready to get up for the day, this message came to me: Practice spirituality outside of the box. That was interesting because I had been thinking about all those people who normally go to church not being able to go. Then I thought of my parents who left the Northlake Lutheran Church in Kenmore, Washington, after the congregation board decided to fire the minister and demand more money from my father. My parents continued in their beliefs and in their dedication to always doing the right thing. Do not get me wrong, I have nothing against organized religion, I am just saying that it is what we do with our beliefs that count. I heard a comedian once say that he would go to church on Sunday and go to hell on Monday. Can you stay on the straight and narrow and be a good person outside of a group setting

155

and without someone watching you or peer pressure? I think we can, and we will because my spirit guides have told me that this current worldwide calamity is also a spiritual crisis. We must all rise to the occasion. And then, think of it, when we return from lockdown and fill the churches, synagogues, mosques, and temples again, or maybe just our own beliefs and practices at home, we will have a new confidence, perspective, and commitment to do what is right and stay on course and follow the light.

"Oh my God, okay. So, hello everybody," I said. My spirit guides were there, but they were quiet.

"Everybody is rather quiet today," I said. Then, Gene stepped forward.

"It's getting pretty dark. Rough times ahead. Be ready," he said.

"Okay. Kind of grim, that's not like you, but thank you, Gene. What do you say, Anzar?" I asked.

"The heavens revolve, life comes, life goes, in a circle," said Anzar. Horrible images of past calamities in history came to mind.

"So, you're saying this is our plague?" I asked.

"Perhaps. But there is hope, the hope is in the light, the salvation of the light. Keep working for the light, in the light," said the ancient alien mystic.

"No one is safe, young or old, we all need to pull together. Selfishness and greed have to give way to love and charity—community action from the ground up," said my friend Gene.

"Thank you, Gene, I know I need to contact the actors, they're a deep feeling and communal people and I know this is a tough time for them," I said.

"Think of the actors, how they need and rely on each other on stage, use that analogy," said Gene.[144]

"Yeah, you're right. If one actor forgets their lines it throws off the whole cast and crew. They're a team that survives each show through teamwork and self-sacrifice. That's why my veteran friends liked being in my plays; they loved the sense of mission, the close teamwork, all that," I said.

"Many people in positions of leadership are beginning to realize more than ever that they need the common people. Calm, steady, reasonable, that is what is needed," said Anzar.

"Thank you, Anzar, Gene, and everybody. *Takk for laget* (thank you for the togetherness)," I said.

"Dear Friends of the Light." That is how I started all my communiqués, and March 31, 2020, was no different. I was going over some notes that morning, and I stumbled across a lecture I gave about the history of warfare. All wars are fought over the same things and in the same places (70 percent of dry land is too cold, too high, or too arid to sustain warfare). Since the beginning, we have primarily fought over:

1. larder (food supplies),
2. territory,
3. revenge (from previous attack or insult), and
4. females.

Our clinging to ancient warring ways does not speak well for our evolutionary progress. On Sunday, March 29, 2020, shoppers jammed into the Brentwood outdoor farmer's market in Los Angeles in the midst of a pandemic and a shelter-at-home order. On my daily spirit walks, I have to dodge people walking their dogs and not supervising their children on bikes who are oblivious to the danger that surrounds us all. Why? It reminds me of an old saying: the teacher will appear when the student is ready to learn. So as these unconscious folks crowd and infect each other, hoard food, strike out at people who point out the truth, and lament about their diminished dating opportunities, their teacher may be preparing some tough lessons.

"All of you are here again?" I said.

"Getting ready, maximum effort," said Anzar.

"Okay. I read that you want us to believe in you, but not too much," I said.[145] I could not remember where I had read that.

"Yes, that is because you must live in your world too. You need to have one foot in each world to survive," said Anzar.

"That makes sense. Looks like you guys are getting ready for battle," I said.

"It is going to be tough, but we can do it together. This is disclosure. I warned you; I told you it was coming, what more did you want?" he said.

"So, this pandemic is part of it?" I asked. Anzar seemed to be getting frustrated with me as I kept asking similar questions.

"Yes, yes, yes. Did you need flying saucers to be flying around the White House, hovering over the Taj Mahal, or landing in Red Square and the Forbidden City for people to believe? Your teachers have told you: experiencing is believing and believing is experiencing. Each experience is at another level, increasing levels," said Anzar.

"I remember Simeon Hein, who told me: 'you are as psychic as you need to be.' We grow with each experience along the way. That makes sense," I said.

"You must keep going, day by day, one foot in front of the other. Back to the basics," said Anzar. Sometimes the pandemic appeared to overwhelm all of us, so taking it day by day and doing all we could each day was our only option. By March 31, 2020, there had been 3170 deaths, and 164,620 cases of COVID-19 in the United States. Testing was not keeping up with demand due to shortages of swabs, test kits, reagents, personal protective equipment (PPE), staff, and machines to run the COVID-19 tests.[146]

April 1, 2020. Cooperation for joint survival. It is as simple as that. By taking care of yourself and your family, and neighbors, you are taking care of the rest of the world. Doing your part to isolate and follow guidelines is not only commendable; it is absolutely necessary. The person who could start a chain reaction of viral infections is the same person who can end it. I always tell my students that the individual matters in history. What we do or do not do matters. For example, America does not go to war, individual Americans do. Our personal experience is not unlike the experiences of our fellow human beings. We are in this together. We rise up together, or we go down together. It is our choice.

"It looks like you are waiting," I said.

"Waiting for things to get worse," said Gene.

"I know they will, some people are just now realizing this, and more have yet to understand the dire situation we face," I said. Then, there was action and movement.

"We can slow down to talk only briefly," said Anzar.

"Thank you. You seem to be moving around a lot now," I said.

"We are busy. Preparations for April," said Anzar.

"I understand," I said.

"This is a spiritual assault, an economic assault, and a health assault. It is of nefarious origins. Unleashed. It is a test," said Anzar.

"I agree," I said.

"Remember, this is a global pandemic that calls for a global solution. It is also an opportunity to come together on other things as well: the environment, ending conflict and hostilities, dismantling, and ceasing production of weapons of mass destruction, and protecting the innocent—all those things," said Anzar.

"Individual action leads to community action, which leads to national action, and that leads to global action," I said, as I felt totally inspired.

"This is exactly what we have been saying: Intervention. This is our last stand. Set up the mechanisms by which all those things can take place and the corresponding protocols," said Anzar.

On April 2, 2020, I posted communiqué number 17. Many people have told me that they enjoy these daily communiqués. These are people whom I admire for their selfless sacrifice and service to humanity. These are loving and caring people. A few have expressed opposite opinions. That is okay, even when they present their opposition vociferously. They may also be loving and caring people (although, honestly, I struggle to muster that thought). Synthesis comes from thesis and antithesis. It can be a messy process. I am referring to the dialectical process devised by the 19th Century German philosopher, G.W.F. Hegel.[147] This dialectical process is all good if people can disagree without being violently disagreeable (as Dr. Martin Luther King, Jr. once said).[148]

My mission is to empower, inform, and nudge my fellow humans into paying attention to what is going on in this world and others as well. Dialogue, even conflictive dialogue, is better than no dialogue at all. Regarding today's exchange with my spirit guides, let me preface it by explaining my framework of understanding how this all works (admittedly, I am only scratching the surface). My theory, supported by scientists and others, is that the spirit world, the alien world, and the quantum world are one in the same.[149] It makes sense when you think about it. Matter can vibrate or phase in and out of this reality and others (according to my scientist friend, Dr. E.M. Young). This is how ghosts suddenly appear out of thin air and pass through walls and doors and how aliens do likewise. In the subatomic world, the world of quantum physics, subatomic particles behave similarly to how ghosts and aliens operate. In my life, I have encountered different types of extraterrestrials (small greys, tall greys, tall bluish/greyish ones like Anzar, reptilians, and insectoids). Stand ready.

"You are all standing there with the doctor, Dr. Bug," I said. Dr. Bug was an insectoid alien I wrote about in my story, "Special Processing," in *Timeless Trinity*. They are all staring at me, especially Dr. Bug, and I am trying not to be frightened.

"Gene, what do you think of him?" I asked.

"Well, I wouldn't go to him if I had a choice of doctors, but he *is* sorry," said Gene.

"He's sorry? Well, I guess I can forgive him, forgive people, even aliens, I suppose. What was the purpose of the procedures and my special processing?" I asked.

"That was just it, special processing, you have a special mission and you had to be fixed so you would survive," said Gene.

"I gotcha, I get it. Very good, okay. What exactly did you do to me?" I asked.

"Altered your genetics, slightly, making you able to survive. Some splicing. Ultimately it was for the better, and good, but rather frightening for you, so we placed a masking memory in your mind through a masking procedure," said Dr. Bug.

"Gene, you believe him?" I asked.

"Yeah," said Gene.

"Anzar?" I asked.

"He *is* sorry," said Anzar. I began to relax a little bit knowing that my spirit friend Gene and my ancient alien mystical advisor trusted him.

"So, he is working with your guys, the good guys?" I asked.

"Yes," said Anzar.

"Well, that's helpful. Okay, I won't call you Dr. Bug anymore, what's your name?" I asked.

"Xotran, Dr. Xotran," said Dr. Bug.

"Are you the same one who worked on my friend Terry?" I asked.

"Yes," said Dr. Xotran.

"And you kept him alive?" I asked.

"Yes. Genetic splicing," said Dr. Xotran.

"But he has a lot of medical conditions," I said.

"Yes, we have been following him, preparing you and him for this moment in time, and many others as well," said Dr. Xotran.

"Okay. Anything else I should be doing?" I asked.

"You are doing what you are supposed to do, and do talk to Yvonne, send her an email with the information, so she can tell George Noory," said Anzar.

"This is all very surprising, I must say. I guess it's all hands on deck," I said. No wonder I have always thought Jerusalem crickets that I find in the yard look so familiar. The same with praying mantis insects.

On April 3, 2020, I posted another communiqué. Something weird happened yesterday that I did not discover until this morning. As most of you know, my communiqués are written the day after my spirit walk so that I can have 24 hours to put together what I have been told. Yesterday, Thursday, I took a new route for my spirit walk because of Ginger's suggestion. On my usual route, I have increasingly encountered folks who are not adhering to social distancing guidelines. This new route is hillier, but shorter, and has the advantage of being mostly free of people. I remember that I was having difficulty concentrating during my walk. Still, I do remember that I started my recording on my mobile phone as usual and began my spirit communication. I recorded for 4 minutes and 17 seconds. When I played it back this morning, there was nothing but some random noises and static. That had never happened before. Thinking that it was a device malfunction, I tested my phone by recording my voice for a few seconds and then played it back. No problem: it worked perfectly. So, what happened? And what did I learn yesterday? I am having trouble remembering, I mean, that is why I take the recorder with me in the first place.

My voice recorder is vital because when I am in my meditative state and speaking with the spirits and alien entities, I often cannot remember much from my contact. Since June 10, 2018, I have made recordings on my spirit walks, and this was the first one that did not record. I listened to the recording carefully, and I heard static along with rhythmic clicks that had two distinct patterns. One clicking pattern was one click per second, then nothing but static. The second clicking pattern was rapid, with multiple clicks, then static. I also heard what sounded like faint higher pitched signals—it reminded me of Morse code on an old ship's radio. How did this happen? Why did this happen? I asked my friend Terry about this recording malfunction incident, and he had a few thoughts:

1. There may be a hidden message in those noises and signals.
2. This may be a missing time incident.

He could be correct on both counts, but I was not able to decipher anything from the static and noises. I do, however, know for a fact that it was not a technical malfunction because the voice recorder works fine. That brings me to the conclusion that my recording was tampered with. Why would somebody, some force, or some entity want to erase my spirit recording? I did remember from my connection yesterday that I asked Anzar about my theories of the pandemic's origins. The three possible explanations I have developed about the source of this pandemic are:

1. China released the virus deliberately.
2. China released the virus accidentally.

3. The virus started organically, but China hid the severity of it and made it worse for all of us and continues to lie about its domestic impact.

I think I recall Anzar saying that China released the virus accidentally and that this virus will be worse than most people imagine, and everything will change. The other thing I now remember from yesterday was that Anzar said that bad alien entities were behind this pandemic and played a role in helping bad human actors. I suppose the bad guys would not want me to remember that. So, there is a motive. This is all very interesting. I will ask my spirit guides on my walk, and hopefully, my phone will record. I will get to the bottom of this and let you all know what I discover. Meanwhile, we have to keep pushing forward, and I know the light will win out.

I wrote up and posted my communiqué on April 4, 2020, based on my spirit walk the day before. Before I reveal what I learned about the missing audio recording, I wanted to share a message that came through early the morning of April 3 as I was getting ready to start the day: Dark avoidance. I did some research and found articles about rats and zebrafish and cockroaches and experiments with both dark and light compartments. None of it seemed to apply to humans (e.g., rats and cockroaches naturally gravitate to the dark to hide their dirty habits). They can be conditioned through electric shocks to avoid dark spaces, or they can be given certain drugs to change their natural behavior as well. All interesting, but not what I was looking for. Fear of darkness seems universal among humans, especially children. In extreme cases, it is known as nyctophobia or achluophobia. Some of this fear may be based on negative experiences, but much of it is instinctual. Scientists believe that it is not the darkness itself that frightens people; it is the fear of what the darkness hides. In the dark, we feel vulnerable and exposed and are unable to detect dangerous threats. Fearing the dark gave our ancestors an evolutionary advantage. I believe the mantra that my spirit guides have given me speaks directly to this phenomenon: stay in the light, be the light.

164

"All of you look genuinely concerned. What happened yesterday, Gene?" I asked.

"Alien intervention," said Gene.

"They erased my recording?" I asked.

"They reprogrammed it, and they took it," said Gene.

"That makes sense; that's why I felt so confused. Okay, alright, why?" I asked.

"Because of what Anzar said. They don't want people to know: How China started the pandemic and how bad the virus is and how bad alien entities are helping bad human actors," said Gene.

"Anything else I should remember?" I asked.

"Keep going. Keep doing what you are doing; get to the bottom of the recording problem," said Gene.

"I gave the erased or reprogramed recording to a friend of mine who runs a recording studio. Hopefully, he can analyze it and learn something," I said. Anzar moved forward, an imposing figure, alien or not.

"Did I have some missing time yesterday?" I asked.

"In a way, you were kind of out of phase, you blinked out, then blinked back in, that's how they were able to stop the recording," said Gene.

"Hey Anzar. Is what Gene said what you told me yesterday?" I asked.

"Yes," said Anzar.

"Who did this…phased me out and in and took the recording?" I asked.

"Reptilians. I increased your protection. They are mad about your *Snarc #2* comic. Hitting too close to home," said Anzar. In my *Snarc* comic books reptilians are the bad guys.[150]

"I think you're right. Anything else I need to know?" I asked.

"You can be phased in and out. You now have extra protection," said Anzar.

I do not fear the dark, I understand its power and respect it, but I will not let it stop me. When you shine the light of truth on the dark forces, their actions and motives are no longer hidden in darkness. I will let you all know what my recording studio friend finds, if anything. The voice recorder worked simply fine the next day, by the way. It was indeed a strange anomaly, and I believe Gene and Anzar. Also, my scientist friend Dr. E.M. Young said that this was an example of interference by the bad guys. He reminded me that when you are doing important work on the lighted path, you are a target. It happened to him when he was talking in public. So that you know, I am undeterred and in the light.

Communiqué number 20, April 5, 2020. I heard the song "Calling All Angels" (2003 hit song by the band Train) playing in my head as I got the following message the night before: All nurses, doctors, healers, medics, and corpsmen in the spirit world, we need you now to help and guide and strengthen our healthcare workers as they combat this horrible virus often without the proper gear. I think I spent half the night last night with this song and thought. Our healthcare workers need all the support we can give them.

I walked my new route again yesterday. The voice recorder worked perfectly once more, providing added proof that it had been tampered with the other day. I cannot return to my old walking route because the people walking and biking were not being careful and following the social distancing guidelines, and I cannot risk infecting my Ginger. None but me wear masks. Maybe they think they are not responsible and not susceptible and that it cannot happen to them and their loved ones? I do not know, but it reminds me of the poem by German Lutheran Pastor Martin Niemöller who wrote about the Nazis' rise to power:

First, they came for the socialists, and I did not speak out—
Because I was not a socialist.
Then they came for the trade unionists, and I did not speak
out—Because I was not a trade unionist.
Then they came for the Jews, and I did not speak out—
Because I was not a Jew.
Then they came for me—and there was no one left to speak
for me.[151]

This virus will touch all of us, either directly or indirectly. We are in this pandemic together—all of humanity.

"Hello everybody, all of you are spread out, some here, some not, moving around," I said. Anzar stepped forward.

"You put out the information," said Anzar.

"Hey Anzar. Yes, I put out the information," I said.

"It was attempted retaliation," he said.

"Yeah, I felt something in my bedroom that night. Was that it?" I asked.

"Yes," said Anzar.

"Thank you for the extra protection. I'll keep doing what I'm doing," I said. I heard lots of sirens in the background, approaching.

"Calamities: Financial, economic, natural disaster, and more," he said.

"I know, you've told me, although I know you can't give me a date. I'm worried about going back to work in the classroom. I can't risk infecting Ginger because of her severe asthma. I should just teach online," I said.

"Testing is needed," said Anzar. Emergency vehicles arrive right in front of me on my route.

"COVID-19 emergency call," he said.

"Scary, really scary," I said.

"People should be scared, take it seriously," said Anzar. The paramedics had already got the person from their home and were loading him on the stretcher. I waited and watched them drive away. The scene played out almost as if to add an exclamation point on what Anzar told me and has been telling me.

"You've told me that COVID-19 is the first calamity, then an economic/financial disaster, then a natural disaster, then violent conflict. What about the October 2020 date that popped into my head the other night?" I asked.

"Possibility of violent conflict. Remember, exact dates are often wrong, too many variables," said Anzar.

"Where?" I asked.

"Spreading around the world. Tough times the next two years or longer. Think of what your parents went through for five years under Nazi occupation in Norway. What did they think at the beginning? Do you think they thought it would not be so bad or that it would be over sooner rather than later? You do not know," he said.

"I get it. I'd like to help more," I said.

"You are helping," said Anzar.

That was it for the day. I thought back to the chorus of the song that I mentioned in the beginning of this communiqué:

Calling all you angels (I won't give up if you don't give up)

Communiqué number 21 was posted April 6, 2020. Make something great and wonderful happen today. That was the message I received as I woke up April 5. What if everyone in the entire world woke up with that thought and then carried it out? We have the ability and the power to do this. Occasionally I read from a book of short stories by Red Elk, who was an inter-tribal Native American medicine man. He wrote: "Over my years, I have met thousands of people.

168

Many in various religions and/or ways of thought. I have seen the good and the ugly. Each is a hologram of my inner self. These are me! My fears. My 'ugly and dark' side…and my Godly side. All 'living projections' on my inner self." Quantum physics reveals to us that everything is connected, like a giant soup in the cosmos of which we are a part. What we see in our daily waking lives is what we have created to make sense of this reality. The quantum world, the spirit world, and the world in which alien beings operate (which are one and the same) is another reality. Or, as Red Elk wrote: "When I tell this is all a dream, I mean it!"[152]

"I'd like to ask about the recent UFO sightings off the southern California coast and in Mexico. Do these sightings have anything to do with our pandemic?" I asked.

"Yes, everything to do with it, and more. They are a sign of the battle that goes on—the struggle above and the struggle below," said Anzar.

"Tell me more," I said.

"Aliens are also arguing about what should be done. Some think humans should be punished for what they have done to the environment and each other. Others are more merciful," said Anzar.

"That makes sense. Anything more about October 2020?" I asked.

"Potential for conflict highest then. Opposing forces both here and above. Prepare," said Anzar.

"Thank you, Anzar. Hello, Gene. I see you're all on a war footing," I said.

"Forces of light and forces of darkness. Be aware of the angels of light. Rescue the angels of light," said Gene.

The following is from my communiqué posted on April 7, 2020. Enthusiasm means: God-inspired, having God in you, or in the presence of God. I did not know that it has such spiritual meaning, but it makes sense when you think about it. As a teacher, I am aware that students know if you are enthusiastic about your subject, in my case, history. They can spot a phony. When I am enthusiastic about history, the students take notice and are inspired and empowered to learn. But I am not special. We are surrounded by everyday people who do not think of themselves as enthusiastic, yet they are. I think of Jason Hargrove, a bus driver in Detroit, who continued to transport folks around the city despite the threat of infection during this pandemic. I am sure that it was not easy for him to get up in the morning and go to work in that dangerous environment, but he did. That is enthusiasm. I also think of Areema Nasreen, an acute care nurse in the UK. She continued to go to work and treat and care for her patients during this pandemic. I am sure it was not easy for her to go to work each day and come face to face with death, but she did. That is enthusiasm. Sadly, both Jason and Areema died from the COVID-19 virus on the frontlines. They are heroes who went to work each day, perhaps somewhat reluctantly but ultimately with enthusiasm, inspired by God, wanting to provide for their families and in service to their fellow human beings.[153]

I did not take a spirit walk on April 6 because I did my meditation at home. This morning I received a message that translates to: "do not take a knife to a gunfight." I interpret that to mean that we must use an appropriate level of force in defending ourselves and in facing challenges in life. No half measures. I know that these communiqués are not popular with everyone, but that is okay. Some think I go too far; others believe I do not go far enough. The fact that folks have a reaction and express their feelings is an indication that something is happening. I am enthusiastic about writing them and compelled to do so. As one psychic said: "It's not about being right or wrong; it's about being helpful."

"I feel that some people in power—government and non-government—have information they are not sharing and that they are confused about what is going on," I said.

"They have technical information but not the spiritual guidance—the spiritual is the most important component. We must fight this virus on a spiritual, economic, and health level," said Anzar. As my mom always said, "It is the little apples that keep the big apples on top of the basket."

I posted communiqué number 23 on April 8, 2020. Late in the evening on April 7 and early on April 8, I had scary dreams. Here they are in sequence. First, I was traveling through a city that was being attacked with explosions everywhere. We got to some type of facility with spacecraft. I was on a circular spacecraft seated low in built-in seating positions with maybe six to eight other people (two of whom I knew). Before I entered the spacecraft, however, I was able to see the propulsion unit, and even carried it for a bit as I walked alongside some scientists. The casing was a round-edged rectangular shape, like a breadbox. The drive was housed inside this casing, but I did not see it. After we were seated, the ship started without a sound. Immediately time and space were distorted in such a way that frightened and shocked me, and I woke up. I do remember someone saying that we were headed to Mars, but the ship did not move. I immediately thought of a passage in Vietnam War helicopter pilot Robert Mason's book *Chickenhawk: Back in the World*: "There's an ancient idea that when a man travels, he does not *go* anywhere. Instead, he performs a series of actions that, if done in the proper sequence, will bring his destination to him." That is what was happening as far as I could tell.[154]

In the second dream, I was in a house I did not recognize when a terrible winter storm started. The snow was blowing with hurricane-force winds. I looked out and could see mountains in the distance. The violence of the storm and the sound of the howling winds was so frightening that I woke up. When I checked Facebook in the morning, I saw posts from my relatives on the island of Andøya in Northern Norway. They had just had a terrible winter storm with the same conditions I had just seen in my nightmare 90 minutes before they posted their videos and photos.

The following is from my spirit walk yesterday. For some reason, there were lots of people out with their dogs yesterday, even though I was using the new route that I thought was less traveled. Only one person of the twelve I encountered was wearing a mask like me.

"Seems brighter today among you all," I said.

"Now, this is not the end. It is not even the beginning of the end. But it is, perhaps, the end of the beginning, as Winston Churchill once said. A long struggle ahead," said Anzar.

"One of my paranormal students asked about Dulce Base, what can you tell me?" I asked.[155]

"Closed down now," said Anzar.

"Okay, good," I said.

"That is all you need to know," he said. Wow, I guess I touched a nerve.

"Okay. What more can you guys tell me?" I asked.

"No time to let up, keep pushing, keep going forward. Expect pushback, that happens. People are frightened and upset," said Anzar.

"I think of what the late Jim Marrs said about the boggle factor where people reach a point where they just can't take in any more information. I'll just keep doing what I'm doing," I said.[156]

"Look at all this beauty in the world, but we're not through this yet. We have a way to go," said Gene.

"Thank you, Gene," I said. The process of disclosure reminds me of the words generally attributed to German philosopher Arthur Schopenhauer. To paraphrase: All truth passes through three stages. First, it is ridiculed. Second, it is violently opposed. Third, it is accepted as being self-evident.[157]

Communiqué number 24 was posted on April 9, 2020. It was a rainy day on April 8 and for the past week here in Southern California. It reminds me of growing up in Seattle, my hometown. My mom always called the rain liquid sunshine to try to cheer me up when I could not go out to play. She tried to be optimistic and often smiled even though she had known tremendous hardship in her life. Eighty years ago, April 9, 1940, Nazi Germany invaded Norway and turned her life upside down. My parents were newlyweds. She would see my dad sent to a labor camp and would also lose her first son, my brother, because the Nazis took all the medicine. My mom was one of eight children who grew up poor and with an alcoholic father who later committed suicide. It is on rainy days that I remember these things. Perhaps a necessary catharsis—rain and tears seem to flow together for me. My dear friend David Willson, my writing mentor, who served in Vietnam and is now suffering from multiple myeloma caused by exposure to Agent Orange, lives south of Seattle. David once told me that the modern wars will bring home a new generation of veterans—veterans who historically have never, ever been treated as promised. From the Revolutionary War veterans who were promised money and land and received nothing to the Global War on Terror veterans who have an astounding suicide rate of 22 per day and now make up nearly one-third of the homeless population in this country, the national shame goes on. As David would say: "If we can't save our heroes, who can we save?"

We know that nurses and doctors are dying on the frontlines of this pandemic, and we can add to that list of fallen heroes, the police officers, firefighters, our military, bus drivers, janitors, and food service workers, and more. These are everyday people who are trying to make an honest living and serve their fellow citizens. I read a story about 27-year-old Leilani Jordan from Maryland, a grocery worker with cerebral palsy. She insisted on working despite her disability and despite the dangers posed by the pandemic. She was particularly motivated to help senior citizens with their groceries. She did not have

173

the proper protection. The virus took her life at the beginning of April—a shame and a tragedy.[158]

"I see all of you," I said.

"Keep going," said Gene.

"Hi, Gene," I said.

"Keep your spirits up, concentrate on the good. You can do it," said Gene.

"I will, thank you, I appreciate it," I said. Anzar then stepped forward to address me as Gene stepped aside.

"Hi, Anzar. Lots of conflicting viewpoints and messages out there," I said.

"People need to slow down a little and focus on what is important. Anti-body testing is critical," said Anzar.

"I agree. How about the good and the bad aliens? How much do the people at the highest level of our government know about them? Do they know what to do?" I asked.

"Some at a high level know, but they cannot formulate a position or get people convinced," said Anzar.

"How about the President?" I asked.

"He is not sure. Even those who know something do not know what to do with the information," he said.

"Okay, thank you," I said.

"Keep those who are vulnerable, protected, and help our heroes— that is everybody's job. Be ready for the bad guys who are taking advantage of this situation," said Anzar.

Many people are quietly helping their friends and neighbors. My Ginger is helping every day. I just discovered yesterday that she paid for a service to provide cat food to our family friend, who is in a very high-risk category and could not get out to buy the food for his beloved animal companion. The service will deliver the food to his doorstep. How many of you out there are doing something similar for those in need? You are the light, and you are my heroes too! As I wrote this, the rain continued to fall, and so did my tears. I wish my mom was still here with us so I could hear her say one more time, "It's okay, Bruce, rain is just God's liquid sunshine."

It continued to rain in Southern California as I wrote and posted my communiqué on April 10, 2020. We need rain, but it is best not to get too much at once. My mom always said that everything should be in moderation. I believe that is true for the paranormal as well—we need to remain midway between panic and complacency and stay in balance. Being balanced takes a great deal of concentration and coordination and can be exhausting. Complacency and inaction, however relaxing it can be, often leads to disaster. Full out panic, of course, is much more tiring and can also lead to a negative outcome. The idea of balance seems to work in nature as well. For example, we can look at how our body responds to the COVID-19 virus. Our immune system kicks into action to take on the virus, but in so doing can cause us great harm in mounting an over-reactive defense. Scientists call this a cytokine storm—a condition where the immune system triggers a runaway response that causes more damage to the patient than to the viral invader it is trying to fight. It reminds me of journalist Peter Arnett's Vietnam War dispatch in 1968 for the Associated Press wherein he quoted an anonymous American major: "It became necessary to destroy the town to save it."[159] The madness of war may have contributed to that statement, but it is illustrative of what can happen when we are out of balance. As my Ginger often says: "Let's keep it together." I decided to conduct my spirit meditation indoors on April 9. It was peaceful and quiet, and I did not get soaked.

"Hello, Anzar. A question from a friend about a military facility near his home (I am not mentioning the name of the facility or his name to maintain his privacy). What do you think about the activity there?" I asked.

"The activity is positive, and there is good work being done on the side of the light and for the good of all," said Anzar. Gene stepped forward.

"Hi, Gene. I'm in contact with the actors about our project. I have to decide on the format. I want to thank you for the positive messages. It means a lot to all of us," I said.

"Heigh-ho, heigh-ho, it's off to work we go," sang Gene.

"Thank you for that song, Gene. That was one of my favorites from *Snow White and the Seven Dwarfs*," I said. Anzar returned.

"You are doing a good job. Remember to tell people that alien entities are not causing this virus. Some of the aliens are on your side, and some are against you, but they did not bring it upon you," said Anzar.

"I discussed this very issue with a friend yesterday, and I know we all have to be careful not to cause panic. I want to help people," I said. We must stay balanced and try to keep our spirits up as Gene reminded me with the song. We can do it.

I posted another communiqué on April 11, 2020. An old dream came back to me with incredible power and clarity yesterday. I know it was a dream I had years ago, but I did not remember until yesterday. I was at my old house in Kenmore, Washington, in the backyard. I cannot remember who was with me, but I do remember that I was digging up things that had been buried behind our family home where I grew up. I found furniture, appliances, bicycles, all kinds of household items, toys, and personal items like clothes and letters. Almost everything I could imagine from my life growing up was buried, and I was uncovering it. Why was this stuff buried? It was shocking and haunting. This old dream disturbed me greatly as I went about my day, then it hit me: could the meaning be that the things we bury from our past are never really gone? Perhaps they are just under the surface, waiting. Is now the time to address the meaning because I am ready? I believe so. There could also be a more literal meaning.

When my father died in 1999, I was in a dark place in my life. I was tasked by my sister with clearing out the old house so it could be sold. I was not getting along with my sister and not communicating with my brother at the time. I was angry and grieving and not in a position to make rational decisions. I threw everything away. I drove the contents of my parent's home to the dump and disposed of it—all the things I grew up with, my stuff, and all my parent's belongings. How dreadful, how horrible, and how unconscionable now that I think about that day. All those precious items from our family's past are buried in the landfill in Seattle. Shameful. Subconsciously I am now unburying those items and dealing with the pain that I could not bear at the time. Such is life, I suppose. Maybe it is a time for healing, redemption, catharsis, and rebirth. Not surprising, I guess, since this is Easter weekend. It was a blustery day, and when the rain stopped temporarily, I went out for my spirit walk.

"Hello, everybody. You're all wearing masks in solidarity—of course, you don't need them," I said. All my spirit friends are looking at me as I called on some deceased relatives of a friend of mine.

"Special request from a friend. What is the meaning of a black feather left on someone's bed?" I asked. The deceased relatives of my friend step forward.

"It is a warning, but not doom and gloom, just a message that we are here and watching you. Take extra precautions; this is not over yet, so do not take any chances," said one of the deceased relatives.

"Thank you," I said.

"Raven feather, black feather, a message or connection from be-yond, not necessarily a bad omen. A message to be careful and that your relatives in the spirit world are expressing concern, extra caution. Be careful; we are with you," said another one of the deceased rela-tives.

"Understood, I will pass that on," I said. They then began whis-tling and singing a happy tune.

"Grey skies are gonna clear up, put on a happy face; brush off the clouds and cheer up, put on a happy face… so spread sunshine all over the place. Just put on a happy face, so, put on a happy face," said the deceased relatives.

"Very nice, thank you," I said. My friend's relatives stepped back, and Anzar stepped forward.

"Transitional weather, transitional times, we shall see what people do, staying home, testing, and so forth. We are near the apex," said Anzar.

"Thank you, Anzar. I see the City of Los Angeles from up here," I said. I was walking an alternate route high in the foothills that allowed a view of the city. Gene stepped forward.

"City of Angels, calling all angels," said Gene.

"Hey, Gene, I see it," I said.

"Hang in there. We'll get through this all together. We're all here, and we're with you," said Gene.

"Thank you, guys," I said.

"There are those acting appropriately, cautiously, always operating from a position of love, that is the key, look for those people, that is who you want to rally behind. Listen to those people who operate from a position of love—that is who you should trust in times of crisis."

"Thank you. My Ginger wrote letters to a bunch of old folks who are in a nursing home. I am so proud of her," I said.

"She is such a person," said Anzar. This is a high compliment for Ginger because she always asks people to "just be a person," meaning to be a kind and decent human being.

It was April 12, 2020, a blustery, cloudy, cool Saturday before Easter. I saw five people on my spirit walk the day before, one was wearing a mask, like me, three had masks but were not wearing them, and one had no mask as she walked her dog and talked on the phone, oblivious to the mandatory order in Los Angeles County. I am not sure which is worse, having a mask with you and not using it, or not having a mask at all. I do not understand. Let us live for one another; let us be careful and not put our healthcare workers at greater risk. Come on, people, let us get it together! We can do it!

Growing up, my mom always made me an Easter basket with a chocolate bunny and other candies. We would go to the Norwegian Lutheran Church in Kenmore, and then later, we would have a delicious Easter dinner (usually ham). I remember Easter egg hunts and how I struggled to gather enough Easter eggs surrounded by overly ambitious kids. I was not quick enough, and I disliked the cut-throat competition to see who could collect the most eggs. There was a lot of pushing and shoving and angry words. Eventually, I would just give up and be satisfied with the few eggs I had and remain calm. It was Easter, after all, a time to be grateful, loving, compassionate, and kind, or so I was told. So, as the roughest, meanest kids gathered their eggs and got a special prize for having snatched up the most, I was satisfied and happy that I had a loving family and cozy home. Does it really matter if you have more eggs than the other person? I think not. Love is not about having more than anyone else; love is about making sure everybody has enough.

"Thank you all for being here. I see some of you are watching other things going on, and some of you are looking at me. Thank you for everything you've done," I said. I noticed a family of hawks is following me and screeching and soaring high in the sky. I smiled thinking that they were likely the family of Hawkeye the redtail hawk, my friend.[160]

"It is essential to focus on the light and the mission, and not on yourself. Do what is right. Understand the sacrifices others have made, appreciate them, and be grateful," said Anzar.

"I understand. In Lutheran Sunday school, I was taught about the ultimate sacrifice that Jesus made for all of us. Who am I to complain about anything," I said. Gene stepped forward.

"Hello," said Gene.

"Hey, Gene. I don't see the City of Angels today, too cloudy. Thank you for being my friend in this world and the next," I said.

"We offer a message of love, brotherhood, sisterhood, compassion, forgiveness, and dedication to the light," he said. Gene's words brought me to tears.

"Thank you, Gene, thank you all," I said. And I am grateful to all of you, my dear readers, you are appreciated and loved.

I wrote communiqué number 28 on April 13, 2020. In America, many of our industries and retailers are shut down, our farmers are plowing under their crops and dumping their milk due to lack of demand, there are shifting shortages of consumer items and commodities, there is growing unrest, uneven and often ineffective government, and fear of drifters and looters. We have been here before. During the Great Depression in the 1930s, these same things happened. But now, we are told, this economic crisis is self-imposed by us trying to stop the spread of the COVID-19 virus. However, when you think about it, was not the Great Depression also self-imposed? It was not the wrath of God that crashed the stock market and shut down our economy beginning in 1929; it was the fault of human beings. In 1929 we had over-production, flat wages, most people living paycheck to paycheck, over-extended credit, a weak banking system, and uneven and ineffective government. The stock market concealed the problems that began as early as 1924. Is this a case of history repeating itself? Yes and no. There was no virus panic in 1929, but the virus is just the straw that broke the camel's back, we were already in trouble before COVID-19 struck. So, if we follow this historical analogy to its logical conclusion, this economic crisis will lead to the rise of authoritarianism around the world and eventual worldwide conflict like it did in the late 1930s. But we do not have to accept that downward spiral as inevitable, we can learn from the past instead of repeating it. We must stand up to authoritarian challenges to the global order and restore democratic principles and stand united with our allies and support our working class, who hold up our economy.

Health care and living wages are desperately needed. Lack of adequate health care and economic disparity are exacerbating this COVID-19 pandemic. As Dr. Martin Luther King, Jr. said in 1968 shortly before he was assassinated: "We read one day, 'We hold these truths to be self-evident, that all men are created equal, that they are endowed by their Creator with certain inalienable Rights, that among these are Life, Liberty, and the pursuit of Happiness.' But if a man does not have a job or an income, he has neither life nor liberty nor the possibility for the pursuit of happiness. He merely exists…It is a crime for people to live in this rich nation and receive starvation wages."[161]

It was Easter Sunday as I made my spirit connection inside our home.

"Thank you for everything you do for us. Hello, everybody. I didn't take my walk today. Can you give us some information?" I asked.

"Stay the course, be logical—compassion and logic together," said Anzar.

"Will there be conflict by October?" I asked.

"The possibility for conflict with authoritarian regimes exists, maybe by October of this year, many variables, hopefully not. There is still time to take the steps necessary to restore hope and prosperity and freedom and avoid violent conflict," said Anzar.

"Okay. Thank you. God bless us all," I said. I do believe that there is still time to do the right thing and restore the vibrancy of this nation, support our allies, and collectively confront authoritarian regimes short of war.

On April 14, 2020, I wrote communiqué number 29 based on my spirit walk the day before. It was on this date, April 14, 1865, that President Abraham Lincoln was shot (he died the next day).[162] It was a sad day, but it is also a happy day. My only daughter turned 24 years old on April 14. Because we are in isolation, I will not be able to hug her, but she will stop by so I can give her the birthday cake I made for her. I am so proud of Caitlin. She is determined, tenacious, and sweet. She is studying to be a nurse, and she will be a great one. I have three sons, one daughter, and two grandsons, and I have my Ginger. I am so lucky, the luckiest. I think my two youngest children may have inherited the paranormal gifts I got from my mother. It will be an exciting journey for them both.

As I took my spirit walk yesterday, I remembered a paranormal event from 1994 that I wrote about in my first *Timeless* book. My girlfriend was having emotional problems, no doubt because she was with me, and was in a mental hospital. I went to visit her, and I met a strange little man named George. He was very hyper and was all over the ward talking and interrupting others. My girlfriend said that he liked to steal women's nightgowns and wear them. After a few minutes of visiting, my girlfriend asked for and got permission to leave the ward and take a walk with me on the hospital grounds. To get off the locked-down psych-ward, she needed a pass and had to check in with the guard posted at the elevator. We got in the elevator and headed down to the first floor. Exiting the elevator, we proceeded to the back door of the hospital that led to a beautiful walking path and garden. As we were walking in the corridor, we saw George walking toward us. He had a lady on each arm. How did he get down to the first floor without permission and ahead of us? Who were these two women? He waved at us and giggled along with his female companions. We asked him how he got down to the first floor and he said: "I flew." Then, he laughed hysterically and skipped down the corridor with his two lady friends. My girlfriend and I were stunned. There was no way for him to get off the ward without going through the security guard and no way that he could have been ahead of us. This incident has perplexed me ever since and is one of the 89 paranormal stories included in my *Timeless* trilogy.[163]

This COVID-19 lockdown has been a surreal experience and has only added to the high strangeness I have experienced in my life. Rest assured, dear readers, we will come out of this stronger and more aware.

"Anzar, what can you tell me about the teleportation incident in 1994 in the Seattle mental hospital? Could the guy do it?" I asked.

"Yes. You saw it with your own eyes, right?" Anzar asked.

"Yeah, but how did he do it?" I asked.

"Attention and intention," said Anzar.

"Could I do it?" I asked.

"Yes, if you wanted to and focused on it. What is stopping you?" he asked.

"Nothing, I suppose. What more can you tell me about what is going on with the powers in Washington?" I asked.

"The President really wants to be reelected, like anyone in that position. They see their personal success as the nation's success. Ego," said Anzar.

"I've read that about presidents and how they personally identify with the office," I said.

"He must realize that the workers need help. The stock market can go up and down, but it is not the true indicator. The key is the workers doing things and making things. It would be wise to cut your dependency on those who are doing you harm and undermining your prosperity, liberty, and democracy," said Anzar.

"Thank you, Anzar. Hi, Gene, thank you for being my friend and for everything," I said.

"Dark days ahead, light in the distance, but you must make the right decisions," said Gene.

"I appreciate your friendship, support, and wisdom. Should I keep doing these blogs?" I asked.

"Yeah, keep doing them as long as you can," he said.

As we celebrate my daughter's birthday in the middle of this lockdown, I will take Anzar and Gene's advice to heart. Set your goals high and believe that the seemingly impossible is possible. Surround yourself with those who empower you to make the right decisions as we all help each other. We will come through this together, tougher and brighter. Then, we can have what President Abraham Lincoln in his 1863 Gettysburg Address called: "A new birth of freedom." Just ask yourself: What is stopping you?

Communiqué number 30 was posted on April 15, 2020. It was warm and sunny yesterday. That always gives me hope, but, realistically, we have a long way to go. I think it is safe to assume that many of us will be locked down until Christmas, at least, and that we will never be able to go back to the way things were before. I keep thinking about shoemakers. I know that seems odd, but think about it, how many shoemakers are out there? Not many, and the ones that still are in business, are probably past retirement. Shoes were made better in the past, and when they wore out, a shoemaker could restore them for us. In our modern world, we just throw them away. Shoemaking is a trade, a skilled trade. For the people who lived during the Great Depression here or abroad (like my mom and dad), there was simply no choice—if you want to have shoes, you fix them or have them fixed. Our modern service economy relies on people not being able to fix things, make things, or even cook their own food. There were no gyms where the general public worked out; most of those gyms were for professional weightlifters or bodybuilders. Many people worked out by working hard at the job or in their garden at home. My dad was a carpenter, and he taught me how to use power tools and build things. I was not a very good carpenter, but I have some of the knowledge. My parents had a garden with raspberries and vegetables. My mom canned fruit and made all our food from scratch. I remember begging my mom to buy Wonder Bread because other kids had it, but she refused. Maybe this virus will teach us to be more self-reliant, both as individuals and as a country. I did not realize how often we ate take-out food or ate out. Not only is it healthier to make your own food, but it is also cheaper in the long run. Dependency on foreign manufacturing has got us in a mess. Let us make things again, let us regain the lost skills, and let us appreciate those who are necessary in our lives and pay them accordingly.

"Thank you for everything, my friends," I said as I saluted the American flag that I pass by every day. It makes me feel proud and grateful.

"Hello," said Gene.

"I see you are all busy, trying to help us figure things out, when we go back to work, and so forth. I don't have to go back until the fall. Probably online then too," I said.

"Safest thing to do. Be careful," he said.

"What do you think, Anzar? Will the virus come in waves?" I asked.

"Yes. There is a chance it will mutate so that the second wave will be the worst of all, and the third wave will be worse than the first," said Anzar. There was some electromagnetic interference. It lasted for almost a minute, and I did not notice it until I played back my recording.

"Be ready," added Anzar.

"I don't see the City of Angels today. Foggy, or smoggy, or haze in the distance. Anything else I should be doing?" I asked.

"Be loving and operate from a position of love," said Anzar.

"Okay, I know, but it's good to be reminded," I said. Gene stepped forward again.

"Teleportation, it's important to bring it up in your next interview. Your experience in 1994," said Gene.

"I will. It's funny that I haven't brought it up in all the interviews I have done the past two years. Thank you," I said. In fact, for some strange reason, the story about my teleportation experience is not listed in the table of contents although it is in the first *Timeless* book. Although we have a long way to go, I know we can do it. Let us face it, these boots (or shoes) are made for walking, so when the time is right, let us get moving America![164]

I published communiqué number 31 on April 16, 2020, after thinking carefully about my spirit walk on April 15. It seems as though the rain has gone away, and warm weather is upon us. I heard lots of birds yesterday during my spirit walk. I did not expect any trouble as I took my peaceful meditative walk, although the four people I encountered were not wearing masks. I recorded my contact with spirit and alien entities as usual on my voice recorder on my phone, a little over five minutes. Then, I tried to play it back. Nothing, just static. I turned on the voice recorder and recorded for 19 seconds. I played it back, and only at the 14-second mark did I hear something— birdsong. My spirit communication was vital yesterday; I was given information about the potential for conflict in October and a very profound observation about life and death by Anzar. None of it recorded. I quickly tried the voice recorder again to document what I could remember. It is not easy to remember what is said during my spirit communication. I have sent the disrupted audio files to a friend of mine who is a scientist to get his opinion, but I already know that the electromagnetic interference was not of terrestrial origin.

When I arrived home, I noticed that the front porch light came on briefly and sporadically, and then went off. Once inside, I tested the switch, and it was off. I switched it on and off a few times, and it functioned perfectly. I suspected I had carried some residual energy from the electromagnetic interference incident with me. On such a beautiful day filled with sunshine and birdsong, I did not suspect that this extra-terrestrial interference would strike again. It was more annoying than frightening. I believe it is significant that the first sound I heard as the recorder began recording again was birdsong. The beauty and purity of the birds singing broke through and reminded me that good does triumph over evil, but evil is always there, lurking, and waiting for an opportunity. Let's all be aware and on guard as we enjoy our precious natural world in the light.

"What more can you tell me about October 2020 so that we can all prepare?" I asked.

"Just before the presidential election, the bad guys will try to take advantage and cause conflict," said Anzar.

"Thank you, I will prepare and spread the word," I said, as Gene stepped forward.

"Love is the answer, love is the most important thing, but not everything can be sweetness and light. I enjoy seeing the City of Angels with you on these walks," said Gene.

"Thank you, Gene, I agree. I like that you can see the view with me," I said.

"Everything is the way it has been for thousands of years. Your space is limited in this life and then is eternal in the next," said Anzar. That was all I could remember from my five-minute exchange with Anzar and Gene. Maybe I will try using my other phone, perhaps even a video. We shall see. What Anzar meant by "our space" is intriguing, and I will be thinking about that one for a while.

It was time for another spirit walk on April 16, 2020, and then I wrote and published my communiqué the next day, April 17. On April 16, at about 4:00 am, my Ginger saw a giant moth-like thing in the corner of the bedroom. It was six to eight inches across. I was sleeping at the time. It eventually disappeared by dropping down out of sight. She said it was light, not a shadow. The last time we had light anomalies in the bedroom, there was an attempted abduction experience soon after. As I have said before, Ginger is not one to jump to a paranormal explanation for such things as she is somewhat skeptical, but I could tell this strange sighting was a little bit disturbing for her. She grounds me and always asks pertinent questions. She made me laugh so hard the other day when she asked about my spirit walks. "You are a smartie…are you sure you are not just talking to yourself out there?" she said. Hilarious! Sure, the thought has run through my mind, but I have had too many instances of affirmation and validation from my contact with the deceased to dismiss the voices I hear and the images I see. And, since I believe that the dead and aliens work in the same realm, I am confident that the alien entities I encounter and communicate with on my spirit walks are not just me talking to myself. Now, it could be that an aspect of Anzar is an aspect of me, as he told me and my friend Lucinda postulated, so I suppose you could say that I may be talking to some part of me out there in the spirit/alien/quantum world. All this brings me back to what Anzar said yesterday, "Your space is limited in this life and then is eternal in the next." What did he mean by space? Does it mean the actual physical space that I occupy in this reality? Does he mean our space-time continuum that I perceive? Could it be both? I am simply not sure, and that is okay because I am lucky enough to have Ginger by my side on this strange journey.

I took the Valley Center route today. All my spirit friends were ready to say something, and I saw Anzar step up.

"Everything will eventually be okay, but the struggle is ongoing. The light will win, but it is not over yet. Not time to let up, not time to relax, or put our guard down, it is a time to stay strong and focused on the good and the light. Although we are helping you, you must realize that you must help yourselves as well," said Anzar.

"That is good, and when you say we, you mean the good ETs?" I asked. Anzar smiled and nodded yes. I then saw my friend, Gene.

"Different route today. Mountains, spirit medicine path, and the beauty of creation," said Gene.

"A change of scenery. I appreciate everything you guys do for me, if there is anything I can do, let me know," I said.

"Help who you can help, save who you can save. Remember, if you save one person, you save all humanity. One person can start this pandemic, and one can end it," said Anzar.

I wrote and posted communiqué number 33 on April 18, 2020, based on my spirit communication the day before. I was working outside with my wife Ginger and my youngest son Leif yesterday—digging holes. I enjoy being grounded and working with my hands out in the fresh air. It is mentally relaxing to do something physical and take a break from my cerebral pursuits. As a result of my "hard labors," I did my spirit communication inside. I remember working for my father as a carpenter and daydreaming about the big questions. My dad would catch me in the middle of such thoughts and get upset. "Do something! Keep moving! What if the owner came by and saw you standing there doing nothing?" I understand now why my dad was mad, but I was not idle, far from it. The ditch-digging, sweeping, and framing work I did caused me to enter into somewhat of a meditative state. Although I did not fully appreciate it at the time, I now think back to how important it was for my intellectual and spiritual growth. We are all physical and ethereal beings.

While Leif and I were digging holes yesterday in the tough, rocky soil in our backyard, we had to use the San Angelo bar—a heavy steel shaft flattened on one end and pointed on the other, used for breaking up rocky soil. The tool is named after the City of San Angelo in West Texas, where the bar was used to break up the hardened top layer of soil to cultivate the land. San Angelo was established in 1867 across the Concho River from Fort Concho, which was the home of the black cavalry known as the Buffalo Soldiers. The town was originally named Santa Angela after the wife of the city's founder, Bart Dewitt. As most of you know, "*santa*" in Spanish means holy or saint. So, as Leif was struggling to punch through the rocky dirt with the San Angelo bar yesterday, I was watching and daydreaming. I finally told Leif and Ginger: "I think San Angelo is the patron saint of frustrated hole diggers." They were amused, slightly. I can only imagine what my dad would have said.

"I see you all there. You're all looking up at the sky, pointing to something—some kind of celestial anomaly," I said.

"You will see it and be sure to get Leif and Ginger to see," said Anzar.

"What is it?" I asked.

"It is a sign of protection," he said.

"We need it. With so much going on in the world now, it's difficult to know who to trust and who not to trust," I said.

"It is simple. Trust those who operate from a position of love," said Anzar.

"Right. Thank you. What was the butterfly object that Ginger saw yesterday?" I asked, as Gene stepped in.

"It was not bad. It was Theodora, your guardian angel, and spirit guide," said Gene.

"Good to know," I said.

"Remember, outer space and inner space are the same. Operate from a position of love," said Anzar. I nodded yes and smiled. Anzar was giving me more clues about the "space" he spoke of the other day. Keep working hard and keep dreaming because we need both.

April 19, 2020. Another day, and another communiqué. A friend and colleague of mine died yesterday. He had cancer. I had a good talk with him last year about his cancer, and he passed on something he had learned from the doctor who first diagnosed his disease. The doctor noticed that his fingernails were clubbing or curving downward. Ken felt fine, but the doctor was concerned, and tests were conducted—he indeed had cancer. It is important to note that clubbed fingernails are not always a sign of cancer, and the disease does not always cause clubbed nails, but it is a warning sign for sure. More importantly, Ken talked to me about working, teaching, and the importance of his family and keeping a positive attitude. He was one of the first people I met when I started at Citrus College in 1998. I will miss him, and I will always remember how kind and helpful he was.

"What more can you tell me about this celestial anomaly you talked about yesterday?" I asked.

"In the heavens, you will see it, it will be clear, and you will know what it means," said Anzar.

"Is it for me or everybody?" I asked.

"It is for everybody, an opportunity for your ultimate protection," said Anzar.

"What about the calamities you warned me about before?" I asked.

"Threats can be seen as rallying points for people to come together and save themselves, so be prepared," he said.

"Understood. Hey Gene, how are you?" I asked as Gene stepped forward.

"Good to hear from you and see you," said Gene.

"I hope we don't get interference today," I said.

"I hope not. My sister and her son work very hard to help people during this pandemic. I want them to know that I'm proud of them," said Gene.

"I'll tell them. What do you think of this anomaly?" I asked.

"It'll be big, no doubt about it. Love is the answer," said Gene. Gene showed me the Beatles poster that he had in his room.

"I remember the Beatles poster. John, Paul, George, and Ringo," I said.

"Remind her," said Gene.

"I will," I said.

Dear readers, it is hard to believe this is the 34th entry. I am learning so much by taking the time to do my spirit communication every day and then transcribing, compiling, and ruminating. Gene mentioning the Beatles was quite insightful. John Lennon wrote the song "Help" in 1965 at the height of Beatlemania when he was grappling with their success. It was a breakthrough in his songwriting, and it was very much a cry for help.

> *Help me if you can, I am feeling down*
> *And I do appreciate you being 'round*
> *Help me get my feet back on the ground*
> *Won't you please, please help me?*

I hope that my sharing helps you all in some small way. Let me help.

I posted communiqué number 35 on April 20, 2020. I started my message on Facebook as I normally do, "Dear Friends of the Light." Today, April 20, 2020, is a special day, and, no, I am not talking about the Four-Twenty celebration of weed. Ginger and I celebrate our anniversary the 20th of every month. We were married on January 20, 2012, the same anniversary as my parents (theirs was January 20, 1940). I would like to take some credit for our relationship being successful, but most of the credit goes to Ginger. She saved me, mostly from myself. It was not an easy transition for either of us, as I can be quite difficult. But then life is about transitions. We are going through many now in this world. Sometimes it feels as if we have no control and no power over these events. I am reminded of a line from Walt

Whitman in *Leaves of Grass*: "That the powerful play goes on, and you will contribute a verse."[165] I love this quote because it acknowledges the enormity of events but also reminds us that we all have a role to play. Famed theatre director and acting teacher Konstantin Stanislavski once said that "there are no small parts, only small actors." Since "all the world's a stage," as Shakespeare wrote, we must embrace our part and do our best as we stay in the light and operate from a position of love.[166] If we were to use a holographic universe framework for reality taken to its extreme where we are all living in a simulation, it seems as though Whitman, Stanislavski, and Shakespeare would probably agree that we are role players in a celestial game.

"Hello, everybody," I said.

"Are you ready for the Big Show?" asked Anzar and Gene together.

"Big Show? I guess so; it depends on what the Big Show is," I said.

"You must be ready," said Anzar.

"Sounds, scary," I said.

"You have been warned," said Anzar.

"Yes, true, and I can do more. Is this connected to this celestial anomaly you've been talking about?" I asked.

"Yes," said Anzar.

"What can I tell my friends?" I asked.

"The calamities are not over, be smart, prepare," he said.

"Be loving and caring—you'll need each other more than you ever thought you would," added Gene.

"Okay. I guess you are right," I said.

"Good," said Anzar. I reached the highest elevation on my spirit walk.

"I see the City of Angels, my favorite part of our spirit walk. The City of Angels, where dreams and nightmares both come true," said Gene.

"Exactly," I said. I moved to Southern California in 1998 and have lived here longer than any other previous place. I thought of the song "Los Angeles," by the band X.

> *She, had to leave Los Angeles ...*
> *She had to get out (get out!)*
> *Get out (get out!)*
> *Get out (get out!)...*
> *The days change at night*
> *Change in an instant*[167]

As we go about our daily routines, we are subject to transitions: morning becomes afternoon and then the evening. Light becomes dark. We cannot have the light without the dark, as Anzar once told me. There is sadness when we lose a loved one, and then happiness replaces the feeling of sorrow. You cannot have happiness without sadness. We must live and take the risk of living in a world of transitions.

I posted yet another communiqué on April 21, 2020. Anti-lockdown protests were spreading across the country. There is a custom in Norway called *dugnad*. The word means support in Norwegian. The concept is that people within a town or village must work together on community projects. It is not a law, but if a citizen does not comply, their neighbors will not think very highly of them. This custom of communal work goes back centuries and is not uncommon in other agricultural societies around the world. A *dugnad* could be tasks like roofing, haymaking, housebuilding, or, in my case, helping put on a theatrical play. I wrote *The Epiphany* based on my parents' experiences during the Nazi occupation of Norway in the Second World

War. The little community of Åse, where my parents lived, came together, and turned their gym into a theater and housed and fed all the American student actors. It was a big success and a beautiful example of what a community can do when they come together. Norwegian national television covered our play, and the experience transformed the fifteen American student actors. They all fell in love with Norway and with the Norwegian people.[168]

We pride ourselves on being rugged individualists here in America. That strength is part of what made us who we are today, the number one power on Earth. However, strengths can often turn out to be weaknesses as well. Americans tend to solve things by conflict and oftentimes conflict is unwarranted, divisive, and destructive. The people who are protesting the lockdown stay-at-home orders on the basis of protecting their individual freedom is clearly an example of this— the individual versus community level of freedom. It strikes right to the soul of America dating back to federalist and anti-federalist arguments among the founding fathers. I grew up with traditional Norwegian values, but I was born in America. I often find myself torn between my sense of rugged individualism and my feeling of communalism. I have finally concluded that the best solution for me is to apply these two strengths as the situation dictates. Sometimes I should be community-oriented, and other times it seems appropriate to go my own way and blaze a trail. Maybe this is my version of Carl Jung's "duality of man."[169] Carl Jung, a protégé of Sigmund Freud, said that all human beings are part warrior and part peacemaker. Instinctually, we are the product of thousands of years of genetic evolution producing survivors who could run and fight—guided by the fight-or-flight mechanism within our brain stems. But most of us would prefer to live in peace. I feel intimately connected to this dichotomy in grappling with my Norwegian heritage, on the one hand, and my American upbringing on the other. Perhaps that is okay, and maybe Theodore Roosevelt was right when he suggested that we should "speak softly and carry a big stick."

"Thank you all for being here. I'm recording my spirit communication inside today because I needed a break from all the people wandering around outside not wearing masks. What more could you say about this celestial anomaly? What can I do?" I asked.

"It will be in the heavens. You will know. There will be time, and there will be a time. The Big Show," said Anzar.

"I think I get it…is this some kind of full disclosure event we are talking about?" I asked.

"It is going to be necessary," said Anzar.

"Okay. Thank you for talking to me. I appreciate it," I said.

I get answers to my questions, but those answers always seem to beg more questions. Will the celestial anomaly be a visible object in the sky, like a supernova, a comet, or perhaps an asteroid hurtling toward Earth? Or will it be a sky full of spaceships? Could it be more audible like a clear signal from some distant alien civilization? Or maybe the heavens will be crowded with angels and our spirit ancestors? I simply do not know. The scientific definition of celestial anomalies includes: the Big Bang, an accelerating universe, dark energy and matter, matter/anti-matter, monopoles, and quasars. Anzar calls it the Big Show, so I am assuming it will not be subtle or that only a handful of people will witness the anomaly. He does say anomaly, not anomalies, so that indicates only one. I guess we just have to wait and see. Anzar provides clues, and today's clue was that there will be time, and there will be a time. I have to think about that for a while. Whatever it is or will be, I am sure that I will need to draw on both my rugged individualism and my communalism to complete my mission.

Communiqué number 37 was released April 22, 2020. The Centers for Disease Control (CDC) Director, Dr. Robert Redfield, warned that the second wave of COVID-19 could be deadlier than the first wave we are currently experiencing. He issued this warning as protesting against stay-at-home orders mount. A typical influenza season can start as early as November and extend until May. In the United States, according to the National Center for Biotechnology Information (NCBI), there are 25 to 50 million documented influenza cases, 225,000 hospitalizations, and approximately 20,000 deaths every year. If the second wave of COVID-19 hits us next flu season, one can see how that would be devastating when the two diseases hit us at the same time. It is no wonder Dr. Redfield and many other medical professionals are concerned. In the 1918 Spanish Flu pandemic, the second wave was the worst, and the third wave was worse than the first. It could be true that there were no antibiotics to treat secondary bacterial infections in those days, and that may have contributed to the high death rate, but a similar pandemic pattern could emerge.

The public health problem must be balanced against the public unemployment problem. Miles-long lines have formed at food banks, and small business loans that were promised have not materialized for most small businesses with the money going instead to larger corporations. As of April 21, 2020, 22 million Americans have filed for unemployment. Farmers are plowing under their crops as people go hungry. My daughter, who is going to college to be a nurse, lost her three part-time jobs and has not received a stimulus check or unemployment. Luckily, even though Ginger and I are in the most vulnerable category and have to stay locked down much longer than other people, I am able to work from home and help my family and friends. The big question emerges: is there a way to protect the most vulnerable and safely put others back to work to get the economy going again?

Many medical and public policy experts say the answer is testing. If a person has already been exposed to COVID-19, then they should be able to work. The problem is that there are not enough antibody tests to test those millions of workers. A few people say it is okay to sacrifice the elderly and the sick and the vulnerable and just open up the economy now and rely on herd immunity. Many healthcare professionals believe we need to shelter-in-place and hold out until we bring the numbers down more and then slowly open the economy when the time is right. It seems clear to me that the answer should come from a position of love. Instead of giving billions to corporations who already have an embarrassment of riches in reserve, put those billions into testing and protective equipment for our healthcare workers and first responders and into the pockets of the unemployed and small businesses. Then, we can put the people who have been exposed back to work. While we do that, protect the vulnerable because that is the right thing to do. Could it really be that simple?

"Hello, everybody, thank you all for being here. It seems very strange outside today. More strange than usual, even in this unusual time. Thank you for letting Ginger see the butterfly anomaly. Maybe she could see a UFO next time?" I asked.

"You shall see," said Anzar.

"I'm interested in the Big Show. Will it be audio, visual, subliminal, spiritual, physical?" I asked.

"Everything," said Anzar.

"I understand. So, there will be no mistaking it, and everybody on Earth will know what is going on?" I asked.

"That is correct," he said.

"That really is a Big Show," I said.

"Be prepared and be ready," said Anzar.

"Okay. Yes, am I doing what I'm supposed to be doing? Writing, posting, radio show, books, comic books, everything?" I asked.

"Yes, that is it," he said. My friend Gene comes forward.

"Hi, Gene. I'll make an extra effort with the actors to get them going on our project," I said.

"Okay. The angels will come," said Gene.

"To Earth? To us?" I asked.

"Yes. And you'll all be contacted and protected," he said.

"Thank you, Gene. I appreciate our continuing friendship. I've always admired and looked up to you," I said, tears forming in my eyes.

"Literally now," said Gene, with a smile that made me laugh.

"Ha, very funny," I said.

The Big Show may not exactly be what we think it is, and then again, it might. Have you ever been through some dramatic event, and then you figure out how significant it was later? In the middle of the incident, maybe we cannot quite comprehend the importance because it is so out of the normal realm of our day-to-day reality. Perhaps the Big Event will be like that. And just like those previous dramatic events in our lives, we are forever changed by them. As Ginger says: "What we think is important today may not hold the same importance tomorrow." Ultimately, I believe the light will shine on us all, the angels will walk among us, and we will be saved.

I posted communiqué number 38 on April 23, 2020. I had a great interview with Dr. Jeffrey Mishlove on his show *New Thinking Allowed*. The two interview segments will be broadcast on May 15. Because Anzar reminded me, I brought up the 1994 paranormal event I experienced at the University of Washington psychiatric ward where a mental patient named George was able to be seemingly in two places at once. What I called teleportation, Dr. Mishlove called a possible example of bilocation. Bilocation is where an entity can be in two locations at once. In quantum physics, it is called superposition.[170] I am not sure exactly how it works, but I will return to my idea that the spirit world, the alien world, and the quantum world are the same. Is it possible for you and me to be in two places at once? I think all of us have experienced something similar. Have you ever been somewhere and zoned out and transported yourself to another place and time in your thoughts? Usually, someone snaps you out of it, and you return to the reality you were in, often with some measure of embarrassment. Sometimes this is called daydreaming. All this points to the

concept of consciousness, of course, since consciousness is fundamental. That leaves us with a world of possibilities. So, maybe we can
all teleport or bilocate. As Anzar told me, you can do it, all you need
is attention and intention.

"Thank you all for being here. Some have asked if aliens are coming as part of the Big Show," I said.

"Yes, but we are already here. It will be visually stunning, audi-
tory, subliminal, spiritual, everything," said Anzar.

"Some have asked me why you need a spacecraft when you can
travel inter-dimensionally," I said.

"For some, it makes it easier," said Anzar.

"Some of the entities we have encountered seem like androids,
usually described as the little greys. Are there spacecraft for them?" I
asked.

"Yes. They are semi-sentient, and we deploy them in smaller
craft. The larger spaceships are for sentient travelers. Remember, we
are not that far away; we are right here, and we always have been,"
he said. Gene stepped closer.

"Thank you, guys. Some researchers are having a debate about the
term "non-human intelligence." If we say non-terrestrial, then that
leaves out ghosts and the spirits of our loved ones. Gene, what do you
think?" I asked.

"I consider myself to be human, of course, what else would I be?"
said Gene.

"Inter-dimensional intelligence. Or, you could say, non- or semi-
corporal inter-dimensional intelligence," said Anzar.

"We do what we can where we are," said Gene.

"I like it. Thank you," I said.

My discussion with my spirit friends was enlightening as usual,
but their answers left me with more questions. If we assume that

teleportation, bilocation or superposition is possible, then it makes sense that an inter-dimensional intelligence would not have to be totally corporal and might present itself as some type of ghost-like image as the process is taking place. This type of presentation is what I have called phasing in and phasing out of our reality. I have seen ghosts and spirits, as well as alien entities, do this. Returning to George, the mental patient, could he have transferred or phased his corporal self to the main floor of the hospital and left a ghost-like image behind on the seventh floor? It would be interesting to know if anyone saw him on the seventh floor when we saw him on the ground floor. Perhaps this bilocation or teleportation is what he meant by saying that he flew. It seems as though if our intention and attention are strong enough, there are no boundaries. We survive death, and we can bilocate at will to accomplish our missions. In other words, as Gene said: "We do what we can where we are."

I posted another communiqué on April 24, 2020. It was number 39 in the series. The word re-accommodation came up in my mind yesterday morning. The last time I heard this word, it was referring to airline passengers being taken off a flight by force. The airline calls this procedure re-accommodation, an amusing euphemism for someone being thrown off an airplane. So, why did this word pop into my mind? Should I take it to mean what the airlines mean, or should I take the more literal meaning, which would be to provide lodging or specific space, again? Ah, there is that word space. What did Anzar say the other day? Oh, yeah, outer space and inner space are the same. He also said, "Your space is limited in this life and then is eternal in the next." Hmm, let us try to put this puzzle together, shall we? The messages I am getting seem to point to something better beyond this life. Gene was clear about how beautiful his spirit existence is, and I believe him. After my mom passed away in 1990, she appeared and told me that "there is a heaven," and that is certainly comforting.

There is an ongoing debate about the term non-human intelligence (referring to aliens, ghosts, and all types of spiritual entities), as I have written about recently. Someone suggested that we should just refer to all these entities as conscious intelligence or CI. I like that simple solution because it does not exclude anything. Now, what if we substitute the word consciousness for space? Outer consciousness is the same as inner consciousness, and your consciousness is limited in this life and then is eternal in the next. Wow! That makes re-accommodation sound less scary, for sure. So, if we get bumped from this flight, maybe I will see you on the next one. Bon voyage!

"Hi, Gene. I know I didn't do much with the actors yesterday, but I'll get them going with some dialogues," I said.

"That will be interesting," said Gene. Sometimes I was not sure if Gene was being sarcastic.

"This idea of re-accommodating. Do you think it's for those who haven't done what they're supposed to do or for those who've done what they're supposed to do?" I asked.

"Those that did, re-accommodated into a different reality," said Gene.

"Thank you, Gene," I said. Anzar stepped forward.

"Hi, Anzar. Some people say we are leaving and going off the planet, perhaps even sooner rather than later," I said.

"An alternate reality where things are better," said Anzar.

"That would be great, but would some stay behind?" I asked.

"That is the re-accommodation," said Anzar.

"I would like to be with my family. Gene has said that in another reality, he has a physical form and is enjoying life with his family. So, can we be re-accommodated without passing away in one of the dimensions?" I asked.

"Unfortunately, not," said Anzar.

"So, something must happen?" I asked.

"Yes," said Anzar.

"Okay. Well, I want to help and play my role. A writer and communicator that is what I'm doing and hopefully that's enough," I said.

"There may be more you will have to do. Do the right things, say the right things, act the right way, and set an example—in this world and the next," said Anzar. I am not sure if I should be excited about what I learned or frightened. Knowledge is power, they say. But they also say that ignorance is bliss. So, is it better to be frightened and empowered or helpless and blissful? I guess I will choose empowered, even if that means I will have some fear. It is comforting to know that my consciousness expands and never diminishes. We are forever, and we are timeless—not a bad re-accommodation.

On April 25, 2020, I published communiqué number 40. I called my communiqués, "News from the Western Front." We were told it was a war against COVID-19, so I published these as a wartime communiqué—it seemed appropriate. What makes a good crisis manager? I believe it is someone who can remain calm and focused and not let their emotions carry them away. Easier said than done. Since I was a little kid, I have always done well in a crisis. I can remain generally calm and do what needs to be done. When I worked in the military prison in Germany and the maximum-security state prison in Minnesota, I was able to stay focused and not overreact in stressful situations like deadly assaults, suicide attempts, rapes, and fires. That does not mean that I was not affected, far from it. The detrimental psychological impact caused by those situations came later. I was only able to delay the onset. I used to call this calm focus, going into my protective bubble. Because my favorite character on *Star Trek* was Spock, I used him as a model for my behavior in traumatic situations. Cool and without emotion. The problem is that life is 99.9% calm and only 0.1% traumatic. My Spock-like persona served me well in those times of trauma but not so well in most situations in ordinary life. It negatively impacted my relationships and my emotional well-being. We can never stop bad things from happening, but we can regulate our emotions in response. We face tough days, weeks, and months ahead. I stand ready to use my wise mind.

"I thank God for every day and for my learning. Thank you all for being here. I am concerned about the Big Show," I said.

"It will be okay," said Anzar.

"Except for the re-accommodation you spoke of yesterday. It all sounds pretty scary," I said.

"Yes, but just keep doing the right thing, and you will be okay," said Anzar.

"I worry more for my family and friends than for myself," I said.

"They will be okay," said Anzar. I nodded yes and half-smiled. Gene stepped forward.

"Hi, Gene, thank you for being my friend and for helping me understand what's going on. I know there is a reason why you asked me to gather the actors and do some readings. I guess it'll be more apparent to me later," I said.

"Yeah, the Big Show will be dramatic, good to be reminded of the dramatic elements—all the world's a stage after all. Be consistent, be persistent, and be at peace," said Gene. Just then, I reached the highest point in my daily walk where you can see downtown Los Angeles.

"Do you see the City of Angels? There it is, a little hazy," I said.

"Yeah. I like it," said Gene.

"I appreciate everything you guys do. Any more you can tell me?" I asked.

"October will be a terrible month," said Anzar. I acknowledged with a nod of my head.

"Remember: the quick light," said Anzar. I was perplexed, but Anzar and Gene had already disconnected.

I am not sure what Anzar meant by the quick light. Could he be referring to bilocation like in the classic dual slit experiment? Photons can appear as particles or waves depending on if they are being observed.[171] This phenomenon is known as wave-particle duality. Or maybe he was just talking about the speed of light or perhaps even the faster than light speed used in *Star Trek* (warp factor). I suppose we shall see as we head into October, and I try to keep my wise mind intact. Maximum warp, Captain!

Communiqué number 41 was posted on April 26, 2020. Approximately 205 years ago, on April 10, 1815, Mt. Tambora in Indonesia erupted. It remains the most massive volcanic eruption in human history. The mountain blew its top off, losing nearly 5000 feet in elevation. Estimates were that 71,000 people were killed, and the explosion caused climate anomalies such as the infamous "year without summer" in 1816. In the Northern Hemisphere, crops failed and livestock died creating the worst famine of the century.

Lightning, tornadoes, and other weather anomalies frighten me. According to the Weather Source website, "When it comes to weather and climate, anomalies are becoming more frequent and the departures from normal more intense."[172] Weather anomalies could come from global warming or a geological event like a volcano. I have had volcano and tornado nightmares for quite some time now. Sometimes I hear gigantic explosions that shake the ground and the house in my semi-dream state. I am not quite sure what to make of all this. It could be a warning of things to come, or it could be merely deep-seated fears rising to the surface from my subconscious mind. In any event, it never hurts to prepare.

"It's Saturday, very hot today, didn't start my spirit walk until almost noon. We have been discussing the Big Show. Sounds like October...is that true?" I asked.

"Approximately, no exact dates," said Anzar.

"What can I do to prepare?" I asked.

"Food and water, generator, remain calm, tenacity, perseverance, and protection. All those things. Be careful. Sunset at midday," said Anzar.

"Okay. That doesn't sound good. Alright. Not sure exactly what that means. How about you, Gene?" I asked.

"Check in with family and friends every day—very important," said Gene.

"What are the bad aliens doing?" I asked.

"Helping cause confusion, so people are driven apart. You must be united. You cannot weather a crisis if you are divided. To divide and conquer is an old trick," said Anzar.

"Will this be like the Rapture?" I asked.

"Not exactly, but a similar concept," said Anzar.

"Okay, lots to think about now. How are you doing, Gene?"

"Great, today is forever!" said Gene, with great enthusiasm.

"Today is forever. I love it! So good to talk to you. Thank you both. Anzar, can you tell me what you mean by quick light?" I asked. Anzar showed me a lightning bolt.

"Lightning? You're showing me a lightning bolt. That gives me a clue. Thank you," I said.

"Weather anomalies could be considered celestial anomalies," he said.

Heaven and Earth. As above, so below. The Big Show is consuming my thinking. I know that we will be okay in the long run, but it sounds pretty frightening. Everything is connected. Perhaps a celestial anomaly will signal the beginning, then a series of calamities will result that are tied together. I do not know. I could be very wrong. I am not making a prediction; I am just relating what I am being told and making preparations. As Anzar says so often, predictions can be wrong, but preparations are always appropriate.

I posted communiqué number 42 on April 27, 2020. The lockdown continues in Southern California and much of the United States and the world. I keep reminding myself of Ginger's wisdom: "What we think is important today may not hold the same importance tomorrow." I have heard that many people are bored and at their wits end as the COVID-19 crisis has shut down "normal" life. I believe people feel that way because this is a paradigm shift and an opportunity for us to find peace within ourselves as the hustle and bustle of daily life has ground to a halt. The rhythm of nature is more important than the artificial time and space we previously lived by day-to-day. Maybe it is time for our focus to be sharper and not try to multitask everything and instead simplify and clarify. That is not to say that it is not a time for action, far from it. We must live by the motto *carpe diem* (seize the day), make it count, and make good things happen. What we are going through is more of a spiritual crisis than and an economic or health crisis. The virus cannot defeat us if we dig deep within ourselves for strength and courage and stand united in spirit and action.

I did my spirit communication inside yesterday; it was pretty hot. Instead of recording what I heard and saw, I wrote it down. That was an exciting process, free-flowing, and very productive.

"Hello, Anzar, what can you tell me?" I asked.

"Welcome the truth, embrace destiny, overcome fear," said Anzar.

"It looks like you're all going somewhere," I said as I noticed Gene. He was smiling as usual.

"We'll be back," said Gene.

"Where are you going?" I asked.

"A short trip to straighten something out," said Gene.

"A signal coming from far away, we shall intercept," said Anzar. I paused for a moment trying to imagine what this signal was.

"I see. Celestial anomalies?" I asked.

"Be patient, be vigilant, be open," said Anzar.

"The truth is here," said Gene.

"The light is open to all," said Anzar. I had to be honest, a lot of the information I was getting could be overwhelming.

"Sometimes, I get confused," I said.

"Listen and watch," said Anzar. Gene stepped forward and stood very close. I knew he had something important to tell me.

"You see me?" said Gene. I nodded my head up and down.

"What do you see?" asked Gene.

"You, Gene," I said.

"Look again," said Gene. I then saw him unfurl magnificent wings. I was dumbfounded. I might have gasped in amazement.

"You've ascended," I said. Gene nodded his head proudly.

"Love and light, answers all questions," said Anzar.

"I'm here," said Gene.

"I know, thank you," I said.

For those of you who are fascinated by my friend Gene (and frankly who would not be), please read more about him in my first *Timeless* book. The story is called: "It's all True!" I was not surprised by his ascendancy. He helped countless people in this life and has done the same in the spirit world. By reporting the things that I hear in my spirit walks and communication, I suppose I run the risk of being accused of creating fear and panic. I understand that, but I believe people are prepared to hear the truth and can adjust. My Ginger has suffered from asthma her entire life. She has been hospitalized hundreds of times and was on a ventilator a few times. When I first met Ginger, I told her how remarkably brave she was. She told me that she just pretends to be brave. Her response surprised me, but it also makes sense. I have interviewed many combat veterans and survivors of trauma, and they all tell me the same thing. Bravery is not the absence of fear; it is overcoming fear to do what you must do. Pretending to be brave is bravery! We have it in us to persevere through this current crisis, and whatever else comes our way, I am convinced of this fact. Carpe diem!

I posted communiqué number 43 on April 28, 2020. Many people are suffering during this pandemic. There is so much sadness that it is all too easy to fall into despair. Harvard psychologist Gordon Allport wrote in the preface to holocaust survivor Viktor Frankl's book, *Man's Search for Meaning*: "To live is to suffer, to survive is to find meaning in the suffering."[173] Despite the torture and pain Frankl suffered at the hands of the Nazis, he refused to give up his humanity, love, hope, and courage. He wanted to be worthy of the suffering. In his autobiography, *Memories, Dreams, Reflections*, psychanalyst Carl Jung wrote: "The world into which we are born is brutal and cruel, and at the same time one of divine beauty." It is good to keep that in mind each day. On my computer at home, I have posted a Latin phrase that Jung had carved above the door to his house in Kusnacht, Switzerland: *Vocatus atque non vocatus deus aderit.*" In English: Called or not called, God will be there.[174] We are not alone in our suffering, so we need to keep going and help others and not lose our humanity.

"Hey Anzar, yeah, looking for a sign. When will it come?" I asked.

"Soon," he said. These type of time answers always remind me of my friend David who said, "You'll find out in the fullness of time." That can often be a long time.

"Okay. Alright. I guess we have enough to deal with right now," I said.

"Consider everything carefully, what you say and what you do," said Anzar.

"I know, Gene has said that before. Okay. Thank you," I said. I was at the high point in my spirit walk so I was looking for the City of Angels in the distance.

"Hey Gene, let's see if the City of Angels is visible today. Tell me about your ascendancy," I said.

"Not that big of a deal, I'm not a big deal, but my job is. I take my job seriously," said Gene in his self-deprecating style.

"Very happy for you, and you're deserving. All the work you do here and in the spirit world," I said. Anzar stepped forward again.

"So, Anzar, what more should I be doing? A lot of things coming up…like October?" I asked.

"It will be terrible, and powerful. Awe-inspiring and terrifying," said Anzar.

"Thank you. I'm looking, Gene. Too smoggy today, can't see the City of Angels," I said.

"But you still see beautiful nature?" asked Gene.

"True. What can you say about October?" I asked.

"We do all we can for the greatest number of people. Not everyone will respond, not everyone will acknowledge and understand," said Gene.

"So, you're saying that I'm helping people to understand the…" I said.

"Transition, re-accommodation, same," said Gene.

"Thank you, Gene. Okay, Anzar. I think I know my mission. To be of service, to help, and guide others in the transition," I said.

The search for meaning in this pandemic is not easy. There are stories of heroism by everyday people, folly by some of our leaders, deviousness by our enemies, and pain and suffering of those losing loved ones and their livelihoods. Perhaps in the transition to this new world after the Big Show we will see the meaning clearly. I take great comfort that my mission will be of some help and that God, whom I call upon, will be there.

April 29, 2020, and another communiqué posting. I am fascinated by stories about baseball, especially the early days known as the "dead-ball era." Ty Cobb was one of the greatest hitters that ever lived, but he had a reputation of not being a nice fellow. He could be generous, though. I read that Cobb supported a few of the old-time players who did not have much in their retirement. He was driven, hard-nosed, and could be vicious in competition. To be fair, that was the way most players played the game. Many of those early players did not make much more money than the coal miners, carpenters, bus drivers, and other working-class folks who watched the games. It was a hard scrabble life for most people and the ballplayers of our national pastime reflected that. Intense competition is the American way. Ty Cobb shared a room with another player, and Cobb would race home to their apartment after a game because he had to be the first one in the bathtub. Nearing death, he lamented that he wished that he had more friends.[175]

In these hard times of isolation, it becomes evident that having friends and family around you is the most important thing. In other words, love. On my daily spirit walks, I see many of the same people. I saw a nice lady who is often out walking yesterday, and we exchanged greetings as usual, and she told me: "It's hard being alone." It broke my heart. I know that I am lucky having my Ginger and my youngest son home with me, even though I miss my daughter, who lives nearby and my two older sons and my grandsons who live in Ohio. I often say that I am the luckiest (listen to the song "The Luckiest" by Ben Folds).

It was a hot day yesterday when I took my spirit walk. I try not to complain about the temperature. When I traveled to Illinois in January 2019, it was below zero, and I complained that it was too cold to be outside. As it happened, I was walking through an old graveyard, and

I heard a spirit say: "You think you're cold, try being dead." Lesson learned.

"You're all standing in a line," I said.

"Waiting," said Anzar.

"Waiting for something to happen, looks like. What's going to happen?" I asked.

"What we told you," said Anzar.

"Okay. What more can I do?" I said.

"Make sure you have secure food sources, keep up your spirits, stay safe, and protected," he said. I nodded my head in agreement, then Anzar showed me a circle.

"It has happened before so it can happen again. I think that's why you showed me a circle," I said. Anzar smiled.

"A good day for a walk, not too hot yet. I would like Ginger to see a UFO, would like to see one with Ginger, that would be great," I said. I got no reaction from Anzar, then he turned his attention to me again.

"It is all too easy to blame others, and hard to take responsibility which is necessary to live a fulfilled life. To be happy, to be good, to be useful," said Anzar. He changed the subject on me, but that was okay.

"Okay, thank you. I keep hearing these explosions in my half-awake state. Is that part of this Big Show?" I asked.

"Maybe," said Anzar. Now I was ready to change the subject. There were rumors that the North Korean dictator, Kim Jong Un, was dead.

"Is Kim Jong Un dead?" I asked.

"Near death," said Anzar.

"Will his sister be worse than him?" I asked.

212

"Yes. It is a problem. That figures into China's plans, having a wild card do their dirty work for them. Then sacrifice them when needed," he said.

"I saw that strategy firsthand at my place of work many years ago," I said. Gene stepped forward.

"Hi, Gene," I said. Gene pointed to the mountains.

"Yeah, the mountain tops, I see them. I miss traveling; I like it. I know you can go wherever you want," I said.

"We have to retreat a bit," said Gene.

"Okay, I understand. Should I keep writing these communiqués?" I asked.

"As long as you can," said Gene. I smiled and nodded my head.

Not only am I lucky to have such beautiful friends and family in this world, but I have lovely friends in the spirit world. Then there is the Creator, of course, always with me. I am never alone. I would not wish loneliness on anyone. I am not exactly sure what is to come, other than I believe it will be dramatic and transitional. Now, more than ever, we need each other.

I posted communiqué number 45 on April 30, 2020. A lot has happened in the past four years. It has been a time of great transition for me, my family, my country, and the world. A few days ago, the Department of Defense officially released videos of military UFO encounters. I had already seen the footage when it leaked in the media, but now the government made its official release acknowledging that the film footage of what they call unidentified aerial phenomena (UAP) was authentic. It did not make much of a ripple in the news cycle, unfortunately. Maybe it was because the footage is gunsight video that is grainy, black and white, and not in ultra-high definition. It is hard to compete with Hollywood production values.

It takes me back to the radio show I was on a few years ago after my first *Timeless* book was released. I shared the evening with another guest, Terry Lovelace. Terry had just published his best-selling book, *Incident at Devil's Den*, that documents his abduction while he was in the US Air Force in 1977. Terry is an impressive person with credentials (a former Assistant Attorney General). He was very believable and credible, and we became friends. I remember thinking to myself, boy I am glad I was never abducted; it is bad enough having seen ghosts and demons and hearing dead people talk to me. As his story sunk in, I began to ask myself deep probing questions about incidents in my life. That led me to contact Yvonne Smith, the world-renowned hypnotherapist. I started the process of piecing together memories of my alien contact through recovered subconscious memories, conscious memories, written historical evidence, and the memories of my childhood friend. It turned out that I had four abduction (I prefer to call reunion) experiences: 1964, 1973, 1977, and 1978. All this was confirmed by my spirit guides later.

One might wonder why such memories would remain in the subconscious and why I did not speak out earlier. Many leading UFO and alien abduction researchers, including the late Dr. John Mack, have written about screen memories. In other words, the alien entities plant false memories to mask the abduction experience. During one of my spirit walks, the alien doctor (Terry and I call him Dr. Bug), admitted to me that he did this to me, but he called it a masking procedure. I did some research and discovered that articles had been published in peer-reviewed academic journals about masking memories (by humans, not aliens).[176] All of this has been shocking, to say the least. If someone had told me five years ago that I would write three books about my paranormal and alien experiences, I would not have believed them. Not that I would have doubted my own experiences, but it would simply be too horrifying to think of publishing about such events in my life. I have no such doubts and fears now. I call this a spiritual reawakening.

"Everybody I encounter today on my walk seems agitated and on edge…the people, not the spirits, you guys are calm as usual, that is comforting," I said.

"Keep working together to solve problems, and come up with solutions bound by love," said Anzar.

"Yeah, I agree. I'm walking past the Freemason Temple and towards the mountains," I said.

"Beautiful mountains. Go up there when you can. You'll find a vision," said Gene. I nodded yes.

"Anzar, was my interpretation of what you meant by the circle correct?" I asked.

"Yes, it happened before, and it can happen again," said Anzar.

"Does that refer to a second and third wave of the virus?" I asked.

"Yes, and other things," said Anzar.

"I took a chance by mentioning the condition of the North Korean leader in my communiqué, based on what you told me," I said.

"Near-death does not mean dead," said Anzar.

"He's a bad guy, but I don't want to wish anybody dead," I said.

"Sometimes wishing people to die because they are bad people and thinking things will be better as a result does not work out like you imagine it will," said Anzar.

"Like Saddam Hussein? I understand. Could you tell me more about October, how can we prepare everybody?" I asked.

"Spirit, health, economics. Prioritize," said Anzar.

"Very good. Okay. Gene, I know you guys have stepped back a little bit, and that's alright," I said.

"We haven't abandoned you, just stepped back," said Gene. I smiled and nodded my head in agreement.

I realize that this communication I have is unusual, and it may cause some people to roll their eyes and keep walking without making eye contact. I get it. But consider this, what will it take for you to believe that aliens exist? Is the Pentagon release of the UAV footage enough? What many scientists and engineers are coming to realize is that consciousness is fundamental, and everything we see depends on this. As I wrote in my first *Timeless* book, "it is not that I believe in ghosts, it is that they believe in me, so I do not have a choice." I feel the same way about aliens. We have been taught that seeing is believing, but what if believing is seeing? As of April 30, on the COVID-19 front, there were 60,966 total deaths, 1.04 million confirmed cases, and 6.25 million tests completed in the United States.[177]

May Day 2020, and it was time to post communiqué number 46 to Facebook. Being sensitive to the paranormal runs in families. My mother was very psychic. My children have all had experiences ranging from UFOs to ghosts. Ultimately, I think this is more of a blessing than a family curse. The gift of insight and intuition is not a bad thing. Being able to communicate with those who have passed on brings great comfort to many folks. If that comes with being able to see scary, dark, shadow people occasionally in the middle of the night, then that is the price to pay. I have spoken to some parents who feel guilty for bringing this upon their children. There is no need to feel guilty, you had no choice, it is natural, and part of a person's destiny. I am helping my children manage their gifts, and hopefully, they avoid the mistakes I have made in my paranormal journey. Some basic rules will keep you going on the righteous path:

1. Your abilities are a gift from the Creator and are to be used to help people.
2. Being of service is more important than being rewarded or receiving accolades.
3. Doing the right thing is imperative.
4. Be grateful and operate from a position of love.
5. Be responsible and humble.

If you follow these simple rules, you should be able to navigate the twists and turns you will encounter. Mistakes will be made, but quickly correct them and learn. Remember, it is all about attention and intention, and consciousness is fundamental. Anything is possible.

"It's Thursday, and I'm conducting my spirit communication inside. Thank you for always being there. Please help us and give us protection. Any more details about October?" I asked.

"Calamities are continuing. They may include geologic disturbances, celestial anomalies of some magnitude, the reappearance or second wave of the virus, and a lot of political instability," said Anzar.

"Thank you. Many people depend on me and would like to be prepared," I said.

"Exact dates are not possible, but October seems likely. That is all we can say for now," said Anzar.

"Thank you," I said.

"Prepare your spirit and soul, be on the side of the good, and be ready. Do the right things, smart things, and make the right decisions. Say prayers. Trust those who operate from a position of love, trust love, for love is the gift from the Creator. Trust yourself. Be the good, be the light," said Anzar. I nodded in acknowledgement.

I do not have all the answers, obviously, but I am receiving some clues that may be helpful. You must decide for yourself what path to take and trust the love you feel. Significant challenges lie ahead, and we must remain steady and keep moving forward. We have free will in an often unfair world filled with dark despair. You may choose wisely and operate from a position of love, but it is almost certain that others will not. Freedom allows for dissent, which can be messy. As Thomas Jefferson once wrote: "The boisterous sea of Liberty is never without a wave."[178]

I could not help myself, I simply had to post yet another communiqué. This one was published on May 2, 2020. My spirit friend Gene has encouraged me to do an online theatre project with my actor friends. Since Gene was the one who persuaded me to write my *Timeless* trilogy, and because he continues to be a dear trusted friend, I decided to follow his advice. I put the following notice on Facebook and many people responded.

> We are going to offer a live performance of my play, *This is My Gun*, online and on many different platforms (YouTube, Facebook, etc.), probably around May 16. The play is a one-act contemporary drama inspired by Goethe's Faust. This is My Gun allows us to examine the issue of gun violence in America without being political and in a dramatic and entertaining way. I was wondering if any of you who are trained in psychology or sociology would like to join the after-performance talk back as there will likely be many questions by audience members. All the actors are performing from home, so we are practicing social distancing. I call this project, Lockdown Theatre. Some of you who are teachers might even want your online students (the only kind we have) to watch the performance. If interested, please email me at bootstobooks@gmail.com, and I will send you the script.

> Thank you!
> Bruce (Locked Down but Not Locked Out)

Writing *Timeless* changed my life, and I think this unique theatre performance will as well. I have witnessed the gun debate going on for decades here in the United States. The most vocal advocates are at polarized opposite opinions: give everyone guns or take everyone's guns away. I believe the problem with gun violence is deeper; it is cultural. Richard Slotkin wrote a book entitled *Gunfighter Nation*.[179] The premise is that we have never really advanced beyond our Wild West days in terms of violence. We are always at war—a warrior culture. We look at everything as conflict and use war terminology in facing our challenges: Trade War, War on Cancer, War on Drugs, War on Poverty, and now, the War against COVID-19. The solution to the gun violence problem in America could take generations to solve, and unfortunately, there are no quick fixes.

"Hello, everybody, thank you for being here. Gene, I see you, the rest of you are taking a step back," I said.

"A lot is going on," said Gene.

"I have some committed actors for our project, but we need more. Unless we have people do double roles," I said.

"That would be cool too," said Gene.

"I'll look into that. Thank you, Gene," I said.

"You're doing a good job," said Gene.

"Well, it's your idea," I said, smiling, which made Gene laugh.

"People will like it. Well, back to work, watching over my family carefully during this time, see you later," said Gene.

"Thank you. Anzar, just wanted to catch you before you go. Many people saw things; what was going on the other night?" I asked.

"Preparations, reorganizing," said Anzar.

"You guys are very busy," I said.

"A lot is going on. Trust yourself to do the right thing. There is something by water, a threat by water, through the water, as well as through the air," said Anzar.

"Okay, I got it. Thank you, guys," I said. I hope to find out more about Anzar's warning. Meanwhile, we must continue to seek peaceful solutions to our complex problems. I am hoping my play promotes understanding and a path to peace.

Communiqué number 48 was posted on May 3, 2020, with little fanfare. The country is opening up again. Experts say a second wave of the virus will arrive in the fall, and we are not even done with the first one. There are armed protesters at some state capitals. Millions of people are still unemployed, and small businesses are failing with government bailouts going to big business. It is all very frightening and strangely familiar. Many years ago, a small tourist island was shocked by an attack by a monster and struggled to balance protecting its citizens and opening for the summer season. A sheriff and a scientist erred on the side of caution and told the local government officials that everybody should remain safe and locked down. Still, the mayor and local businesses disagreed and did not even think the threat was real or that great. Of course, you know the movie *Jaws* is what I am talking about, and we all know what happened in that story.[180]

"I see everybody, and it looks like you're heading out. I wanted to say hello," I said.

"We are very busy," said Anzar.

"I see that, and I hate to bother you, but I had to do my spirit walk this evening instead of earlier this morning," I said.

"Hello," said Gene.

"Gene, we had a good meeting and read through with the actors, it'll be great! All because of you," I said. Gene gave me two thumbs up and a big smile. "Thank you, Gene. I'm doing a rewrite, any suggestions?" I asked.

"Make them read in between the lines, not too on the nose," said Gene.

"Anything you can share about celestial anomalies or October or what Anzar said yesterday?" I asked.

"Submarines are a threat by water and air. In and over the ocean, in the air," said Gene. That was a scary thought.

"Yeah, you're right. Thank you. I want to see the City of Angels with you. There we go. Coming up. We'll see it. There you go," I said as I approached the high point of my spirit walk and Los Angeles came into view and I could see Gene smile.

"Alright! Thank you. Angels to guide us, watch over us, and protect us," he said.

"We need them. Hey, Anzar, Gene told me of the threat. Can you add anything?" I asked.

"Submarines, ships, missiles. Watch out. Be careful," said Anzar.

"In October, the fall?" I asked.

"Hard to say, October is dangerous. Threats and aggression are prompted by vulnerability, like with the wolf and other predators," said Anzar.

"Anything else you can tell me?" I asked.

"Good time to reexamine your life, cut out things that are no longer important, and enhance those things that are," he said, as I nodded in agreement.

"Thank you. I know you're busy; I appreciate it," I said.

"Guard the innocent and protect them. Forgive the wicked," said Anzar.

"I know, it is not easy sometimes, but I understand. Thank you, Gene, and Anzar," I said. If we continue with my *Jaws* analogy, then we must take the threat seriously and not act shortsightedly. It must be the right time to go safely back into the water, and meanwhile, we may need a bigger boat.

My communiqué posted on May 4, 2020, started with sadness. Certain anniversaries in our lives can have profound effects on us. This is a tough one to write. Fifty years ago, on May 4, 1970, four young students at Kent State University in Ohio were shot and killed by equally young National Guardsmen. Although the Vietnam War was winding down and troops were being sent home, President Richard Nixon decided to expand the war into Cambodia. Campus protests increased. On May 1, 1970, there was a violent protest in Kent between protesters and local police. On May 4, the protests continued on the campus at Kent State University, where there was a small militant chapter of Students for a Democratic Society (SDS). Earlier in the day, the 1000 National Guardsmen were confronting protesters who were hurling rocks and tear gas was used. The National Guard retreated to a hill on campus as the confrontation escalated. Then 28 Guardsmen fired 61 shots into the crowd killing four unarmed students: Allison Krause, Jeffrey Miller, Sandra Scheuer, and William Schroeder. Nine others were wounded.[181]

The Scranton Commission, in October 1970, found that "The indiscriminate firing of rifles into a crowd of students and the deaths that followed were unnecessary, unwarranted, and inexcusable." Later in 1975, a federal judge dismissed a criminal case against eight guardsmen. Larry Shafer, who was part of the National Guard's G Troop and fired his weapon at students, remained quiet for years. He later admitted that he had remorse over the shooting, but felt his life was in jeopardy. He died in 2013 after a long career in public service. Someone gave the order for those young soldiers to fire, but to this day, no one knows for sure who did.[182]

After the Kent State shooting, I remember my mom said that it did not matter if your boy was in Vietnam or back home, there was no safe place. In 1970, my brother was starting his second tour of duty in Vietnam and had turned against the war. He protested in his own way while he fought in Vietnam. He wore a peace symbol patch on the top of his boonie hat and signed his letters home with peace symbols. My brother came back home in November 1971, but he was forever changed by the war and is now a disabled veteran haunted by memories and suffering from Agent Orange-related leukemia and heart problems. On the twentieth anniversary of the Kent State shooting, on May 4, 1990, my mom died after a brief battle with cancer. I was in graduate school at Bowling Green State University in Ohio. Vietnam still haunts us, and there is a little bit of that faraway place in all of us. The date of May 4 is imprinted indelibly in my mind. A terrible date in both our nation's history when we lost four precious young people and in my personal history when I lost my dear mother. The feeling of safety at home was lost forever.

"Testing, 1, 2, 3. Interference again, oh good, now it's working—a Sunday evening. Hello Anzar. Everybody is more still, but not relaxed, looks like you're planning something. What's going on?" I asked.

"You can see it yourself. Things are coming apart and leading up to an October crescendo of things falling apart. Be ready" said Anzar.

"You didn't sugarcoat that one. That's awful. What more can I do?" I asked.

"Stand by and be ready," said Anzar.

"Yeah, when I saw those people confronting the police in Sacramento and around the country, I had a flashback to the 1960s and 1970s, and civil unrest over the Vietnam War. It looked like the protesters weren't being rational. Nobody's wearing a mask when I take my walks," I said. I reached the point in my spirit walk where I can see downtown Los Angeles.

"Hi Gene, about to see, there it is—the City of Angels," I said.

"Yeah, I see it, wonderful, thank you," said Gene.

"There's a helicopter coming, let's see what happens, here it comes." I said as a helicopter flew low-level over my head.

"R44, yeah, okay. It's an R44, not sure whose it is. Gene, what can you tell me?" I asked.

"People aren't rational; they're driven by outside forces," said Gene.

"Who? Aliens?" I asked.

"Partly," said Gene.

"You must ask yourself who thrives best under chaos? Who thrives the best under anarchy? And then you will have your answer," said Anzar.

"It seems like the wheels are coming off the wagon. You guys mentioned submarines yesterday, frightening prospect," I said.

"They can be anywhere off the coast," said Gene.

"A lot to think about. Thank you both," I said.

Ginger noticed that I was depressed yesterday. I did not even see it myself. She is tuned in quite well, and I am lucky to have her. Sometimes anniversaries of events sneak up on me, and my body feels it even before I consciously acknowledge the impact. Even though I try just commemorating my mom's birthday on August 12, the date of May 4 hits me hard every year. My psychic teachers have told me that our bodies retain memories. They are right. So, today, I remember the loss of my mom in this physical realm, but she is still with me in the spirit realm and helps guide me day-to-day.

I released communiqué number 50 on May 5, 2020. In some ways, it would be a lot easier if the paranormal stuff was not part of my life. I tried to push it back and ignore it for decades, but my paranormal experiences kept coming back. Finally, it re-emerged for good when I had my vision with Gene in October 2016, and he encouraged me to write my *Timeless* trilogy of books. I had to accept the fact that I have a paranormal life, and it was time to share it with the world. Gene has helped me put all this into perspective. When I was struggling with alien contact and abduction, Gene said: "Is it so hard to believe in one more miraculous thing when you already believe in so many extraordinary things?" He was right. Gene had already reminded me that experiencing is believing and believing is experiencing. His wisdom cuts through all my fears and apprehensions about our place in the infinite universe. Still, I have my moments of doubt and grapple with reconciling my spiritual foundation and belief in God with aliens and ghosts. I was taught that God created Heaven and Earth, so that must mean that God created aliens as well. Never once has my ancient alien mystic advisor Anzar said that he was God or, like a god. He acknowledges his subordinate role to the Creator of all things—the mind of God, the ultimate consciousness, or the super implicate reality as physicist David Bohm described. You see, it is not that I believe in aliens, it is that they believe in me. The paranormal events in my life are part of who I am. My experiences have brought me here to this place in time, where I am trying to comprehend and report on the magnificence of creation and the love that binds it all together. We each have a piece of the puzzle, and it is time to share.

"Hello. What's going on?" I asked.

"We told you, the Big Show is coming," said Anzar.

"Can you tell me more?" I asked.

"Geological, biological, cultural, spiritual, political, celestial. All fronts," he said.

"Some of my friends have asked if it will be an alien invasion," I said.

"No, alien involvement, yes. Remember, we are already here," said Anzar. Gene stepped forward.

"We are the aliens," said Gene.

"Gene, thank you for helping me. The play is going well. We'll perform May 16, live. The actors have great drive and commitment and passion for the project." I said.

"Give them my love and encouragement," said Gene.

"Yes. Is there more, Gene?" I asked.

"Hold your family and friends close. Approach everything from a position of love. Protect the innocent and the vulnerable," said Gene. Anzar stepped back in front.

"Am I part of the Big Show? Am I supposed to help?" I asked.

"You are playing a role and helping prepare," said Anzar.

"Where are you guys?" I asked.

"Between Heaven and Earth," said Anzar.

"Is God helping us?" I asked.

"Yes, and us, all of us. The darkness is intense, but not stronger than the light. Be the light," said Anzar.

I have thought about how long I should continue to write these communiqués. My spirit friends have told me to keep writing them as long as I can, but I know that they will end someday. I can see doing this through the fall, the time of the Big Show. I cannot stop now because my mission is to help prepare us for the upcoming event or events. Just precisely how all this will play out, I am not sure, but we are on this journey together, and I know that ultimately, we will be okay. We just have to prepare our souls for what I believe will be the next step in our evolution.

On May 6, 2020, I was writing my communiqué based on my spirit walk the day before and my thoughts after. Phil Red Eagle, a Lakota and Vietnam War veteran, spoke to my Vietnam War class more than 25 years ago when I taught at Green River Community College in Auburn, Washington. I remember telling him that I had some good luck in my job searches. "Define good luck," he said. "Good luck is when you get something unexpectedly," I said. He shook his head. "Not in our native tradition. Good luck is when you have an opportunity, and a means to help somebody," he said sternly. He was right.

A few days ago, Ginger and I sent in a donation to the Oceti Wakan organization; they help Lakota children on the Pine Ridge Indian Reservation in South Dakota, which has been hit especially hard by COVID-19. The other day, I read that Native American tribes severely impacted by this terrible virus have received $2 million in donations from Ireland. You see, more than 170 years ago during the

226

Irish Potato Famine, the Choctaw Nation sent money to Ireland. That is how good luck works.

"Thank you all for being here and for everything you do. Beautiful day, mountains, and walking on the magic highway. I am incredibly grateful to have a flexible job and be in a position to help people. Anything more on the Big Show?" I asked.

"The Big Show is coming," said Anzar.

"I will keep doing the communiqués through October. Or whenever the Big Show is. Any advice you can give me?" I asked.

"Take inventory of the most precious things in your life and preserve them. You will find relationships are the most precious," said Anzar.

"Thank you. I keep using David Bohm's three levels of reality (explicate, implicate, and super implicate) in my radio interviews, does it make sense?" I asked.

"Yes, the trinity," said Anzar.

"What more can I tell my friends?" I asked.

"Express yourself from the position of love, not from hate or anger, or frustration. Love is how you solve problems," said Anzar.

I often say that I am the luckiest. That is truly how I feel. And what gives me the greatest good feeling? Helping others—there is nothing better. It is the reason we are here on this Earth. Thank you all for reading these daily communiqués and doing your part.

I posted communiqué number 52 on May 7, 2020. I watched the film *The King's Speech* again yesterday. I like the movie and can identify with the main character, King George VI. Like the King, I am also a stutterer. I have learned to overcome this affliction, but it is always there beneath the surface. According to the National Stuttering Association, "no one speaks perfectly all the time—we all experience disruptions in our speech. For people who stutter, these disruptions, or disfluencies, are more severe and experienced more consistently. For some, stuttering goes away in childhood, for others, it persists throughout adulthood." Researchers contend that stuttering is caused by various factors including, genetics, language development, environment, trauma, and the way a person's brain functions in speech. For me, it began at age six and persisted for many years. I believe it is related to having had my first alien contact at six years old. For two years, I was taken out of class each day for speech therapy. I was eventually able to somewhat overcome my impediment and the speech therapy was discontinued. It was so bad at one point that I did not want to talk, and it may have also hindered my learning to read because I refused to read out loud in class because of the teasing by classmates. The bottom line is, I would never have imagined that one day I would be a college professor and speak in front of many people each day or host a radio program. I have learned some tricks to avoid getting hung up on certain words that would trigger stammering. I do this instinctively now. One method I use is to listen to myself say what I am going to say in my head, first, and then I express my thought out loud. It all happens very quickly. We can all overcome whatever challenges we are presented with and figure out how to achieve our goals in different and creative ways.

"Thank you, everybody, for being here. It is a very confusing time for people. Many folks were clamoring about the isolation and they wanted to get back to work or some kind of normal life. Now that the great majority of states have opened up to some degree, people are still apprehensive, even afraid, and there are still no real solutions on how to effectively deal with the virus and get the economy up and running again. Any advice you can give me, Anzar?" I asked.

"Balance is the key. Stay the course, be cautious, make smart decisions, take guidance from above, and practice love down below. Multiply the blessings, geometrically," said Anzar.

"Thank you. I know that we keep talking about October. Not wanting to be predictive and instead concentrate on a more preparatory mode, how can we prepare for what is to come?" I asked.

"Spiritual and psychological impacts will be the greatest, but that will lead to economic, cultural, and political effects. There will be a series of natural and human-made disasters that will remind everybody how fragile this earth is and how we need to work together," said Anzar. Anzar showed me a little boat on the ocean in a terrible storm with huge waves.

"I get it, no time to argue and fight; we need to work together to survive and reach the safety of the shore. I feel the ocean in my blood often. I feel at home on the sea," I said. I noticed that Gene was stepping forward.

"The actors are really into what we're doing, and I came up with a dedication to you that we'll probably show at the end," I said.

"Just remember, I'm not dead, you know," said Gene.

"I know you're not dead, just passed on to a different reality and dimension. You're very active behind the scenes in this project. Anything to pass on to the actors?" I asked.

"The anguish of one life lost, is the same, no matter the circumstance. The parents of the victims and the perpetrators are both suffering," said Gene. I nodded in acknowledgement.

I have a lot to learn, and I know that. Every day presents new challenges and new opportunities for growth. When I approach everything from a position of love, things seem to go better. People sense where you are coming from, and they respond. I am not ashamed of being a stutterer, or even upset that it happened to me, I see it instead as an asset. I think very carefully about what I say. It helps me be a better writer, as well. I have found meaning in the suffering and taken on the challenge of overcoming what stood in the way of my destiny.

So, unlock your destiny and step boldly into your dreams and make them manifest.

I wanted to keep rolling with my communiqués, so I posted number 53 on May 8, 2020. What happens when things come together? I am excited about the live theatre performance of my play—*This is My Gun*—coming up on May 16 for many reasons. First, it was inspired by my friend, Gene. Second, it brings together talented actors and brilliant technical people who all need a creative and collaborative outlet during our lockdown. Third, it deals with the issue of violence in America that is vitally important to the health and safety of us all but especially our young people. Fourth, it showcases an exciting new way to bring live theatre to folks around the world. Fifth, it helps with my own healing from our near miss school shooter lockdown in January 2019. I was able to recruit two friends of mine who are healthcare professionals to take part in our after-show talkback with the online audience—Dr. Christianson and Dr. Bigby. They are both caring, compassionate, experts on the issues the play brings up, and very experienced. Joining us also will be a police officer who is a former veteran student.

I often say that I do not choose what to write; it chooses me. Consequently, this project is not about me, it is about the mission, and people are ready to share in the experience and begin the journey of healing. Interestingly, I wrote this play about a school shooter one year before we had our own lockdown incident at Citrus College. The time is right to bring polarized factions in our society together to address the problem of gun violence. "The play's the thing," as Shakespeare wrote, and I believe this play is the thing that can bring us together.

"Thursday, warm day. Welcome to all of you, thank you for being here with me. Hoping that it'll be a successful day. Getting a lot done with the project," I said. I see both Gene and Anzar who nod their heads in agreement.

"There was a question, is the Big Show going to happen just here or everywhere?" I asked.

"The whole world, definitely," said Anzar.

"Any more information or what I can do?" I asked.

"Disclosure is a process, and you are part of the process—writing, speaking, the paranormal course, the play, and the radio show. All preparation," said Anzar.

"Thank you," I said.

"Energy manifests in material constructs of our reality, and we can help and shape that reality. We can not only be good; we can actually make good things happen. Unfortunately, those of evil intent can make bad things happen. In a way, it is a contest, so stay on the side of the light and be the light," said Anzar.

"Thank you, excellent stuff," I said. I noticed Gene as he stepped forward to look around. The Los Angeles skyline came into view.

"There it is, the City of Angels, barely visible," I said.

"I'm keeping a careful eye on my family. We're doing this for the good of humanity—to help stop the violence and bring reason and love back. We can work it out, the Beatles," he said. Gene started singing.

> *We can work it out*
> *We can work it out*
> *Life is very short, and there's no time*
> *For fussing and fighting, my friend*
> *Yes, indeed, my friends, we can work it out*
> *And things are coming together, right now*[183]

My communiqués continued as I posted number 54 on May 9, 2020. Lately, I cannot help but feel like we are living in a movie—some mashup of *The Grapes of Wrath* and *The Andromeda Strain*. *The Grapes of Wrath*, starring Henry Fonda, came out in 1940 and was based on John Steinbeck's Pulitzer Prize-winning novel published in 1939. *The Andromeda Strain* was a science fiction film that premiered in 1971 based on Michael Crichton's book published in 1969. *The Grapes of Wrath* follows an Oklahoma farm family devastated by the dust bowl as they come to California and struggle during the Great Depression. *The Andromeda Strain* deals with how a deadly extraterrestrial organism is brought back by a satellite and kills all but two inhabitants of a small town. A team of scientists rush to discover what the organism is and how to stop it. I remembered how the film frightened me when I first saw it on our old TV set in the recreation room.

They say when you have your health, you have everything. But what if you do not have a job or an income? We are now arguing about how to balance stopping the spread of the virus and putting people back to work. And it will have to be a balanced solution with protection for the most vulnerable while we hold on for the vaccine and better treatments. Meanwhile, my spirit friends are preparing us for more.

"Hello everybody, why is it so dark?" I asked.

"Are you ready?" asked Anzar.

"For what?" I asked.

"For what is to come," said Anzar.

"A test? Or do you mean this is it? I thought you said in October," I said.

"Time is immaterial here," said Anzar. I noticed that Gene was in the area.

"Gene, help!" I said.

"You're okay, only a test. Like the old emergency broadcast system on our TVs and radios. A warning to see who's prepared and listening," said Gene.

"Remember your army training? Train like you fight, and fight like you train. Readiness is key," said Anzar.

"Okay, I remember. So, we'll be fighting?" I asked.

"Not exactly. When love answers, will you remember the question?" asked Anzar. I scratched my head contemplating his question.

"Careful consideration, good comes of it. There will be push back and resistance. Be the light. There can be no light without the dark, as I told you long ago," said Anzar.

"Be prepared, like in the theatre. Nervousness turns to excitement which enhances your performance. Fear is part of bravery," said Gene.

"God help us," I said.

During the Great Depression, the Hoover administration told frightened and unemployed Americans that prosperity was just around the corner and that we would be okay in the long run. The problem was, we do not eat in the long run, we eat every day. They had long bread and food lines back then, and we have them again today. Significant changes are required and are coming. I have got a feeling that this theatre performance of my play on May 16 is not just for entertainment; it is training and preparation. Training and preparing to fight the battles that lie in front of us. Our group of young actors, technicians, producers, and directors are working together, but apart, and blazing the path forward. It can be done, and we are doing it, my friends.

I skipped a day and posted communiqué number 55 on May 11, 2020. I am sorry that I did not post yesterday. We were celebrating Mother's Day with Ginger's mom and thinking of my mom in heaven. I have tried not to let sadness overtake me on Mother's Day and instead find joy in the memories and the celestial connection. We had a full cast rehearsal Saturday for our live online performance this coming Saturday, May 16. The actors were magnificent, and the tech crew was brilliant. It will be a great show, not the Big Show as outlined by Anzar, but a great show. The significance of what we are doing is sinking in. Think about it; we are taking a performance that is ordinarily done in a crowded theatre on stage and packaging it live and streaming to the world. Actors will be performing from the safety of their own homes and yet collaborating and bringing you the magic moments you would expect in live theatre. I am beyond excited to help bring this story and this production to all of you. Beyond that, it shows how we can survive and even thrive in lockdown. The virus cannot stop us; nothing can stop us. I have been watching small comic book shops who have had to close their brick-and-mortar stores convert to online live sales on Facebook. I love how people take what they are given and run with it and shine.

"Try to be the audience and see what they see and experience what they experience, then make changes through collaboration, and have fun," said Gene.

"Thank you, Gene. Any more information about this test?" I asked.

"Beginning of the test, a fortnight. The play is the thing, essential for understanding everything," said Anzar.

"I think you're right, we're using war and conflict terminology, like trade war, or the war against COVID-19. I'll keep that in mind as we prepare for performance," I said. I reached the peak elevation in my spirit walk.

"No City of Angels today. Beautiful day, though," said Gene.

"Hazy, yeah. Any more advice for actors and crew?" I asked.

"Mission focus, lay it all out, leaving nothing behind, leave nothing in the tank," said Gene. I nodded in agreement. "If you're going to do it, do it all the way and be all in," said Gene.

"Yeah. Anzar, any more wisdom?" I asked.

"Solitude has its place so you can find the peace within you and then share that peace with the world," said Anzar.

"Thank you, Anzar. What's going to happen in the next 10 days?" I asked. There was no answer. I assumed that you are not supposed to receive answers to the test.

"Remember what I said, I just look scary, but I am not the bad one," said Anzar.

"I remember. And I've also learned that demons tend to take the form of little girls to trick us. Never judge a book by its cover," I said. Gene stepped forward.

"The play is important, and it'll help guide the way," said Gene.

"No test today, but the real thing is coming. Be ready," said Anzar.

"Thank you both for your help and inspiration for the play. I think I understand it more now and what can be done," I said.

Everything we do has a purpose and effect. My motivation is to help people and share the connection I have. We all have free will, so not everyone will cooperate or listen. We must be patient with them and always operate from a position of love. That is not to say that we cannot defend ourselves or our loved ones, but that is as a last resort when all other efforts have failed. As the late John Keegan (British military historian) wrote: "War is a bankruptcy of policy."[184]

I posted communiqué number 56 on May 12, 2020. I think I know why this play is all coming together so quickly. We need its message to help guide us into the future. We had a shooter-on-campus lockdown at Citrus College in January 2019. I was locked down with 43 of my students in silent darkness for three and a half hours, and nearly six hours in total. Luckily, no one was injured, physically. I tried to convince our administration that we needed to make changes to prepare for the future and learn from the experience. Some changes were made, but not enough, in my opinion. I was frustrated. Then I remembered, when you cannot work through the bureaucracy, you use art to affect change. "Art is not a mirror held up to reality but a hammer with which to shape it," as German playwright Bertolt Brecht once said.[185]

So, when my spirit friend Gene suggested that I gather the actors together to perform a play, I knew precisely which play to choose—*This is My Gun*. I have taught college history for 30 years and have always worried about my school being a target. In 2018, a year before our lockdown at Citrus, I wrote the first draft of *This is My Gun*—foreshadowing the January 2019 incident. Now, the play's time has come. As I told my fellow staff members and our administrators in January 2019, we were lucky because this incident was a warning, and we will not get another one.

"Thank you all for being here," I said.

"Good job," said Gene.

"It's not me, it's you guys," I said.

"A worthy cause to help people understand gun violence in America," said Gene.

"We have a police officer and two therapists on our post-performance forum. We have great actors and tech design crew," I said.

"Great accomplishment and responsibility. Live, meaningful, dramatic, and thought-provoking," said Anzar.

"Thank you both," I said.

"People must prepare with a survival mindset. Psychotic behavior must be exposed and then cleansed before its awful impact. You must preserve life. The truth is not always pleasant," said Anzar.

"I know, we need universal mental health care in this country. People are going crazy as they come out of lockdown. They can't accept that normal life has changed. We need healing and help," I said.

"Create change and make the change happen. Be the light of change," said Anzar.

I had a dream vision last night, where not only had our world changed, but it had gone from bad to worse. Every aspect of life on Earth, including the air we breathe, had been degraded. It was murky and dusty, acrid, and most desolate. I woke up in a panic and feeling horrible. I think it was a warning. I believe we have a chance to change that bleak vision of the future and instead create a promising, healthy, and joyful one. It is up to us to make good things happen for ourselves and future generations.

The world premiere of our first streamplay was only three days away when I posted communiqué number 57 on May 13, 2020.

> *And when the night is cloudy,*
> *There is still a light that shines on me,*
> *Shine on until tomorrow, let it be.*

My mom loved the Beatles. Her favorite song was "Norwegian Wood," but she also loved this song. Her middle name was Marie, by the way. There are two origin stories for "Let it Be," one told by Paul McCartney and one told by the late Malcolm Evans, who was an original Beatles tour manager. According to Sir Paul, the song was inspired by a dream he had of his late mother, Mary, who came to him and said, "let it be." Malcolm agreed that Paul had a dream, but he contended that it was of him saying "let it be," not Paul's mother. In an outtake from a White Album studio session, supposedly, you can hear Paul McCartney sing, "Brother Malcolm comes to me." Although I tend to believe Paul McCartney's version, it does not matter because it is a beautiful song.[186]

"Thank you, everybody, for being here, and thank you for all your messages, guidance, and love," I said. My spirit friends were smiling.

"Coming up to the performance soon and there's a lot of work to do. I think the latest written revision is good, and the actors and tech folks are doing a great job. Many things have to go right on May 16, but I am confident it will," I said.

"Yes, it will," said Gene.

"I'm still concerned about the bleak vision of the world I received yesterday. It was a post-apocalyptic vision and not good. I've had lots of military dreams too," I said.

"It is not too late if you take action and work together to turn that around," said Anzar.

"The American people are divided. I'm not a partisan political person, because I like to be friends with everyone. What do you think? Who can we trust?" I asked.

"Some people are agents of change. Someone can be such an agent either wittingly or unwittingly, and often that change can ultimately lead to good results, or it can lead to bad results. As such, good people can do good things, bad people can do bad things, good people can do bad things, and bad people can do good things," said Anzar.

"That last part seems like a paradox," I said. Anzar nodded yes.

"It reminds me of what my mom always said: 'Your friends are never really as good as you think they are, and your enemies are never really as bad as you believe them to be,'" I said. Gene nodded in agreement.

"Gene and Anzar, thank you for helping me bring all this together, please help me to do a good job in the preshow narrative and say the right things," I said.

"Speak the truth, and people will listen," said Gene.

"I've been teaching for 30 years, and I've often thought about school attacks. I wrote my play a year before our January 2019 lockdown at Citrus College. I also had a nightmare dream of a school shooter in my classroom just before the incident took place," I said.

"Talk about the incident and your personal experience," said Gene.

"I will, thank you. Truthfully, the play is somewhat autobiographical. Although I've never contemplated such extreme acts of violence

238

as depicted in *This is My Gun,* I've been in a very dark place emotionally and spiritually. I was lucky enough to have good and loving people around me to help me and even divine intervention. In my "hour of darkness," a light came upon me and warmed my heart and soul and made me understand that I had a choice between doing the right thing and doing the wrong thing. I chose correctly, thank God, but I understand the descent into darkness," I said.

"There is no light without the dark," said Anzar.

"Everybody needs a lifeline and a life raft every once in a while," said Gene.

"Thank you both. Any more on the UFO and alien front?" I asked.

"Some help, some are indifferent, and then some are not helpful," said Anzar.

"Gene, anything you want me to pass on to the actors today?" I asked.

"Front-load your performance," said Gene.

"Not sure what you mean," I said.

"Like a good hitter in baseball. You coil and load up and then explode as you hit the ball. That is what you do to deliver a powerful performance," said Gene.

"That's how you knock it out of the park! That makes sense, thank you, guys," I said.

Do not despair, my friends, even though there will inevitably be dark days ahead. Remember, we have the light. We can all make a powerful impact on this world, even if it is only one step and one day at a time. Meanwhile, we can take comfort in the lyrics from this eternally beautiful song.

> *When I find myself in times of trouble*
> *Mother Mary comes to me*
> *Speaking words of wisdom, let it be.*

And in my hour of darkness
She is standing right in front of me
Speaking words of wisdom, let it be.
Let it be, let it be.
Whisper words of wisdom, let it be.

Because of the performance of my play *This is My Gun* on May 16, I had to take a brief hiatus and did not post communiqué number 58 until May 18, 2020. I did have two spirit walks during that hiatus, and those will be documented below. You can now watch the recorded version of the play on YouTube. We assembled quite a team, so we are already talking about our next project. Stay tuned. Ginger finally got to see a UFO, but it was anti-climactic. Anzar said we would see one that night (May 15), and we did. I do not think Ginger was convinced at that time, but now a few days later, and after I told her that I tried hard to debunk the sighting, I believe she thinks it just might have been a UFO. The sighting occurred at 9:05 pm pacific time on Friday, May 15, 2020. I spotted the UFO moving from the southwest to the northeast heading toward the San Gabriel Mountains; I estimated the altitude to be around 80,000 to 100,000 feet. It was as bright as Venus and moving steadily and quite rapidly. My estimate would be nearly Mach 1. I called both Ginger and Leif, and they both came out and witnessed the UFO until it disappeared behind the mountains. It was too high up to be an airplane and too low to be a satellite. Here is the exchange I had with Gene and Anzar on my May 15 spirit walk.

"Saturday is our big show, but not the Big Show," I said. Anzar and Gene smiled.

"I know this play is important for many reasons: proof of concept for the technology, a way to help young actors and technical directors, and to provide exposure for the issues raised during the play and in the after-show forum. Inspired by you, Gene. Thank you all," I said.

"Very proud," said Gene.

"It does seem like things are getting darker every day. Weird feeling. I don't want you guys to be right, but I know you are. What more can we do to prepare?" I asked.

"Be ready in case your hours get cut. Branch out with Zoom for all your classes, including the paranormal course, maybe in fall. Probably a permanent thing," said Anzar.

"I hear you. Adapt, improvise, overcome," I said.

"Stay healthy, stay strong, keep working on projects, writing, communicating, always from a position of love, always," said Gene.

"Consciousness is expanding for those who are prepared and ready; the invitation is coming," said Anzar.

"Universal consciousness?" I asked. Anzar nodded yes.

"UFOs?" I asked.

"Sure, if you want to see it, we can do it," said Anzar.

"I have seen it, but maybe for Ginger and Leif. We're making good things happen," I said. That was the conclusion of my spirit communication from May 15, and here is the contact I had during my spirit walk on May 17.

"Sunday, *17. Mai. Hurra.* It's Norwegian Constitution Day! Hello and welcome to everybody, thank you for helping everything work out. We had a little YouTube trouble, but the show was incredible. Thank you, Gene, for everything you did," I said. Gene was smiling.

"I think we'll go farther with it, dedicated team. Yet another thing to fall back on. Can you confirm our UFO sighting?" I asked.

"You were seeing a UFO," said Anzar.

"Who was it?" I asked.

"We do not know, could be anybody," he said.

"But can you confirm that it wasn't in the current earth inventory and was extra-terrestrial in origin?" I asked.

"Correct," said Anzar.

"Not one of you guys?" I asked.

"No. They were transitioning," said Anzar.

"So, they didn't have to be seen, but they chose it for some reason?" I asked.

"Transitioning through this dimension, you just happened to glimpse that," said Anzar.

"It was the same time as our UFO sighting last year on March 14, 9:05 pm. Anzar, you called it, right?" I asked.

"Yes, you wanted to see one; you saw it," said Anzar.

"I don't think Ginger was convinced," I said.

"That is okay; she will be, and she is better prepared now," said Anzar. I noticed that Gene had returned.

"Thank you, guys. Any more you can tell me about October or fall timeframe?" I asked.

"Be prepared, very prepared," said Anzar.

"Keep the fire going with this creative pool of talent; do not let it slip away. It is possible, so it is doable. Keep up the good work," said Gene, who was smiling. That was it, sorry that I was delayed in this communiqué. Experiencing is believing and believing is experiencing, as Gene and Anzar always say. Ginger is better prepared for what I wonder? Maybe for October? Perhaps for more dramatic sightings of UFOs? I am not sure. On the day of the play, I listened to "Family Snapshot" by Peter Gabriel. It is a hauntingly beautiful song about gun violence and the JFK assassination. Although I do not subscribe to the lone gunman theory, the song is poignant and powerful.

> *Today is different*
> *Today is not the same*
> *Today I make the action*

Take snapshot into the light, snapshot into the light
I am shooting into the light[187]

I posted communiqué number 59 on May 19, 2020. I have always loved the song "The Sound of Silence" by Paul Simon and Art Garfunkel. I like the updated cover by the metal group Disturbed as well. I think it perfectly describes what we are all going to have to deal with soon.

Hello darkness, my old friend
I have come to talk with you again
Because a vision softly creeping
Left its seeds while I was sleeping
And the vision that was planted in my brain
Still remains
Within the sound of silence[188]

In his book, *A New World*, Whitley Strieber writes that the aliens (visitors as he calls them) can see a glow around some people, and that is how they identify who to contact. I believe the same is true for spirits in the spirit world. It makes sense, because the spirit world, the alien world, and the quantum world are the same. In fact, Strieber also wrote that, "maybe where the aliens are in the mirror universe is where our dead go?" Those people who accept the invitation to the universal consciousness will serve as a bright light for their fellow humans and signal to the visitors that they are ready. Darkness must give way to light. There is no reason to curse the darkness because, without it, there is no light.[189]

"Monday afternoon, a cool day with rain in the morning. The other day, you mentioned a higher universal consciousness coming to those who are prepared," I said.

"Yes, it has begun, and the test is almost over," said Anzar.

"Will we see more UFOs, and maybe you'll appear to Ginger and Leif?" I asked.

"Yes, and we shall see. Dark cloud around October. Have medicine, be prepared," said Anzar. As I was on my spirit walk, I noticed someone listening to me as they sat in their truck. I began to speak in Norwegian so he could not understand me.

In 1997, Anzar came to me as the Progenitor. I tell the story in my second *Timeless* book, *Timeless Deja Vu*. Of the many things he told me, Anzar said that without anguish, there is no joy. I understand. How can we appreciate what we have unless we have known what it is like to suffer? I always think of President Franklin D. Roosevelt (FDR) when I think about rising through adversity. When he was struck by polio in the 1920s, he thought his life in politics was over. His wife, Eleanor, convinced him to keep going despite his not being able to walk. Before his illness, Franklin was likable and charismatic and successful, but he had trouble connecting to the working class. He had been born into wealth and had never suffered much.[190]

After he returned to politics and began public speaking again after his paralysis caused by polio, Franklin was a changed man. He was able to convey sincerity when talking about the plight of the working class, and people believed and trusted him. They sensed that he knew what suffering was. Franklin Roosevelt capitalized on that strength he had gained and led us brilliantly through the Great Depression and World War II. Admirable. Whatever adversity that we have now and that will likely come in the fall will motivate us to work harder to raise the universal consciousness of our fellow human beings and work toward the preservation of our planet. This paradigm shift in understanding our place in the universe is what I believe the visitors or aliens want to see in us so that we can then take the next step in our evolution.

I posted communiqué number 60 on May 21, 2020. I often wake up between 3:00 and 4:00 am. I then go outside and look at the night sky. Early this morning at about 3:00 am, I saw a bright flash directly above me in the heavens. It was not a meteorite or an airplane or a satellite. It was only visible for an instant. I believe it was a message of inspiration, knowledge, and a direct spiritual connection.

We are interviewing Cindy Catches of the Pine Ridge Indian Reservation on Tuesday, May 26, on our *Timeless Esoterica* radio show. She has helped develop a curriculum for young Lakota children based on the sacred medicine wheel of their people. She was married to Peter Catches, who was a 38th generation medicine man. They started an organization called Oceti Wakan or a sacred fireplace. I watched Peter Catches explaining what the organization will do and was blown away by the ancient wisdom he possessed. He said that Oceti Wakan would bring a different light of understanding to people that will help heal. He explained that the great mystery revealed by the Great Spirit is one of love and that our natural state is to be always expanding. This growth is not just for helping yourself but for helping others as well. "We all have a place in creation," he said.[191]

"What is God?" I asked.

"You are on a sacred path, you know, you have been touched by God. You are dwelling on this earth with your consciousness in heaven," said Anzar.

"Help me to understand," I said.

"Yes, help is here," said Anzar. I nodded my head in acknowledgement. Gene stepped forward.

"Another project, Gene," I said.

"I like it, good work. Prepare them, the actors, but really, everyone, it's all tied together," said Gene.

"You have an important interview next Tuesday. It will reinforce your mission and open a broader and deeper dialogue and consciousness. Free will and destiny. The archetypes, the hero's journey. The energy is there to do good and make peace. Always from a position of love. October is the trial, and you must prevail," said Anzar.

245

"What about my war dreams? Last night I was fighting with an old bolt-action rifle?" I asked.

"Symbolic of the coming conflict where the old ways of thought are no longer sufficient. You must all evolve to your higher consciousness," said Anzar.

The bright light in the heavens was a sign of my spiritual connection and commitment to making good things happen. Different spirits have told me, and in different ways, the same message. Our mission in life is to help alleviate the suffering of others.

I posted communiqué number 61 on May 22, 2020. "The world breaks everyone and afterward many are strong at the broken places." This quote is from Ernest Hemingway in *A Farewell to Arms*.[192] If there is one thing I have learned, it is that all writing is autobiographical. During rehearsal yesterday for a streamplay called *The Bridge* that we are working on for Lockdown Theatre, one of our actors asked: "Do you ever write any comedies?" He had a point. *The Bridge* is about two very different people randomly meeting on the Golden Gate Bridge in San Francisco. They are each holding a secret—they are there to jump. The last streamplay we did was *This is My Gun*, which is about a school shooter. *The Bronze Star* from 2012 was about the Vietnam War, and the suicide of my veteran friend. *The Epiphany* in 2016 was about the Nazi invasion of Norway in 1940. None of these are comedies, yet I did weave some comedic moments into these theatrical plays and streamplays. Even villains can be amusing. The truth is that life is both tragic and funny, cruel, and beautiful. I know these characters in my plays because they are part of me. I can identify in some way with all of them and their broken places. Strength and character come from continuing and moving forward despite the obstacles and tragedies that befall us. As Neil Weiss, one of my writing mentors, once said, "nobody wants to see a play about happy people living in happy town." The following is from my walk yesterday evening.

"*Torsdag*. Thor's Day. Viking stuff," I said.

"Very proud of you," said Gene.

"We have three Seattle people in our current production, Gene," I said.

"That makes me happy," said Gene.

"Me too. It's your legacy. I hope it's successful for them and their careers, and us and our concept," I said.

"It will be," said Gene. Anzar stepped up.

"Anzar, I'm concerned about the dark cloud of October. Any more you can say?" I asked.

"Not much you can do to stop it, you just must weather through it," said Anzar. He showed me a frightening image of the ocean during a big storm.

"Like big storm waves on the ocean, you must ride through it and not get caught broadside," said Anzar.

"My dad taught me that. He was an old-time sailor and traveled around the world as a young man. He said to approach a big wave diagonally," I said.

"Yes, and be as prepared as you can be," said Anzar.

"I'm thankful for your help. All of you," I said.

"There is a spiritual drought, and when the rains of truth come, they will be powerful, and people must be ready to accept the flood of enlightenment and the paradigm shift that follows," said Anzar.

"Ginger says that what is important today may not hold the same importance tomorrow," I said. Anzar nodded yes.

"The bright light over my head the other night, what was that?" I asked.

"Communication, saying hello," said Anzar.

"It was quick," I said.

"That is all you needed, right?" said Anzar.

"Yeah, I know you are there, and I know you are helping us. I have confidence in you," I said.

"Have confidence in yourself," said Anzar.

"Were you on a ship or just reaching out?" I asked.

"Just reaching out," said Anzar. I came to a viewpoint on the walk.

"Thank you, Anzar. Okay, Gene, here's the City of Angels. There are a lot of LA-based people in this project. We're going to make it happen for a lot of people," I said.

"Take what you're given and make the best you can out of it. Make something beautiful," said Gene.

"Thank you, Gene. Any advice for *The Bridge*?" I asked.

"Establish the Golden Gate Bridge as a character immediately and end with it," said Gene.

In *The Divine Comedy*, Dante has a sudden flash of clarity that is almost beyond comprehension. Finally, he understands the nature of the Trinity, and his soul becomes aligned with God's love.

> *But already my desire and my will*
> *were being turned like a wheel, all at one speed,*
> *by the Love which moves the sun and the other stars.*[193]

There is no humor without sadness. There is no light without the dark. I keep getting reminded of that fact. We can all establish our own light, and have it burn bright for as long as we can, not only for ourselves but for others as well, like a lighthouse warning passing ships of danger and refuge. The two go hand in hand.[194]

On May 23, 2020, I posted communiqué number 62. Anzar once told me that love is what we do. I guess there are different ways to look at that statement. Perhaps it means that we are in the love business? Or does he mean that saying "I love you" is not as important as demonstrating that I love you? Maybe, although I think that both are necessary. The song "Love Me Do" by The Beatles comes to mind. Paul McCartney wrote the song in 1958 while he skipped school one day. John Lennon later added the bridge or middle eight. It was the Beatles' debut single in 1962 and reached number 17 on the British charts, and in 1964 hit number one in America.

"Hello. Nice day today. Just saw two large bucks, that was cool. At the top road of my walk. Significance?" I asked.

"Good luck. Good fortune. Gentleness and strength in combination. There is a lot you must do to make good and do good," said Anzar. I noticed that Gene had stepped closer.

"Thank you. We cast *The Bridge*. It is an important play," I said.

"People have to know to choose life and give tomorrow a chance. You might be broken, but don't give up. Fix yourself," said Gene.

"Thank you. Hey Anzar, can we see another UFO?" I asked.

"You got it," said Anzar.

"What does it mean?" I asked.

"That we are watching, we are here, and not to worry. Have faith, love, humanity, universal humanity," said Anzar. Just after he spoke, a strong gust of wind almost blew me over.

"Thank you. I feel the wind that adds importance to your words," I said.

"There might be something bad that happens in October, but good will come," said Gene.

"I will always keep love in my heart," I said.

I was listening to an audio book, *The Lakota Way* by Joseph M. Marshall, III, and he told a story about how a young Native American boy was targeted for bullying and called every horrible thing imaginable. He went to his grandfather for help. "Do you believe what those other boys said about you is true?" the grandfather asked. The boy said he did not believe it was true. "Then let the wind of their insults blow through you, and you will be unharmed by them. You may feel it, but do not let it catch your anger or your pride. It will pass," the grandfather said. That is a story of love and how to approach a conflict situation with love and wisdom. Love guides us in all things, and it is what we must do.[195]

I posted communiqué number 63 on May 25, 2020. Memorial Day. A day to remember those who have given their lives in service to their country. But, when you think about it, they gave their lives in service to us, the people. Putting on a uniform is not just for parades; it is an honor and a symbol of a sacred commitment to be willing to give your life for another. Fewer than one percent of Americans have served, and more than one million have died in war in our history. American poet, journalist, and soldier Edwin Rolfe (who served in the Spanish Civil War as a volunteer and in World War II) in his poem "City of Anguish" wrote: "War is your comrade struck dead beside you; his shared cigarette still alive in your lips."[196]

"Thank you all for being here. What do you think the blue light was in the corner of the bedroom the other night, around 3:00 am?" I asked.

"A spirit," said Anzar.

"Whose spirit?" I asked. Anzar and my spirit friends were consulting.

"What do you think of what a friend told me that we shouldn't worry?" I asked.

"He is right; worrying does not help, just prepare and advise others to prepare. You are doing your job," said Anzar.

"Alright. I'd still like to know who that spirit was. I'm sure that it was somebody trying to contact me. I know it wasn't a bad thing," I said. Gene stepped forward to talk.

"Hey, Gene, I rewrote *Tough Trip Through Hell*, a dramatic-comedy play I wrote based on my friend David Willson's unpublished novel about Virginia City, Montana. It'll be great for my friend David to see it and hear it. It'll be a challenge to produce," I said.[197]

"I'm proud of you," said Gene.

"I'm proud of us—for what we've done, and what this team has done," I said.

"The mountains are citadels for the struggle that is coming. You might have to go to the mountain tops," said Anzar.

"Okay, you'll let me know, right?" I asked.

"Yes. And remember the river," said Anzar.

"I wrote a poem about rivers," I said.

"The nature of reality," he said.

It is funny how Anzar throws these non sequiturs at me, but then later, I figure out how it is connected to what we were talking about or what I was thinking. Memorial Day, citadels, plays, rivers, the nature of reality? My friend David is a veteran of the Vietnam War and has been suffering from agent orange related cancer for years. He always tells me that politicians are quick to send us to war, but we are then left with the butcher's bill. To see his unpublished novel produced as a play would mean the world to him. It is also a reminder that veterans die from their wounds, injuries, and illnesses long after their wars are over. A citadel is considered a fortress, and mountains certainly can appear to be fortresses, but what does Anzar mean? I know that when I stand on a mountain top, I gain perspective and understanding and feel as if I can handle anything that happens down below. Rivers are of great interest to me, so many years ago, I wrote a poem called "A River."

> *Passing through a wilderness one day*
> *I found a dry riverbed.*
> *Rocks, gravel, and sand*
> *beneath my feet where water once flowed.*
> *What is a river?*

A river is water,
but water can be a lake, a pond, an ocean, or a baby's tear.
So, water alone is not a river.
A river is the channel of rocks and sand.
But rocks and sand can be a mountain, a beach, or
life's shadows captured in a fossil,
or a dune in the desert.
Rocks and sand, then, are not a river.
Maybe, a river is where it is going.
A river flows and has direction,
not always straight,
sometimes raging,
sometimes meandering,
but always a destination.
Standing in a dry riverbed one day, I knew.

That poem reminds me that we are like a river in that we all have a destination, and it is our consciousness that survives and lives forever. The old saying is what you see is what you get. I believe there is more, and we just have to keep going, like a river, to find out what that is. Have a peaceful Memorial Day.

I posted communiqué number 64 on May 26, 2020. The nature of time is fascinating, but do we really know what it is? I read an article yesterday entitled: "Time's Passage is Probably an Illusion."[198] Scientists and philosophers do not really know what time is. A thought popped into my head early this morning—long ago was just now. I was thinking of what will happen in the future and of an event in the past, and then I thought that at that moment in the past, I was probably thinking of another event further in the past and an event in the future. So, where are we? When I think of past events, I see a movie playing in my head. The same thing happens when I think of the future. Is it the same movie? Is the present a frame in that film? Can I run the film backward and forward? Who really knows? Albert Einstein once wrote to a friend: "The past, present, and future are only illusions, even if stubborn ones." If we combine my early morning thought, "long ago was just now," with a popular advertising slogan, "the future is now," then everything would be now! That idea is precisely what my friend Gene told me about the afterlife: "There is no past, there is no future; there is only the eternal now."

"I see you are all concerned," I said.

"Second wave," said Anzar.

"I know, I'm doing all I can, but things will happen. A critic wrote anonymously that I was just a fiction writer, and he doesn't believe me. I usually just ignore critics unless they attack others. What do you think?" I asked.

"Stay that way, approach everything from a position of love and humility," said Anzar.

"Memorial Day is always sad. Wars continue and will likely continue," I said.

"The lessons are still being learned," said Anzar.

"We have to protect ourselves, right?" I asked.

"When necessary, but there is always a price to be paid," said Anzar.

"No City of Angels today, well there is, but you can't see it," I said as I reached the high point of my spirit walk.

"But you know it's there. The nature of things, just because you can't see it does not mean it's not there," said Gene.

"True. Thank you. Anzar, you talked about citadels, mountains, is it a metaphor?" I asked.

"Take it in the way that is most appropriate," said Anzar.

"Maybe we'll take a drive to the mountain top. I think we'll learn something," I said.

Just one day before he was assassinated on April 3, 1968, in Memphis, Dr. Martin Luther King, Jr. said:

> Well, I do not know what will happen now. We have got some difficult days ahead. But it really does not matter with me now, because I have been to the mountaintop. And I do not mind. Like anybody, I would like to live–a long life; longevity has its place. But I am not concerned about that now. I just want to do God's will. And He's allowed me to go up to the mountain. And I have looked over. And I have seen the Promised Land. I may not get there with you. But I want you to know tonight, that we, as a people, will get to the Promised Land. So, I am happy, tonight. I am not worried about anything. I am not fearing any man. Mine eyes have seen the glory of the coming of the Lord.[199]

King made the biblical reference (*Deuteronomy 34:1–4)* to Moses climbing to the top of Mount Nebo, where he saw the promised land. God told Moses that he would not cross over into it. Very prophetic since Moses died shortly after, just as King died the next day after his speech. Dr. King seemed to know what would happen, or to put it another way; he remembered the future. Here is a poem named "Remembering the Future" that I wrote long ago, or maybe it was just now?

If we remember the future
time runs both ways
If time runs backward
rivers head back to the mountains
old become young
broken hearts become whole again
wars return to peace
leaves of autumn leap back green to their limbs
crashing waves on the shore return to the sea
lovers become strangers
departed loved ones return to us

If we remember the future
time is circular
We are born, we live, we die
born, live, and die
Endlessly
If we remember the future
there is no present
there is no frozen moment
Even a memory is like a film
playing, replaying, forward and backward
Direction, movement, the universe
we are all in motion
atoms of our bodies
air that we inhale
constant motion
For what is before the beginning?
Or after the end?
If there is no end
we have nothing to fear
as we listen to the endless whisper of time

My next communiqué, number 65, was posted on May 28, 2020. When is bad news, good news? I was reminded of the Rolling Stones' song "You Can't Always Get What You Want" released in 1969.[200]

You can't always get what you want
but if you try some time
you just might find
you get what you need.

Ultimately, if we get what we need, then we are very lucky indeed. But for many people, they want more, and unrealistic expectations can lead to heartbreak and disaster. I understand the power of our consciousness and how we can manifest things and events. However, often the results are not exactly what we had in mind. Not getting everything you want is the bad news, but we must keep in mind that

255

having is often not as great as wanting. The good news is that we can influence events and do good work that is needed for others and for our souls. The following connection was from May 26.

"Thank you all for being here. Anzar, it looks like you are busy. I see you, Gene," I said.

"Wonderful," said Gene.

"I wrote about time the other day; I always quote you," I said.

"Yes, you've helped a lot of people," said Gene.

"I'm just using your words, my friend. I think we'll do *The Bridge* next and then *The Briefcase*. The production team is pumped, and the actors are excited," I said.

"That's great!" said Gene.

"Then we'll produce *Tough Trip Through Hell*, my friend David's dramatic-comedy western. It is more challenging to produce than the others, so we have to establish some frameworks first: logistically and artistically," I said.

"Samuel L. Jackson," said Gene.

"I'd love to have him be in one of our productions," I said.

"Doesn't hurt to ask," said Gene.

"True, but we already have great actors, even if they're not as well-known, yet," I said. Anzar stepped forward.

"Hey, Anzar, anymore you can tell me?" I asked.

"Prepare, everything is very fluid right now, things will just lie dormant then all of a sudden explode out of nowhere, be ready," said Anzar.

"Thank you. Yeah, I would like to use my psychic energy, even more, to make things happen," I said.

"Be very clear what it is you are trying to manifest," said Anzar. That was good advice since he had already told me that we manifest our own reality.

The following spirit connection was from my May 27 spirit walk. Protests over the death of George Floyd in police custody in Minneapolis, Minnesota had begun on May 26, and were spreading around the country.

"Hello, everybody. Kind of dark where you guys are. How is everybody? Like to ask for your help to keep us all safe and protected. Please let us see a UFO," I said

"You got it, but you must stay awake long enough to spot them," said Anzar.

"I know, very funny, thank you," I said, knowing that he was referring to my going to bed early almost every night.

"Turbulent times ahead, so hang on. The good, do the good for your people, and all others will do good for their people, then we all do good for each other," said Anzar.

"I understand. Hi, Gene. Can you see the City of Angels?" I asked.

"Just barely, a little hazy," said Gene.

"God bless all of us," I said.

"Yeah, thank you. A lot of good people involved in trying to do good," said Gene.

"This thing about time is interesting. I know what you said, Gene, it's all in the now," I said.

"Like a floating now," said Gene.

"Sometimes the magic works, sometimes it does not." That is what Old Lodge Skins said in *Little Big Man*, one of my favorite movies of all time.[201] Manifesting good things is important business, but we do not always see the good we do. Also, other people may not see the results. It is easy to get upset and expect thanks and gratitude. We

257

should manifest and do the right thing without any expectations. It does not always happen exactly the way we want it to, so it is best just quietly to do your good work and move on. Easier said than done. These words came to me early this morning: "Let them into your heart: the strong, the foolish, the weak, and the wise—all of them. And do not let your heart harden." To me, it means that we must accept people for who they are and what they do and love them regardless. This acceptance goes hand in hand with operating from a position of love. It does not mean that we allow ourselves or others to be fooled or hurt; it just means that we do not pass judgements on others. We may never know the real reasons for what people do, and they may not either. All we can do is be grateful for having what we need, do the best we can, and let our hearts be free to love and be loved.

I posted communiqué number 66 on May 30, 2020. In 1994, I began to watch *The Power of Myth*, a documentary about Joseph Campbell, the American mythologist and professor of literature. Many events can have an impact on our lives, but that video and Campbell's books changed the trajectory of my life. I remember him saying that: "People say that what we are all seeking is a meaning for life. I think what we are seeking is an experience of being alive." It made so much sense to me. Instead of stumbling around in the dark without a purpose, or reason, waiting for someone to put me on the right path, I had to fully explore life, and find my own path. I started writing poetry again and even attended poetry readings. Not surprisingly, it was only three years after watching the *The Power of Myth* that I had my first encounter with Anzar, the Progenitor.[202]

Lucinda Laughing Eagle (Luci) and I interviewed Cindy Catches on our *Timeless Esoterica Radio Show*. Cindy was married to Peter Catches, who was a Lakota medicine man and the son of Pete Catches. They were 38th and 37th generation medicine men, respectively. Cindy runs Oceti Wakan (the Sacred Fireplace), an organization that helps promote traditional Lakota values for children on the Pine Ridge Indian reservation. Pete Catches brought back the Sundance ceremony that had been made illegal by the government. I deeply respect what she is trying to do for the Lakota people, but it is really for all of us. We have lost our way in modern society. The twelve core values in the Lakota way of life are bravery, fortitude, generosity, wisdom, respect, honor, perseverance, love, humility, sacrifice, truth, and compassion. These should not be new to any of us since that is what our own elders have also taught us. I believe We are more alike than different. We must return to our true selves to put things back in balance on Earth. By making the invisible world visible through expanding our consciousness, hopefully, it will allow us to see the light within us. The following is from my May 28 spirit walk.

"Thursday evening, it was a warm day. So nice to see all of you, bright and shiny. I will try to stay awake long enough tonight to see a UFO," I said, smiling. Anzar and all my other spirit friends laughed.

"Anzar, a lot of people worried about what you said yesterday," I said.

"You can see how things can explode, but they were just below the surface the whole time. Be careful, disruption and conflict could pop up anywhere, be on guard, and be rational," said Anzar.

"Thank you for always helping us," I said.

"Do what you know is right in your heart," said Anzar.

"Thank you. It's been working, yeah. Not letting negative things catch on my anger or my pride, just doing my work, job, and mission," I said. Gene approached.

"Not only with the actors and play production, but with your students and VA group too," said Gene.

"Thank you," I said. The following is from my spirit walk on May 29. The civil unrest was worsening in the nation and the White House was put on lockdown as demonstrators rallied nearby.[203]

"Friday morning, cooler today. Hello everybody. Almost June. Hard to believe. I know you guys are going to be working overtime.

There is an unraveling with seams coming undone in society," I said, as Anzar showed me images of killing, riots and unrest, anger, sadness, and pain.

"Use your wise mind; use that technique. Lots of emotion and logic mind going on, not a lot of wise mind. Balance, put things in balance, that would be helpful to everybody," said Anzar.

"I agree, I keep falling asleep before I can see another UFO. I will try again. I'm sorry. Thank you all for helping," I said.

"It would be a good idea to have a read through for the *Tough Trip Through Hell* streamplay. Get the actors going on that too," said Gene.

"I know, I want David to see it produced since it is based on his unpublished novel, and he is very ill," I said.

"Your play *The Bridge* was an important play that could help people. But racism is an important issue and especially right now, and *Tough Trip Through Hell* will help with that," said Gene.

"Let me know what else I can do," I said.

"Safety for family and friends," said Gene.

"The unraveling will occur more rapidly as we approach the fall. Many things colliding at once. You must be ready," said Anzar.

"The breaking apart at the seams analogy, I get it. Thank you for all your help," I said, with tears in my eyes. I know that my spirit friends have been warning me of what is happening, but now that it has accelerated, it still seems unbelievable. How can you stop a runaway train? Negative forces are in motion. I see fear in the world, and fear is probably the greatest motivator of human behavior. Fear must be replaced with love, for if you have love in your heart, you have no room for fear. Maybe if we can help people to remember the basic values that we all know to be true, the Lakota values, the values for all humankind, then we can slow down that runaway train and let people off and back to safety. At the end of May 2020, 103,781 people had died from COVID-19.[204]

I published yet another communiqué (number 67) on June 1, 2020. "Are you a republican or a democrat?" I am often asked. "I am an American," is always my reply. As a historian, I have seen that partisan politics can often interfere with historical analysis. From a historical perspective, what is going on today in America, as disturbing as it seems, makes sense. We have been in a period of transition since the 2016 election, which is now leading to a profound political paradigm shift. We are in a 40-year cycle; the last shift was the conservative revolution in 1980. Whoever is elected president in 2020 will have an opportunity to move the entire political system like Ronald Reagan, and Franklin D. Roosevelt before him. It comes down to classic political theory: how much change do you want in society, and how quickly do you want it? In a classical sense, conservatives want very little if any change and they are in no hurry. Liberals want substantial change, and they want it sooner rather than later. Radicals want complete change, and they want it now. What we do not know is in which direction the center of politics in America will move. Compared to other modern democratic nations, our political system is rather conservative or right of center. Even our recent liberal presidents Bill Clinton and Barack Obama were not that liberal, especially compared to Roosevelt. As a result of our 2020 presidential election, the political system could move to the center, it could go far left, or it could go further right.

Adding to the anxiety caused by COVID-19, and the coming political paradigm shift, is the long-simmering racial tension in America. Dr. Martin Luther King, Jr. spent the last year of his life protesting the Vietnam War and working on his poor people's campaign. He wanted to fundamentally change our socio-economic system to help all poor working-class people attain a living wage and dignity. King saw the connection between racism, poverty, and conflict. By challenging the very power structure of American society, he put himself

261

in great jeopardy and was ultimately assassinated by those who recognized the threat he posed to what President Dwight D. Eisenhower called the Military-Industrial Complex.

Many people today are invoking Dr. King's name and cherry-picking his words and speeches. Still, nobody that I have heard has mentioned his poor people's campaign and call for a change to our socio-economic system. I believe what we have today is a movement to fulfill the original goals of Reconstruction after the Civil War. Reconstruction sought to bring the North and South back together and integrate former slaves into the mainstream of American society.

In my view, we must strive to fulfill the promise of full integration to heal the wounds of slavery and obtain a sense of balance. If you are a person of color, or if you are friends with a person of color, or you are simply paying attention, you know that the echoes of segregation and slavery still haunt our nation, and the sting of racial and ethnic prejudice is ever-present. If we all listen to one another, really listen, we will hear the anguish, feel the pain, and will be compelled to make positive change happen now. In so doing, we will live up to the words in the Declaration of Independence. "We hold these truths to be self-evident, that all men are created equal, that they are endowed by their Creator with certain unalienable Rights, that among these are Life, Liberty and the pursuit of Happiness." This is not about being left, right, democrat, or republican; it is about doing the right thing to restore the American dream to its people. In the words of American political scientist Samuel P. Huntington: "Critics say that America is a lie because its reality falls so short of its ideals. They are wrong. America is not a lie; it is a disappointment. But it can be a dis-appointment only because it is also a hope."[205]

"Hello everybody, terrible last couple of nights, people losing control, unrest throughout the country. I'm afraid the verdict in the pending trial of the Minneapolis police officers responsible for the death of George Floyd won't be what many people want," I said.

"This is just the first wave of protests. There are more calamities to come: The celestial anomaly, natural disasters, a second wave of the virus, and a possible political rebellion in the fall," said Anzar.

"I was afraid of that. Thank you. On a lighter note, Gene, let's see if we can see the City of Angels," I said.

"Yes, but it's hazy. I'm worried about my family," said Gene.

"I know they read what I write, and they're prepared," I said.

"There needs to be socio-economic changes; that's the root of the problem," said Gene.

"I agree. We need to listen to the original complete vision of Dr. Martin Luther King, Jr., not just the abridged version," I said. My mom and dad stepped forward, which is very unusual.

"Hi Mom and Dad," I said.

"Take care of each other, family and friends. If someone isn't listening, they can't understand. Help them to understand," said my mom.

"Yes, Mom," I said.

"Believe in love. Believe in the good," said Anzar.

I had more military dreams this morning. In one dream, I was at a funeral home and looking at many bodies in frozen contorted poses. It was so frightening. Then, my mom showed up, walking right next to me. She told me she did not like this place. I think the place she did not like symbolized the world we are living in today. We have got to do better and make things right. It may seem impossible, but it is possible to make good things happen. All it takes is attention and intention and the patience to do the hard work. Justice and good things do not happen automatically; it takes dedication and hard work by good people.

My next communiqué (number 68) was published on June 3, 2020. I support people. I support first amendment protesters, the police, firefighters, journalists, healthcare workers, all workers, small business owners, and all people who work for good each day. It appears that the legitimate process of airing grievances in a public forum is being hijacked by those who want anarchy and chaos to further divide us along racial, ethnic, and political lines. Can we believe our political leaders? The media? Maybe we should stop or at least slow down for a moment and try to find the truth behind these rapidly evolving events rather than reacting instantly and emotionally. Can we work together for solutions and work out our differences? As Dr. Martin Luther King, Jr. said: "We need to learn to disagree without being violently disagreeable." There are some lessons to be learned by those who came before us. As Mexican author Don Miguel Ruiz wrote in his book *The Four Agreements*:

1. Be impeccable with your word.
2. Do not take anything personally.
3. Do not make assumptions.
4. Always do your best.[206]

Ancient Persian poet and mystic Rumi gave us good advice. "Before you speak, let your words pass through three gates: At the first gate, ask yourself, "Is it true?" At the second gate, ask, "Is it necessary?" At the third gate, ask, "Is it kind?" Think of how much better our world would be if we could follow this timeless wisdom.[207]

These events of the past week have taken me back to 1968 after Dr. Martin Luther King, Jr. was assassinated. I remember talking to my mom about the tragedy.

"When we came to this country from Norway, my aunt told me not to speak Norwegian in public," Mom said.

"Why, Mom?" I asked.

"Because if we didn't speak, others wouldn't know we were immigrants, and wouldn't make fun of us and treat us differently," she said.

"Oh," I said.

"But black people can't hide who they are," she said. Her words have stuck with me for all these years. It was one of the many lessons she taught me. She only had a sixth-grade education, but she was smart and wise.

"Thank you all for being here. Mom and Dad are here too," I said.

"Hello," said Mom.

"Hi, Mom, and Dad," I said.

"Protect family and friends. Keep love in your heart. Keep Norway close. Teach the truth," said Mom.

"I will, thank you, Mom and Dad," I said. My mom and dad stepped back, and Gene stepped forward.

"Hey Gene, first official rehearsal for *The Bridge* tomorrow," I said.

"It'll have a big impact," said Gene.

"Then *Tough Trip Through Hell* after that, in September," I said.

"Big challenge," said Gene.

"I agree, but very rewarding for everybody. Looking forward to these two productions, thank you for making it happen," I said.

"Stay away from crowds," said Gene.

"I understand, I know it'll be hard for your sister and nephew because of their jobs, but I'll check in on them and mention that. Thank you, Gene," I said.

"Make the complicated simpler to understand through the arts, through theatre, and through your writing," said Gene.

"I will," I said. Anzar stepped closer.

"Hey, Anzar. Thank you for your help with everything," I said.

"Do not dwell on predictions, stress preparations," said Anzar.

"What else can we do?" I asked.

"Think about Norway. A refuge," he said.

"Okay, at what point?" I asked.

"Make preparations," said Anzar.

"Thank you. Alright. Do you think it will get that bad?" I asked. I was frightened by the apocalyptic vision in my head.

"It could," said Anzar.

"I was taught sensitive differentiation and trying to walk in another person's shoes. We all need to do better with that," I said. Anzar nodded in agreement.

"One of my friends asked about armed conflict with China," I said.

"Hard to know for sure, but certainly skirmishes are a potential. Neither side wants a big war, but all this could happen very suddenly," he said.

"Another reason to think about Norway. Maybe not a good time to buy a house. Listen to Ginger's instincts," I said.

My youngest son Leif and I watched the *Grant* miniseries on the History Channel. It is interesting how our perception of General/President Ulysses S. Grant has changed over time. He was second only to Abraham Lincoln as the most famous American for many years. Unfortunately, in a rush to heal the wounds of the Civil War, the southern perspective not only led to the disabling of reconstruction and the rise of segregation but also tarnished the reputation of Grant and elevated Confederate General Robert E. Lee.[208] It reminds me of what my friend and Pulitzer Prize-winning author Viet Thanh Nguyen said: All wars are fought twice, the first time on the battlefield, the second time in memory."[209] My volcano nightmare this morning is a clear warning in addition to Anzar's shocking words. We are in trouble. We must seek the truth and keep love in our hearts, or we will all descend into chaos, despair, division, and conflict.

I did not post a communiqué, but I took a spirit walk on Thursday, June 4, 2020. I had more disturbing military dreams again last night.

"Hello everybody. You're all wearing white. Not sure what that means," I said.

"June 4 might be a very significant day," said Anzar.

"What can you guys tell me?" I asked.

"House of cards is collapsing. Hang on through the chaos and confusion. Hang on. You are protected in more ways than one. Lines are forming, sides are being taken. Possible civil war," said Anzar.

"Anzar, that doesn't sound like good news, everything seems pretty grim and out of control. We have to come out on the right side of history," I said.

"Hard to know, lines are blurred. You know what is in your heart, that is not blurred. Position of love, love in your heart," said Anzar.

"I was worried because my daughter Caitlin wanted to go to the George Floyd protests in Los Angeles. I told her that I didn't want her to go," I said.

"Okay, she has a lot of spirit," said Anzar.

As it turned out, she did march and one of the marchers threw water bottles at the police and law enforcement returned fire with rubber bullets. My daughter was not injured. She decided not to go to any more protests, and I was grateful for that decision.

I published my last communiqué, number 69, on June 6, 2020. As the political situation grew more tense approaching the election and with the George Floyd protests spreading across the country and abroad, my communiqués were drawing negative comments from an increasingly polarized readership. It was not worth it to continue, at least not on Facebook.

This will be my last communiqué for the time being. I continue to have upsetting military dreams almost every night. I believe I have said what needed to be said. This is the 76th anniversary of D-Day. I will share Dwight D. Eisenhower's message to the invasion force.

Soldiers, Sailors, and Airmen of the Allied Expeditionary Force!

You are about to embark upon the Great Crusade, toward which we have striven these many months. The eyes of the world are upon you. The hope and prayers of liberty-loving people everywhere march with you. In company with our brave Allies and brothers-in-arms on other Fronts, you will bring about the destruction of the German war machine, the elimination of Nazi tyranny over the oppressed peoples of Europe, and security for ourselves in a free world.

Your task will not be an easy one. Your enemy is well trained, well equipped and battle-hardened. He will fight savagely.

But this is the year 1944! Much has happened since the Nazi triumphs of 1940-41. The United Nations have inflicted upon the Germans great defeats, in open battle, man-to-man. Our air offensive has seriously reduced their strength in the air and their capacity to wage war on the ground. Our Home Fronts have given us an overwhelming superiority in weapons and munitions of war and placed at our disposal great reserves of trained fighting men. The tide has turned! The freemen of the world are marching together to Victory!

I have full confidence in your courage, devotion to duty and skill in battle. We will accept nothing less than full Victory!

Good luck! And let us beseech the blessing of Almighty God upon this great and noble undertaking. [210]

My parents lived through World War II under Nazi occupation in Norway. My dad was put in a Nazi labor camp and my eldest brother died during the war because the Nazis took all the medicine. Whatever hardships I have faced as a result of COVID-19, does not compare to the pain and suffering my parents endured in World War II.

Spirit Walks, June to December 2020

I switched back to my regular spirit walks after communiqué number 69. The political climate in the United States was causing people to react in strange and angry ways to my helpful and loving public postings on Facebook. To continue posting my communiqués seemed to be non-productive, and I was not certain that I was helping more than I was contributing to the consternation. On warm, Saturday morning, June 13, 2020, I took a spirit walk. There had been another shooting on Friday, in Atlanta. It seemed as though the public had gone mad and those who were unstable to begin with, were acting out. Most of the people I encountered on my walk were not wearing masks. I was ready to connect with my spirit friends.

"Are we right or is everybody else right?" I asked.

"I think you are correct and there is not much you can do about other people. You must protect yourself. Keep love in your heart, approach everything from a position of love and remind folks of the same as you go through this series of calamities, catastrophes," said Anzar.

"What is in the hearts of the looters and rioters, certainly not love?" I asked. Shortly after I spoke, I thought I saw a UFO flash in the sky.

"Sharing, and being vulnerable is what empowers others, that is how we grow, and love each other," said Anzar.

"I'm trying not to be full of hate, with the riots, and with our president not saying the right thing, I pray for our leaders to make good decisions," I said.

"Take money out of the hands of terrorists, and your enemies. You are a good people, redeemable, you are redeemable. There are disappointments, but you do not have to start over. Tearing down all the monuments will not help you heal. Put them in context, learn from history. October will be a reckoning. There are only certain things we can do. Do the best we can. Do not respond to the crazy negative people, they must seek their own solutions, just put out positive messages," said Anzar.

"Thank you. I think it's possible for us all to come together, probably if we all face a common threat and realize it as such," I said. The easiest way to control the masses is through anger and fear. We are not very smart when we are angry or afraid. I am sharing this poem that I wrote to remind us all that anger has consequences. I wrote "Waiting for Reconciliation" after I lost custody of my two older boys back in the 1990s. If you have problems with rage and anger, please seek help before it is too late.

> *Six months down and gone*
> *judge said no contact*
> *listening to Erik Satie*
> *ringing footsteps in the rain*
> *riding silently by their house*
> *waiting for reconciliation.*
> *Six months down and gone*
> *in a small town, the last image remains*
> *handcuffed shuffle*
> *vacant no-tear stares*
> *daddy's a bad man*
> *waiting for reconciliation.*
> *Six months down and gone*
> *never again the daddy*
> *the other man moved into house and heart*
> *I am sitting alone*
> *on the other side of town*
> *waiting for reconciliation.*

It was June 14, 2020, and instead of a spirit walk, I had some thoughts that came to me. It is time for all of us to think about the America we know and love and how we can make progress toward forming a more perfect union promised in our constitution. I have been teaching American history for 30 years, and one of the things I have come to believe is that black voices can help provide the conscience for our nation. All nations are ultimately judged by how they treat their indigenous and ethnic minority citizens. We are a good people, and I believe we can and will do better. God bless us all.

In my 30 years of teaching, I have noticed a falling off of academic preparation and, more importantly, emotional development. It makes me sad and worried about our future. I spend as much time counseling my students as I do teaching them history and empowering them to work hard to make things better for everyone. What I mean by conscience in context is a real understanding of what is going on and a moral compass to help us all to do the right thing. Many people do not listen to their conscience and what it is trying to tell them. I believe this is as much a spiritual crisis as a political and cultural one. We are taught to treat people fairly and equally as children, but then life beats people down, and they adopt toxic beliefs that erase the innate sense of fairness we had as children. The suffering from the original sin of slavery in this country persists, and our conscience (led in large part by the voices of black people) are trying to help us all understand and guide us. Many white people are refusing to listen or only pay lip service and pretend to care but ultimately do nothing to help.

On June 15, 2020, I took another spirit walk in our neighborhood. It was a Monday morning. I had a nightmare recently and I wanted to ask my spirit friends about its meaning. In the nightmare a little person in a spacesuit, and protective gear, was spraying something. I thought it was Ginger at first, at my old house in Kenmore, Washington. Then it really shocked me, when I realized it was an alien.

"Hello everybody. I see that everybody is working," I said.

"A lot going on," said Anzar.

"Appreciate all you do. Hi, Gene, thanks for helping me understand what happens when we pass from this world. Don't know what I'd do without you," I said. Gene smiled as Anzar stepped forward.

"My nightmare, was it real?" I asked.

"Yes. Premonition of a traumatic memory. That same person is coming back, whoever it is," said Anzar. His answer was somewhat helpful, but I wanted more.

"Who was it," I asked.

"Just what you saw, an alien entity," he said.

"What were they spraying?" I asked.

"It was for decontamination," said Anzar.

"Were they good, bad, or neutral," I asked.

"Neutral," he said.

"I understand, thank you," I said. I wonder what kind of contamination the alien being was decontaminating. It was a frightening nightmare. No one wants to see anyone in a space-age hazmat suit spraying around their house.

It was Tuesday, June 16, 2020, and time for another spirit walk. The cars were especially loud today. I must keep love in my heart and not give in to road rage. Yes, it is true, in my younger days I have had road rage just walking without being in a car.

"Thank you everybody. For being here. Much of the time I must keep my own counsel, try to do the best I can, help others. Sometimes I hear others say good things about me and it bounces off and doesn't stick. I have to learn to let it stick and not let the bad things stick," I said.

"Let the bad things bounce off, good things stick," said Anzar.

"Good advice. Some in the ufology community have developed a cult-like following. I've always tried to avoid that and gently ushered people away who saw me in that way," I said.

"Not good for people, only leads to disempowerment, the power must come from within and from good, not some external fake philosopher and charlatan. Shame on them. People ask for spectacular proof, I understand. They do not want to be taken in. I understand perfectly. All I can offer them is preparation and advice and they must find the truth themselves, spiritual crisis, the answers are not provided by another person, they are provided from within and by God, and then you internalize that knowledge," said Anzar.

"Any more about October?" I asked.

"Why, not bad enough already? Preparation, communication, have you thought about it. Power, communication, food, water," said Anzar. I have prepared but not to the extent that I think I should. Some preparation is better than none I suppose.

Sometimes I dreaded my spirit walk for fear of learning something scary and unsettling. But truth is the truth, and it is better to be aware and prepared than clueless and helpless. With that in mind, I set out on my spirit walk, Friday, June 19, 2020.

"June Gloom they call it. Hello everybody, all very busy, dressed in black. What is going to happen? My job?" I asked.

"You already know because you will make it happen," said Anzar.

"Keep my head down, don't be a fool, do what I'm told, I can't teach in the classroom until we get properly immunized. I'll keep doing what I'm doing, the best I can. But what about our country?" I asked. I did not wait for an answer as my mind was racing. A major election, revolutionary activity in October, we will sort it out. President Trump will have served his purpose as a transitional president leading to a paradigm shift. Will Joe Biden and Kamala Harris be as progressive as people think?

"More agitation. Other calamities. How much detail do you want?" said Anzar.

"Enough so we can be prepared," I said.

"Think of food, water, medicine, safety, power, and communication. Then you will be ready. Immunization will be your liberation point. Remember, there is a sucker born every minute," said Anzar. The thought of Anzar quoting P.T. Barnum made me laugh.[211]

"I don't want to take advantage of people, but many do, they'll grab all they can get regardless of whether it hurts other people," I said. Crisis points bring out the best and worst in people. The key is to keep love in my heart and operate from a position of love.

"How about disclosure stuff?" I asked.

"Ongoing, spiritual in nature," said Anzar. I guess it is time for all of us to open our eyes and see what is real and what is already here.

On June 20, 2020, I had two nightmares. In the first dream, we (friends and family) were all wearing gas masks and were lying down in tents. Then we were ushered through decontamination chambers with radiological warning lights and alarms. In the second dream I was on a sinking ship and had to swim to shore. Not a restful night of sleep.

I took my spirit walk on a cool, nice Saturday morning. Ginger and I always celebrate the 20th of every month as our anniversary day (our actual anniversary is January 20, 2012). President Trump was having a big campaign rally in Tulsa today, his first since March.

"Hello everyone, June Gloom day.[212] What was the meaning of my two dreams last night?" I asked.

"It is a warning, but not necessarily to be taken literally. It indicates a transition, the end of one era and the beginning of a new one," said Anzar.

"The end of the American experiment?" I asked.

"Yes, at least the way it was, yes," said Anzar. I had been telling my students for years that every 40 years or so there is a paradigm shift in the American political system, but this time, it could be combined with a corresponding decline of our hegemonic power in the world as well.

I had yet another nightmare on June 21, 2020. There was a volcanic eruption and then a giant mudslide hit my college. The building I was in was shaking violently. The next day, June 22, 2020, I took a spirit walk on a cool Monday morning.

"Thank you everybody for being here. Please help me keep love in my heart and approach everything from a position of love," I said. I say this every day because we live in turbulent and transitional times.

"Things seem to be falling apart quickly," I said. Anzar stepped forward.

"The seams are coming apart in society. Extremists exploit that. Some otherwise normal and rational people side with extremists to preserve what they have. You must stand up with reason and love," said Anzar. I was glad that my spirit friends offer such wise and uplifting advice and observations on the state of the world.

"The virus is coming back with a vengeance in the fall and winter," said Anzar. Things are coming apart faster than I thought.

"Propane tanks and masks. Important. Respirators. Survival. Canned foods, water, and a way to decontaminate water. Medicines, power. Lay low, do not expose yourself," said Anzar with a staccato delivery.

Tuesday morning, June 23, 2020, it was a cool, cloudy morning as I took my spirit walk hoping to hear some brighter news from my spirit friends.

"Welcome to everybody, crazy times that we live in. Anzar, my friend Lucinda said that you're really me and I'm really you in the quantum world, past, present, and future together. Is she right?" I asked.

"Yes, an aspect of you is an aspect of me. Still a separate entity now, part of a greater whole," said Anzar.

"Thank you. Do you guys think I'll go back to in-person teaching?" I asked.

"Probably not soon," said Anzar.

"Okay. I want to keep Ginger and everybody safe. That is important. How bad will this whole disintegration of our country get?" I asked.

"Really bad. Threat will unify you, aliens, war, series of threats, that will do it, yet to come," he said.

"Thank you," I said. It does not get much scarier than that.

For my spirit walk on Wednesday morning, June 24, 2020, it was hot.

"Hey Anzar, I spoke to someone in the UFO community who gets a lot of sightings and confirmations. Would I be able to get that?" I asked.

"Okay," said Anzar.

"If you could give me a sign that we are communicating right now. Maybe show me a UFO over the mountains I'm looking at. Not sure what that was, a light over by that tree," I said. Then, I thought more about my request. Was it for my amusement or to show off to someone? I had a change of heart.

"Okay. It's alright. The main thing is that I know I'm talking to you with or without other types of confirmation. Still working on preparations, things changing fast, the new normal, I guess," I said.

"Continue to take the virus seriously," said Anzar.

"Yes, we will. Thank you everybody. I appreciate everything you all have done, the warnings, the wisdom," I said.

"Synchronicities?" asked Anzar.

"Yes, those too," I said.

This is a compilation of my spirit walks through the end of June 2020. I thought a lot about my cousin Eva Solheim who died a few years ago. She was my first cousin and was also a writer. I had never spoken to her in the spirit world so I thought I should give it a try.

"Return to your roots. The sea. Always return to the sea," she said. That made sense for me because we are from a remote island in Northern Norway and our ancestors have all been connected to the sea.

I talked to Anzar about the upcoming election. He had suggested that neither Biden nor Trump would ultimately be president. I was worried about the health of Joe Biden.

"What is Joe Biden's condition?" I asked.

"Signs of senility, but with the coming crises, it does not matter who is elected because either one would be equally ineffective. The system is so corrupt that it needs to be purged on both sides," said Anzar. Joe Biden looks very weak. Suddenly I was reminded of the "Patterns of Force" episode from the original *Star Trek* TV series. In that episode, a Federation officer suggested and helped implement a Nazi system of government for the inhabitants of the planet Ekos. The Federation officer was then set up as the Führer even though he was only a puppet leader who was kept heavily medicated. A scary thought indeed.

"Let's hope Americans don't have to suffer for it," I said.

"There is always suffering," said Anzar.

"COVID-19?" I asked.

"Out of control, second wave will be bad," he said. Gene stepped up to speak.

277

"Proud of you for sending 1000 *Snarc* comics to the school children at the Pine Ridge Reservation," said Gene. Ginger and I had also sent *Snarc* comics to US service members serving in the Middle East and to the VA hospital in Long Beach, and St. Jude's Children's Hospital.

"Thank you, Gene," I said. Anzar stepped forward again.

"Prepare for a few hard years. Calamities will continue," said Anzar.

I continued to have military dreams, but I was not sure if it was just based on my having served for six years in the US Army or some indicator of something yet to come. I also had a dream about visiting Brad Pitt in his home. There was a long tunnel you had to go through to get to his house. I saw a total mess with kids running around, a dog, and Angelina Jolie cooking something. Pitt was hyperkinetic and I was just me.

I spoke to Anzar again.

"Settle down for a couple of years of turmoil, at least," said Anzar. The COVID-19 death toll in the United States stood at 126,140 at the end of June.

The following is a compilation of my spirit walks and thoughts for July 2020. I felt like things were going crazy in the world, like a psychological operation (psyop) in the military. Everything was changing so fast. The power of the Black Lives Matter movement is undeniable and growing. The news media was promoting Juneteenth, and the Black National Anthem, and I had never heard of either of them. I have been teaching US history since 1990 and was totally unaware of these things. The media acted as if these things have always been promoted widely but were ignored by a racist US population. There could be some truth to that, or maybe the American media was pretending to be on the band wagon and were responding to pressure. I am not sure, but I do care about black people and all people. Weird. I am worried about my birth country. Not sure what will happen.

"Anzar, whatever guidance or help you can give me would be great. Disinformation is a huge problem, manipulation of information. Propaganda. I don't have any political leanings, I just want what is best for everybody," I said.

"Things are falling apart faster than we thought. October still three months away. Acceleration of the disintegration. Keep Norway in mind. Defunding the police is a bad idea, but reforming is a good idea. Demilitarizing okay," he said.

"How do the aliens fit into all this?" I asked.

"We are all the aliens. We are all connected that is why we are trying to help but not interfere, survival is the goal, but you may not thrive," said Anzar. Honesty is always best. If it is bad news, just tell me and we will deal with it and figure it out. I want progressive reform, but I am not radical. The problem is that people are acting in bizarre, violent, and unloving ways.

"What more can you tell me about what's going on?" I asked. They are not saying very much, then Anzar stepped forward.

"Disintegration. They will need people like you to pick up the pieces," said Anzar.

"Who will listen to me?" I said.

"After alien exposure, reveal, they will. They need kindhearted, loving people to help. That is the key," said Anzar.

"Any more information on what in particular is going to happen and what about the report of UFOs over Iranian nuclear sites?" I asked.

"All the calamities we discussed. Make sure you have propane, water, communication. You know the connection with nuclear sites. A little bit of insurance, safety patrol, to keep a lid on things, giving peace a chance," said Anzar. That made me laugh, Anzar quoting John Lennon.

On a warm Friday morning in July, I was on a spirit walk when I saw my mom on top of a mountain near our home on Andøya. She was waving and picking blueberries. It was such a peaceful and wonderful image. Then I connected with Anzar.

"Time is just eternal, no passage of time, it just is. Like you are looking at the whole picture not just one part of it. Your viewpoint is omniscient instead of narrowly focused," said Anzar.

"Is it possible to be both infinitely large and infinitely small?" I asked.

"Yes, and mission focus," he said. Even though his response was mixed, I understood. I knew that I was learning at a rapid rate but needed to stay focused.

"What do you think of this dialogue I want to start with an African American my own age, working class?" I asked.

"Like Malcolm X said, everybody needs to put their cards on the table, speak the truth," said Anzar. We are at another level and everyday people are nervous as others are taking advantage from all angles, profiteers, charlatans. It would be just two guys speaking honestly.

"Sounds good. It might help. Might go viral and promote the other projects and the mission," said Anzar. I know that I am supposed to help Terry Lovelace and now Kevin Hines who survived jumping from the Golden Gate Bridge and has dedicated his life to preventing suicide. It is a miracle, intervention, miraculous intervention, that we came to meet.

As July dragged on, I had to shorten my spirit walks and keep them closer to home because so many people were not wearing masks and were not being careful. Terrible calamities coming up. Please help keep me on the good path.

"Civil unrest bordering on civil war, economic collapse, violence, international conflict. All those things. Stay sharp, stay together, and you can do it," said Anzar. I noticed Gene in the background as I approached the apex of my spirit walk route.

"Hey, Gene, City of Angels coming up, hard to see, dark smog or smoke. Can see it just barely," I said.

"Thank you, my friend," said Gene.

"Trying to be safe, so many not being safe, walking where there are no people, doing my best. UFOs, that would be great," I said.

"Any more you can say, Anzar?" I ask.

"Be careful, others are not being careful," said Anzar. Gene nodded in agreement. Anzar was front and center.

"Anzar, Lucinda is the only one who has seen you other than me," I said.

"Yes, and say hello to her," said Anzar. I nodded my head yes.

"Good move, you will know it when you see it, the sun will let you know, you will get a sign," said Anzar. I was not exactly sure what he was talking about, but he was gone before I could ask him.

My spirit walks continued throughout July 2020, and as the weather heated up more each day, I had to start earlier in the morning.

"Hello everybody. I'm glad you could all be here. Big things in UFO world, like the MUFON debacle and their president being arrested. What do you have to say?" I asked.

"The government knew what he was doing, and when he was ready to reveal something they did not like, they got him. He was a security risk," said Anzar.

"Is comet Neowise the celestial anomaly?" I asked.[213]

"Yes. Only discovered in March, I told you of it earlier than that. Keep love in your heart and approach everything from a position of love—only then can you make the world whole," said Anzar. To make the world whole, that would be nice. Neowise will be back in 6,800 years, maybe we will have it figured out by then.

Later in July, an airplane was flying low overhead. These are very interesting times we are living in. There was a ufology-related panel discussion that I planned to attend but did not. It was recommended by Kit Green, a CIA-connected doctor who is well known in the ufology community. I am not sure if the MUFON director who was arrested is guilty, but it seems to me that he was ready to disclose something that was important and perhaps even considered a national security threat. There was supposedly a *New York Times* article that was coming out, but who knows for sure.

"How is TTSA involved?" I asked.[214]

"They are a buffer, made a deal, between the UFO community and the government. One foot in each world," said Anzar.

More information kept drifting in during my late July spirit walks.

"Greatest accomplishment coming. Enlightenment. Full disclosure. Acknowledgement, threat, but will be protected. Angelic hosts, protection, cooperation, triumph through adversity, significant," was what came in, mostly from Anzar, but also from other unidentified sources.

"Ultimate disclosure," said Anzar.

"Alright," I said. I had to unpack what Anzar told me in this rapid download. I assumed he was talking about the Big Show and its aftermath.

Approaching the end of July 2020, and I made contact with Anzar. I felt like I needed to be careful what I wrote on Facebook. I did not want to cause a panic.

"Anzar, October?" I asked.

"Unraveling, look to the sky, something between the US and China, potential of limited nuclear exchange, not on the mainland," said Anzar.

"That is terrifying," I said. I was thinking that maybe Anzar and other alien forces might be able to neutralize nuclear weapons.

"Catastrophes will happen, then the rally around the flag, and we will learn more lessons. Be ready, do not say anything officially that is political," said Anzar.

"I'm very worried about what is going on in our cities and in our country...seems like many have been brought to the point of insanity. I will listen free-form now," I said. With free-form, I just tune in and forget about any questions and reactions of mine.

"Armed rebellion, civil war, contested election, strife, calm down by March, must bring in federal troops to quell rioting, martial law. Really bad, crisis. Food shortages, gas lines, power grid disruptions, natural disasters, uncertainty, and continuing pandemic crisis," said Anzar. Not exactly a relaxing meditative walk when you hear that type of stuff.

A few days later, I spoke to Gene.

"Gene, what do you have to say about the Fox News report last night: the government has UAVs not of this earth, more evidence, proof of alien life. Some think it is not true, but it was in the *New York Times* as well, and other news sources," I said.

"Some of it is hype, some is real, we have known this for some time, reports, testimonies, people have been discredited. If they attack the messenger, you know it's important. There is something to it, but lots of false info too. But it is true that we're all the aliens because we're all connected, future visitors too, quantum reality, when we break through in the future," said Gene. That was a lot of information from Gene that I had to digest.

"Hi, Anzar, do you agree with Gene?" I asked.

"Yes, absolutely, startling information, but maybe not to those familiar with what has been going on, but it is confirmation, and others will be scared and frightened. Advantageous for the government to release information now. There is a lot at stake. Important to release information for all humankind. But be careful with information because contained within it is deception," said Anzar.

"Please help me figure it out, so I can understand and help others understand," I said.

"Believe in yourself," said Anzar.

"Ok, I will. Thank you. A lot of stuff," I said.

A day later, on Saturday, July 25, 2020, I had to reach out to Anzar again because I was very worried.

"Thank you everybody for being here. Grim news yesterday," I said.

"Not better today, in fact, worse," said Anzar.

"Okay. What else can we do to prepare based on what you mentioned yesterday," I asked.

"Keep doing what you are doing, you know what is coming, take care of family and friends, take care of what you have to take care of. Assuage their fears," he said.

A few days later, Anzar showed me the image of a hand.

"All the answers are here," he said. I remember using the hand analogy when describing how the Nordic countries survived during the Cold War. Each country had its own approach to the superpowers, the United States, and the Soviet Union, yet they were together, like the fingers of a hand operating on their own but attached to the palm.[215]

In a strange dream, I was in a Pentagon briefing room speaking Norwegian to other officers who were from Norway, Denmark, and Sweden. Then, one of the big wigs asked, "Why did you not become an analyst?" I answered: "I decided to have two bad marriages instead." They laughed. It was partially true in that I had an opportunity with the CIA as an archivist, and I had also applied with the NSA, but was turned down because my wife at the time was a national security risk, unbeknownst to me.

"Anzar, was I correct in my interpretation of the hand symbol?" I asked.

"Strength and flexibility, like the Nordic countries, dexterity, strength, common purpose, it is what you have to do to meet the challenges ahead," he said.

Early in the morning of July 29, 2020, I had a powerful dream vision. I flew in an alien spacecraft, it was us, we are the aliens. Essentially, I was read in, as they say in the intelligence world. The officer who was explaining the craft told me that when the graphite rod base is removed, then it moves. "It's alive," he said. The officer explained that we got it from an alien source. He noted that you cannot kill with it; you can only observe, and no one sees you. Invisible, in other words. It had a simple controller and there was nothing fancy inside. The spacecraft is made of a material that you see through and it can reshape as anything you want it to look like. The briefing officer told me that it displaces time, and you can travel instantly. It had no control surfaces. We flew over streets and highways with people and cars, and no one knew we were there. We flew out of a US Air Force base and others on base did not know what we were doing. "It's alive and integrated with the pilot," said the briefing officer.[216]

On my early morning long walk after my dream vision, it was hot and sunny, and I was feeling especially connected and spacey. I decided to do another free-form connection to Anzar without me interrupting with questions.

"Cosmic explosion, lightning speed, conversation, establish conversation, coordinated attack, strife, age of disillusionment, android, okay. Things will come to pass quickly, change reaction," said Anzar. That was it, a very rapid download.

"Hey, Anzar, CERO meeting yesterday, they took the warnings seriously, doing what they feel they must do. Can you give me more information about the hand?" I asked.

"Hand of friendship, helping hand, with my own hands, do it, lend a hand," he said.

On my last spirit walk on July 30, 2020, it was an early Thursday morning when I reached the high point and decided to talk to my spirit friend Gene.

"Hey, Gene, can't see the City of Angels, sorry. How are you?" I asked.

"Great, on a mountaintop with a golden crown," he said. I smiled.

"Wonderful. Advice?" I asked.

"Steady as she goes, keep plugging away, stay on top, stay ahead, don't look back, embrace the moment, it will be great. Do good, always do good," said Gene, and then he faded away.

"Anzar, I want to talk about the dream I had the night before," I said.

"Not a spacecraft, it is a transport zone. It envelops you and you become part of it, semi-organic. Fits around you, forms, becomes what you want it to be, can go anywhere and anytime, wherever and whenever, can be seen or not be seen, your choice, transmute, transform, flying saucer or whatever you want it to look like," said Anzar.

"Does the US government have these things?" I asked.

"Earlier versions, scouts, we are now much more advanced. We have what our senses allow us to understand and see. That is the ship we see," he said.

"Interesting, if nuts and bolts is what you need to see, that is what you see. If a spiritual dimension is what you imagine and see, then that is what you see," I said.

"Always keep love in your heart, operate from a position of love, work with people and help them, be calm and rational, so many people are angry and do not even know why. Not a matter of good and bad, it is a matter of decisions on how to think, the motivations people have, their object, intention, all entities have that," said Anzar. His words reminded me of one of Ginger's favorite exploratory questions: "What does it want?" Whether it is a person or a thing, everybody and everything wants something. The CDC called for reopening American schools, but it was unclear how that could be done safely. More than 25,000 Americans died from COVID-19 in July bringing total deaths to 150,000 in the United States.[217]

I took my spirit walk on an early Saturday morning on August 1, 2020. Foothill Boulevard and Valley Center Avenue were very busy, but I did not let that distract me because I felt very connected, like I was slipping through time and space.

"Glad that all of you are with me and helping me. There is a lot going on so I will do some free-form connection," I said.

"Convolution, ecstatic news, careful consideration, magnificent revelation," said Anzar.

"What do you think of the spacecraft traveling dream? Is it what I call an inter-dimensional vortex?" I asked.

"Yes. Any shape you want it to be. Very true, that is what you see, that is what you do not see. Friends, count your friends and blessings. Keep love in your heart and operate from a position of love. See the truth through the fog, through the lies, through the deception, truth has a ring to it, your gut tells you," said Anzar.

On August 2, 2020, a hot Sunday, I took my spirit walk. I was able to make a connection to Anzar, my ancient alien mystic friend.

"What can I do to help?" I asked.

"Keep doing what you are doing. Post helpful things for people. Do good. In your dream vision, the technology, it cannot be used to harm others, we will shut it down," said Anzar. What Anzar explained reminded me of that original *Star Trek* episode, "Errand of Mercy." In that episode, Captain Kirk tries to convince the placid Organians to resist the Klingons, but they do not. In the end, it is revealed that the Organians do not want anyone to fight and are powerful beings of pure energy that stop the Klingon and Federation fleets from engaging in an armed conflict.[218] I will try to keep that in mind and only do good. As far as the spacecraft I saw in my vision, semi-organic, controlled by the participant in the travel through space and time, I remembered Sue Richards' invisible jet in *The Fantastic Four* comic book series. Maybe Jack Kirby, the creator and artist, and Stan Lee, writer, publisher, and co-creator, understood a similar concept.[219]

"What about the election?" I asked.

"Unclear who will win, lots of variables, voting irregularities, conflict, legal challenges, dissent, turmoil, civil unrest, challenges from malevolent powers, China, Russia, and Iran," said Anzar. Not a pretty picture of what is to come, for sure.

I continued my spirit walks and contact throughout August. I was reminded that we all manifest our own realities. I did some more free-form contact.

"Open the skies, guard the innocent, travesties will occur, protect, do the best, look for friends, forgive your enemies," said Anzar. I love doing the free-form, but often it takes some time to interpret what Anzar means with his words. My take is that we have to open our eyes and our consciousness to knowledge. Looking for friends is always important. You can never have enough friends. Forgiving your enemies is hard, very hard, but it is essential. I always think of what Ginger says, "What does it want?" Your enemies wanted something, and by understanding what that is, maybe we can avoid conflict. I also thought of what my mom used to say: "Your friends are never really as good as you think they are, and your enemies are never really as bad as you believe them to be." I know I have mentioned it before, but it bears repeating. It was time for more questions.

"Hey, Anzar, any more on the calamities, natural, man-made, coming and already here?" I asked.

"Civil unrest, maybe one of the worst," said Anzar.

"Alien stuff?" I asked.

"The knows and the do-not-knows. They know what they do not know. And they do not know what they know," he said. I love the way Anzar challenges my understanding of the world and reality. It made me think of another original *Star Trek* episode, "The Way to Eden." In that episode, a renegade group of space hippies hijack a spaceship and are in search of the mythical planet of Eden. It was not the first mention of Eden in the series, by the way. The leader of the space hippies, Dr. Severin, is like a cult leader and they make a triangle shape with their hands that they call "The One." They seek to simplify existence and live in a more natural way. Spock is interested in their understanding of "The One," but does not support their activities. Unfortunately, the Planet Eden is not a paradise, and most of the hippies get poisoned eating fruit high in corrosive acids. I believe "The One" is the one true consciousness, the super implicate order, or the mind of God.[220]

The dog days of summer. My spirit walks in August were hot, and exhausting. I was concerned about the upcoming presidential election and the aftermath in addition to the dire warnings Anzar had issued. In terms of aliens and UFOs, their existence will be hard for those in power to accept, but they will be responsible for maintaining order in society. That coupled with other calamities, concerns me a great deal. I had a lucid dream where I was walking up to and around my old house in Kenmore. It was nighttime and I had to urinate in the back of the house in the grass. I could hear my parents inside the house calling for me. As I woke up, I saw two images of the dream as if I were two people having the same dream. Bilocation? Somewhat mind-blowing. The foundation of our understanding of life is based on our experiences as children. My first contact with an alien entity took place at that house. I sought council from Anzar.

"It will keep getting worse before it gets better. Relaying the truth. Warning for preparation. Civil unrest guaranteed, no matter who wins the election. It will be contested. Some aliens trying to help, some are neutral, some are cheering on the consternation. Technology? What can you manifest? What can you dream up or think of? That is what you can manifest as real," said Anzar. I appreciated his wisdom.

Late-night dream. My mom came to me and told me that when I was six or seven years old, I told her that someone name Gerson Benjaminsen spoke to me in my dreams. It was a very powerful dream vision of my mom. I did some research and asked my Norwegian relatives about that name. No one had heard of a Gerson, but the last name Benjaminsen was well-known on our home island of Andøya in northern Norway. I then asked them about Geir, a more common name.

On a hot Sunday morning in August 2020, I took another spirit walk. I tried to not let the heat distract me from my mission of contacting my spirit friends.

"Good morning everybody. You are all wearing dark clothing, and sunglasses, not sure what that means. Can you tell me?" I asked.

"Mourning. Crises that have happened, are happening, and will happen," said Anzar.

"Can you tell me about something coming up?" I asked.

"Military provocation against us in Korea, and in the Middle East, sponsored by China and Russia against us," said Anzar. I understood that we were headed for trouble. It seems to me that Senator Kamala

Harris would be Biden's pick as a running mate. Not sure if that would be good or bad.

"Turmoil is worsening, tumultuous election, panic, disorder, chaos, by March okay. Alien interdiction, more reveals, just what we have said. Many variables," said Anzar. He has said that things will calm down by March a few times, but does he mean March 2021, 2022, or when?

As we approach the middle of August, we now know that Senator Harris is Biden's running mate.

"Hey, Anzar, what do you think of the Biden VP pick?" I asked.

"The plan is that she is to be the next president, even if they lose," said Anzar.

"What difference does it make?" I asked.

"Some. In terms of calamities, not much difference. Hang on, be cautious and liberal in thought, conservative in actions, and be calm," said Anzar.

On August 15, 2020, early morning, around 20 minutes after midnight, I saw an orb the size of a grapefruit in our bedroom. It appeared in the middle of the room, moved erratically, then darted off into our walk-in closet and disappeared. I got a good feeling from it, probably my mom, looking out for us. I had been dreaming about my spirit experiences, and then I woke up and saw the orb. I needed to consult with Anzar.

"The light anomaly in our bedroom, early morning, what was it?" I asked.

"Your mom, looking out for you," said Anzar. I am convinced that all the politicians in Washington care about is power, the struggle for power, with each side using whatever dirty tricks they can. Then, they rely on us to back them up, blindly, in a partisan fashion, willfully ignorant of the truth. There may be some honest ones among them, but it is hard to sort them out.

291

"The most corrupt will fall," said Anzar. We can only hope. There are so many irresponsible people in positions of power.

Later in August, I had a lucid dream with my mom. We were in a nice waterfront home with large windows. Ginger came up to me and said: "There's someone here to see you." I asked who it was. "Your mom," she said. I then looked outside and sure enough my mom was out on the patio in a nice yard with grass. I ran to her and hugged her as I cried.

"I miss you so much, Mom," I said. She was rather unemotional and business-like.

"You have to let me go and get on with life. I'm okay. I know it sounds a little mean, but you have to let me go," she said. I was in shock. She moved back into the house and without saying another word, she disappeared into a heat register in the floor. It was a bizarre dream vision.

A few days later I had a nightmare where I was walking on a city street, in a post-apocalyptic setting, and people were running around afraid and desperate. There was a downed plane in the middle of the street, and the presence of radiation. The prevalence of my military and disaster dreams could be taken literally or it could be symbolic or maybe both.

"Anzar, please help me understand what's going on," I said.

"Transition, tables turning, powers are shifting, adapt, improvise, and overcome. A lot is going to happen between now and October. Do your best to understand, and help people deal with civil unrest, economic problems, disclosure issues, and keep love in your heart, and operate from a position of love. It is fundamental to everything," said Anzar.

We were getting nearer to the end of August 2020. I asked for Anzar's advice about what my mom told me in the vision from a week or so ago.

"My mom said to let her go. In what way?" I asked.

"Realize that you are your own man, you do not need her help, but you can still ask for help from time to time. You can walk on your own," said Anzar. I do remember one more part of the vision, my mom told me not to be so *avhenge* (which in Norwegian means dependent). I think that is good advice for everyone.

"Watch news, but do not be consumed by it, realize that there are lots of variables, be cool and calm, rational, liberal in thinking and conservative in action. Idealistic in thinking and realistic in action. Good combination. As for the alien stuff, it is always there, and always has been, always will be," said Anzar. I think I am finally waking up to the fact that we are the one.

"You are in the quantum world, you have the power to manifest good things, you have the power to make good things happen," said Anzar. Talk about empowering! He also told me that aliens present themselves in a very physical way at first and then do not need to after that. The trail has been blazed; the shortcut made. There may also be changes in the DNA of experiencers.

I received more downloads from Anzar and my other spirit guides.

"Combine independent mindedness and communal spirit. You need independent capabilities within a communal spirit framework— a perfect blending of rugged individualism and service to the community," said Anzar. He went on to say:

"Pressure building in society, people are going crazy, lashing out violently, and they do not even know why. We must help guide people with calmness, firmness, and wisdom, as it is going to get worse, you see that daily. There is also a disclosure narrative that will emerge more and more. It might be used by those in power," said Anzar. All of this reminded me of what I have learned about propaganda. Propaganda is made by taking complex problems and finding a phrase or concept in the fewest words possible that seems to solve this complex problem (they do not have to be true). Then you repeat the phrase over and over. The formula must be simple enough so that even the least ingenious person can understand. The purpose of propaganda is to get people to believe something and then take action based on that belief. We had come to the end of August 2020, averaging 904 deaths per day and a total death count of 174,298.

It was an early Wednesday morning on September 2, 2020, when I took my next spirit walk.

"Anzar, I see that things are still going off the rails," I said.

"Stay in the middle, be kind, compassionate, firm, calm, considerate, and logical. More bad things will happen between now and election and between election and March. Potential for civil war. Rhetoric has to calm down, those who promote violence should all be ashamed of themselves," said Anzar. A few days later, I contacted Anzar again after I had given a lecture.

"Thank you all for being here. What did you think of my lecture?" I asked.

"Well-balanced, people trying to get you to take a side. There is only one side, the side of love and humanity, love is the answer," said Anzar.

Several days later in mid-September, I contacted Anzar from the comfort of my own home.

"Anzar, what is going on?" I asked.

"What I told you. It will get worse," he said.

"I see, what else, specifically?" I asked.

"Unrest, civil war almost, a contested election, environmental problems worldwide, a celestial anomaly. Disease is still spreading, uncertainty, rise of authoritarian hegemony," said Anzar. I know that good will happen when good people do good, and do not expect acknowledgement or praise.

As we approached the end of September 2020, I contacted Anzar on my spirit walk, as the air was still filled with smoke from wildfires in Southern California.

"Hello everybody. Anzar, you told me we're going to get blown away by what will happen. What does it mean?" I asked.

"Shock and awe, what will happen between now and March, especially October," he said.

"Specifics?" I asked.

"Lots of variables, volatile, maybe extremely so, but volatile none the less. The message does not hit you in the face, it signals your soul, touches your soul, not didactic and pedantic. It will appeal to your humanity. Stay on top of things, keep people honest," said Anzar. I was curious about what Anzar meant by message. In a recent dream, Ginger and I were watching an electrical storm, and there were tornadoes in the distance by the mountains. Then, Ginger is gone. After a few minutes I see her getting into a car with her friend and they speed away. Maybe the message is the truth of love, that lies deep within our hearts. It is a song that we have heard and felt since birth.

On my spirit walk the final day of September 2020, Anzar was still advising me that we were on the brink of civil war and that there would be more alien disclosures, and more revelations that would be religious or spiritual in nature.

"You can offer healing and solutions through the arts, emotional expression in art reaches everyone and touches all souls," said Anzar. I am utterly convinced of that. I know that during the Harlem Renaissance in the 1920s, African Americans had the opportunity to express themselves through the arts and attained white patronage.[221] This movement was centered in Harlem. The stock market crash and the subsequent Great Depression of the 1930s ended the Harlem Renaissance but did not totally do away with the focus on learning from each other through the arts.

"What about the celestial anomaly?" I asked.

"Yes, and more calamities, along with the election debacle. Stay calm," said Anzar. By the end of September 2020, America had lost 199,080 people to COVID-19.

The big news on October 2, 2020, was that both President Trump and his wife Melania had COVID-19 disease. I took my spirit walk that Friday morning and reached out to Anzar and my spirit guides for information and advice.

"Hello everybody, already the things you told me about are happening. What will happen with the president and his wife?" I asked.

"Could be deadly, major health crisis, far reaching ramifications. It could spur conflict with adversaries, financial turmoil, shortages, natural disasters, civil strife, civil unrest nearing civil war, public anxiety, a celestial anomaly panic, and the worsening of a COVID-19 second wave," said Anzar. I was getting more and more nervous about October and beyond. Anzar always reminds me that predictions can be wrong, but preparations are never wrong. There are simply too many variables. This much is clear, the road ahead is looking rough.

On a Sunday morning, October 4, 2020, the temperature was pleasant as I took my spirit walk up Valley Center Avenue.

"Anzar, what can you tell me?"

"President will survive but will be sick for a while. Close election, neither one will ultimately be president. Second wave of COVID-19 will be worse, so be careful," said Anzar. I was perplexed by his comment about the presidency. You would assume that one of them would have to win, but his words were carefully chosen. What does he mean by ultimately? I guess we will have to wait to find out.

A few days later I decided to try my free-form communication with Anzar again, even though it is often hard to understand.

"Spiritual path, always walk the spiritual path and keep love in your heart and operate from a position of love. Considerate, kind, thoughtful, fair. Round and round it goes, we do not know where this will go, lots of variables. Possibly, very bad or mildly bad, in between. Biggest concern is fear and irrationality, what we need to face down fears and irrational behavior. Rely on your conscience. Always the best. Do not be afraid," said Anzar, in his rapid-fire download. The process of free-form contact requires that I totally let go, almost like physical mediumship. The words and images come at me so fast I have no time to react and reformulate or contaminate the flow with my own perceptions, thoughts, and opinions. It reminds me of those fast-talking legal announcements at the end of commercials. What really stuck with me was his warning about fear and irrationality. People who are afraid or angry are not smart, they are in the fight-or-flight mode. Anzar had more to say.

"Messages are coming, and the messengers are coming," he said. That certainly made me take notice. Most people realize that times are changing quickly, and this causes anxiety. I see my mission as helping to calm people and have them act rationally and with love in their hearts. The Great Leap of Consciousness is upon us.

As we approached the middle of October, I grew more and more anxious. Anzar kept mentioning the possibility of more civil unrest, natural disasters, and a life-threatening celestial anomaly. But would these things happen sooner or later? He also said that we would have increased contact with visitors and messengers. I assumed that he meant aliens and maybe some celestial beings. He reminded me of something one day when I was really missing my mom, dad, sister, Gene, and so many loved ones who had passed on.

"The spirit is the most essential thing, that is what touches you when you are not physically together, it is the most essential part," said Anzar. I realized how lucky I was, and it was becoming clear that transcendency was necessary as we all move beyond the physical and embrace our spiritual nature.

"An imbalance, things coming back to balance, can create instability in the spirit world and on Earth. Forces will be aligned," said

Anzar. He reminded me that there would be an increased awareness of information on UFOs and aliens and my mission would have to come first ahead of my own selfish desires.

On a cool Sunday morning, October 18, 2020, I made contact as I watched my country and the world suffer.

"Every day something bad happens. Historically, in presidential elections there are October surprises, certainly President Trump getting sick with COVID-19 was one of them, and the news about Joe Biden's son is another example," I said.

"COVID-19 will get worse, second wave, be prepared. More people will have contact, more hints dropped in the bucket," said Anzar. No matter what people say, I have to hold on to love in spite of pain and suffering. It occurred to me that people in my past seem so different than I remember them. So much has happened and what was important then is no longer important now. I suppose it demonstrates how we all change over time. Anzar was not finished and stepped closer.

"Insurrection, chaos, intervention, clarity. Stand by, stand ready to help," said Anzar.[222] Once again, some ominous words to contemplate.

I had a vivid nightmare on October 20, 2020. A giant grizzly bear was running after me causing rocks to roll down from the mountain. I was on the mountain top, in terrain that reminded me of eastern Washington State. The beastly bruin emerged from the cascade of collapsing boulders, and as he rumbled toward me it felt like an earthquake. He was running right for me and I had nowhere to go. I woke up just as his open jaws grabbed me. I was able to fall back asleep only to enter another vivid dream. It was wartime and I was part of a salvage crew getting valuable equipment from burning naval ships. People spoke in a British accent. What did all this mean? I would have to ask my ancient alien mystic advisor, Anzar.

"What was the grizzly bear dream about?" I asked.

"Fears, handling your fears, dealing with crises, dealing with a major crisis," said Anzar.

"What can you tell me about what is coming up?" I asked.

"Everything we said that you know already, maybe a little more, or a little less, time to understand your spiritual self, everyone, they should work on that. This is a time of reckoning, be careful, be guarded with who you trust, but keep love in your heart, and operate from a position of love," said Anzar.

Only a few days left in October 2020. Anzar has downloaded what he called the Era of Reconversion into my thoughts.

"I received your download, but what more can you tell me?" I asked. Anzar decided to deliver his response in rapid-fire free-form style.

"Convoluted, everything, expression, departure, insurrection, un-decided, nobody will know, mini-revolution, pocket revolution. Movement, think of movement in your action and motivation," said Anzar. This was followed up with a nightmare the next evening. I was meeting with some people about a play we were doing and a remake of my play, *The Bronze Star*. Then, I heard a cracking in the wall next to me when I looked outside, I saw the whole world moving horizontally past the large window. It was so loud, like a thousand tornadoes and earthquakes at the same time. At the end of October 2020, we had lost 222,625 Americans to COVID-19.[223]

The beginning of November and Joe Biden was elected President of the United States. Legal challenges were immediately started by the Trump campaign in battleground states. I had a strange dream where we suffered a temporary loss of gravity in the world. Anzar told me that we are entering a Reconversion Era. In another strange dream I was back in the US Army, this time as a sniper. I was forced to hide out in an old, dingy, broken down hotel filled with criminal types. Ginger was with me and we had to climb many stairs. She finally told me that she was not going to make it to the top (more than

37 floors to go). Ginger decided to go down to the ground floor again where there were rich people and doctors.

The strange dreams and Anzar's Reconversion Era pronouncement left me perplexed. My assumption was that we were going to return to our roots in terms of consciousness, like indigenous humans. As for the dreams, I was not sure. On November 10, my sister, who had passed away in 2014, spoke to me in a vision in the middle of the night.

"Hey, it's Bjørg...I'm awake," she said. Hearing her voice so clearly and seeing her ghostly visage was both joyful and frightening. I tried communicating with her some more, but she did not respond. When I was on my spirit walk, I connected with Anzar and my spirit friends.

"I'm hoping you guys can help me figure out what that all means. I feel guardedly optimistic that things will calm down and a vaccine will be available to everyone soon," I said.

"There will be troubles through the spring. Be prepared, I told you it was not a prediction it was a warning for preparation. Challenges, big challenges to come. Cool heads prevail, people will need guidance," said Anzar.

I took a short spirit walk on November 11, 2020, Veterans Day. I felt that trouble was brewing so I asked Anzar for clarification.

"Power struggle, disenchanted people rioting, a pocket revolution. The power is inside, unlimited power, of perception, wisdom, unleash it, untether it," said Anzar. I am sure that those in power do not want everyday people to know the power they have. A few days later Anzar told me to keep in a safe and neutral position, and let the turmoil play out.

On my long spirit walk on Thursday, November 19, 2020, I spoke to Anzar and my spirit friends again.

"A leap of consciousness instead of a leap of faith," said Anzar.

300

"Leap of consciousness and reconversion, are they tied together?" I asked.

"Yes. You will figure it out. COVID-19 second wave bad, third wave worse than first, but not as bad as second one," he said.

"Celestial anomaly?" I asked.

"Not always timed perfectly, but it is coming. A leap of consciousness…bridled versus unbridled reality. Hard to accept, but it is reality, nonetheless. Comfortable reality is not true reality, to see the world and universe as it really is through enlightenment does not come easy," said Anzar.

I was walking up Valley Center Avenue on a sunny, warm Saturday on November 21, 2020. The mountains looked especially beautiful, and I was ready to talk to Anzar, my ancient alien mystical friend.

"Proliferation of violence as people seek quick remedies to their problems. Stand guard and stand ready with reason and light. Shine your light into the darkness, to penetrate the darkness and to bring healing and love. Remind government officials that alien technology is to be used for peaceful purposes, not war, to help all of us," said Anzar. I sure was glad to hear that because a hostile power possessing unlimited cosmic power would quickly annihilate us all.

"Common cause, people need it to move together for common decency. Existential universal threat will bring people together, a celestial anomaly could cause that," said Anzar.

"I understand, but how does all this tie into the leap of consciousness and the reconversion era?" I asked.

"Ancient people were close to the earth and knew who they were," said Anzar. I have had contact with Native Americans throughout my life and often feel that Anzar reminds me of native people I have met.

Tuesday, November 24, 2020, was a sunny, mildly warm day in our neighborhood—a perfect day for a spirit walk up Valley Center Avenue.

"I wish there was solitude outside, but I can develop solitude inside," I said. After I said it, I wondered why I thought that. Why would I want seclusion or loneliness? But then I thought of how people are in Northern Norway. When you pass them by on the street you do not greet them if you do not know them. It is not a sign of being rude, it is a sign of respect for a person's privacy. So maybe that is what I meant, I need privacy outside, so I can have privacy inside. In the digital age, no one seems to have such solitude.

"Reaction. Interaction. Manifest the good through interaction with love in your heart," said Anzar. Our interaction with others should be based on love, but often that is not our first reaction in a busy and conflict-ridden world.

On November 27, 2020, I tried something different for my spirit walk. I went live on Facebook during my connection with Anzar and my spirit friends.

"Ancient Medicine Road, based on what I have experienced, where I do my spirit communication. Start with Anzar," I said.

"As I told you before, keep love in your heart, always operate from a position of love. Trials and tribulations, calamities, will occur, will sort themselves out by March 2021 give or take a month or so," said Anzar.

"Presidency in USA?" I asked.

"Neither Biden nor Trump will ultimately be president," said Anzar.

"Not really sure what that means, maybe an interim period, or power behind the throne situation, sounds tumultuous," I said. I continued my spirit walk and decided to help my listeners understand a little about Anzar's background.

"Many ask who you are," I said.

"An ancient alien, progenitor, first contact, here to help you, guide you. Here to remind you that all of us are related. You are related to those you call aliens, ETs, all the same consciousness, all connected to what you call God," said Anzar.

"Why do they (the aliens) want to contact us?" I asked.

"Because we are all related. Do you not care what happens to your relatives? For others as well? All creatures on Earth? That is why we are here. There are those from the future and those from the past because in the quantum world there is no future or past, only the eternal now," said Anzar. Interesting that those are the words my friend Gene used as well.

"Will these cataclysms be the end of us on Earth?" I asked.

"No, but serious enough so that everyone will have to work together to survive," said Anzar.

"Thank you. I speak for many that say hello and thank you for your connection, and I'm humbled to hear your words, humble thanks," I said. By the end of November 2020, we had lost 259,690 Americans due to the COVID-19 pandemic.

I did another live Facebook spirit walk on December 1, 2020. It was a cool, Tuesday morning. We are about to get a stay-at-home order.

"I believe in God, consider myself a Christian, open minded, and I love all people. We need to love one another and compromise to share our pieces of the puzzle. Anzar, what can you tell us?" I asked.

"Cool and calm. That is the way to proceed. Overcome anger, the pain of the past, and grasp the love of the moment, the future, and the promise. Everyone has pain, recognizing that pain in others leads to having love in your heart, which leads to good deeds, because you have to love yourself," said Anzar.

"Furthering contact with ETs?" I asked.

"A big year, 2021. A leap of consciousness, not necessarily a leap of faith. Where you evolve, your connection to everybody, everywhere in this universe. That is the key," said Anzar.

One of my spirit advisors is Leon; I met him camping near Mt. Adams in Washington State.[224] It was a powerful moment. Not sure when Leon lived, but in this world, he passed away a number of years ago. For some of you this is a lot to accept, it is a matter of experience. My spirit friend Gene always said, "experiencing is believing and believing is experiencing." Sometimes something has to be believed to be seen.

On Thursday, December 3, 2020, it was time for another spirit walk. A thought came to me the other day, the old saying, "God will find a way." Then, a voice, probably Anzar, told me, God will help you find a way. God could be your higher power or whatever you want to call this force. I walked past the Glendora Masonic Temple where they have performed magical rituals for years on Valley Center Avenue, the ancient Native American medicine road. I was lucky enough to see the majestic San Gabriel Mountains in the background as I climbed the almost mile-long steeply graded road to Sierra Madre Avenue. So, God will help you find a way. That means we must play an active role. We cannot be passive or expect that things will be done for us. You must work hard to manifest things. Your higher power, or God, will help you find the strength, and the perseverance, to create, heal, and love, and we can amplify that with our own actions. It was time to connect to Anzar and my other spirit friends.

"Crows follow me around as if they are telling me something. If only I spoke fluent crow, but I get the gist. When I was little, I spoke to animals, but as we grow up people convince us that it is not real. Gets pushed aside. Later in life, I realized this wisdom that was in me since I was born. Now, I tapped into it again. I am not more special than anyone else, we all have it. I always like to be prepared for what is to come," I said.

"A reconversion, realignment of consciousness, we all have to do our part. Declassified briefing, US military investigating UAPs (UFOs)," said Anzar. He has told me that this reconversion is to our true selves, the ultimate consciousness, that which unites all of us throughout the universe. We are all the aliens, according to Gene and Anzar. We are all connected. Brothers and sisters. Leon said that this ancient medicine road still has the magic and that is why it is easier to make the connection. We must make good and wonderful things happen today.

On a cool Saturday evening, December 5, 2020, I connected to my spirit friends after saying my prayers of protection. As this was a Facebook live broadcast, I spoke first to my listeners.

"Wishing you all peace, health, happiness, in these dark days. But there are bright lights, you can be one of them. That is why I say be the light. Do this for everyone. Making our dark times brighter," I said. I had an image come to me of stones, flat, black and grey, stratified, striped, of varying sizes. Layers of black and grey.

"Great significance and power for peaceful purposes. Could be the missing element," said Anzar. I wonder if Anzar is talking about the element 115 that Bob Lazar wrote about in his book *Dreamland*.[225]

"Navy and Air Force disclosures, military people do not make silly reports, it's a big concern, because they know UAPs are real, and they're afraid that this alien tech will fall into enemy hands," I said.

"Sure, that is what your enemy thinks as well. What government officials do not know and do not want to believe, is that the alien technology is not to be used to harm people. Trying to weaponize this ET technology will not work, that is not what it is for," said Anzar.

"If ETs were malevolent, they would've already hurt us, logically," I said.

305

"The year 2021 will be a realignment, reconversion, a paradigm shift for humans as they evolve. This will not come without conflict," said Anzar.

One of my mentors, Dr. Bernard Sternsher, said that "history is forces for change and forces against change over time." Bernie was a World War II veteran who survived his ship sinking in the Atlantic while they were chasing a German U-boat. That experience informed the lesson he taught us: "to survive, we must hold on together."[226]

We must survive as we experience this reconversion. Will we see more UFOs more ghosts, more of everything?" I asked.

"Maybe, but they have always been there. You will see them as you open your 'doors of perception' as William Blake, said. The only way to survive through these coming calamities and take a leap of consciousness is to keep love in your heart and operate from a position of love," said Anzar.[227]

I took another spirit walk on December 16, 2020. It was my youngest son Leif's 21st birthday. It was time to connect to my ancient alien mystic advisor, Anzar, and my other spirit friends.

"Hey, Anzar," I said.

"The pocket revolution, civil unrest, bordering on civil war, President Trump not going away, powerful following," said Anzar.

"And what about Haim Eshed, the Israeli general and former head of their space program, who talked about agreements with ETs and contracts? Intergalactic contracts?" I asked. [228]

"No, there were words, and thoughts expressed, and agreements based on honor," said Anzar.

We were coming to end of a tumultuous year of 2020. I sought the advice of Anzar as the outlook for 2021 did not look good.

"Hey, Anzar, what will happen with President Trump?"

"An ugly ending, he will not go away easily. Pockets of resistance, violence, turmoil, maybe settled down by March," said Anzar. Thinking back on the last year, there was something he did do right—he pushed for the rapid development of the vaccine. I compare President Trump to the wealthy and unscrupulous businessmen who arranged and profited from the building of the transcontinental railroad. The true heroes of that venture were the workers including Irish and Chinese immigrants, former slaves, and civil war veterans. The true heroes of the Operation Warp Speed were the scientists, doctors, researchers, and volunteer test subjects.[229]

"Convergence tomorrow. Reconversion already begun. Leap of consciousness," said Anzar. I wonder what it will be.

I took a regular spirit walk up Valley Center Avenue on December 22, 2020, and immediately noticed something strange. On top of the mountain in front of me was a bright light. I know there are not any structures that high up and it could not have been car headlights as there was only one light and it was too bright. It was very strange.

"Anzar. Unusual thing up there. Truck?"

"No," he said.

"Right there. What is that bright, shiny thing? Weird. What do you guys think it is? Reflective surface or a light? Terrestrial origin?" I asked.

"Maybe not. Very bright, does not change based on angle," said Anzar. Hopefully, we will find out more. Crows were following me again.

"Rough transition, disruptive, pocket revolution, unrest," said Anzar.

It was December 25, 2020, Christmas Day, and the last spirit walk of 2020. Where do I begin? People show their true colors around the holidays and under crisis. I felt it was time to connect with my mom.

"Mom, what can you tell me about UFOs and aliens? Did you have experiences? Did you know I had them?" I asked.

"I knew," said Mom. I could sense she was reluctant to talk to me about this subject.

"Yeah, I understand, hard to talk about for you so it would be hard to talk about them with me. Especially with Dad not wanting to talk about anything paranormal. I do not blame you Mom. What you did for me was wonderful. I could not have asked for a better mother or father. Very lucky," I said.

"Power is about dividing; love is about cooperating for joint survival. Stay on the old medicine road. Powerful medicine. Healing. Spiritual connections, connection to the source," said Anzar. I understand more, so much more to understand. More than I did before, but there is so much more. On the last day of 2020, New Year's Eve, 336,802 of my fellow Americans had lost their lives to the COVID-19 pandemic. I was not celebrating.

Spirit Walks, 2021

On January 4th, I was told again about the coming pocket revolution, bordering on civil war. Anzar told me about precognition and how some events being so impactful that they reverberate back in time. The words strife and rebellion came to me and Anzar had already mentioned an insurrection on October 18, 2020.

On January 6th, early in the morning, I had a nightmare. I was in the military again, in combat (I was never in combat in real life), and we were fighting in a large round structure on top of a hill. There was a huge circular center area where there were a lot of people gathered. I remember there were columns surrounding the center area. I remember having to climb up steep walls to get to this circular area. We saw airstrikes coming in, but no explosions. It was terrible. I lost my primary weapon and picked up another. I looked closely at who I thought was the enemy, and they were everyday Americans, men, women, children. We were fighting ourselves! As it turned out, this was the day of the attack on the US Capitol building. This event on January 6, 2021, has come to be known as the insurrection, as Anzar had predicted. This is an example of subjective psi experience déjà vu because it combines the profound experience of having seen and dreamt of the event before it happened along with knowing what would happen next during the event (a distortion in time) along with precognitive elements. As it played out in real time on TV, I remembered my nightmare.

One of my friends, that has intelligence agency ties, said that there were warnings to agencies about trouble on the 6th. Now the government is saying that they had no such warnings. It reminds me of the old saying: "The first victim of war is the truth."[230] I am now doing spirit walks every other day. Dark days ahead. God bless us all.

After having an odd dream about a riot on my college campus, I took my spirit walk on January 12, 2021. I spoke in Norwegian to my mom and dad. My mom told me that I would always have Norway, my home place. She was worried about how things are going in the United States. According to my sister, Mom did not want to come to America in 1948 and would often cry about how much she missed her homeland and her mother. It is heartbreaking to think about this. But, after my dad retired in the early 1980s, he wanted them to move back to Norway to live out their retirement years. Mom refused, she told Dad that America was now her home, but she wanted to visit Norway every year. Mom passed away in 1990 and dad in 1999. They are both buried on the island in northern Norway where they were born. My plan is to visit Norway every summer in my retirement, just as my parents did.

Anzar, looking rather grim, then stepped up closer to me. I was not looking forward to what he was about to say.

"Anzar, what do you want to say?" I said.

"Be prepared. Much is coming. Most not good. Instability, insurrection for reality. As you would say," said Anzar.

"You've said before that President Biden wouldn't last very long," I said.

"Lots of variables, beware, take care. Alien involvement. Well, there are those who want to help, are helping to mitigate. There are also those who are merely observing, and there are those who would like to see things go badly. I am not among those, I am here to help, help you specifically," he said.

"Thank you, Anzar," I said.

"Many ships will come. You will see them; many will see them. Some will understand, many will not, you must help them," said Anzar.

"Leap of consciousness?" I asked.

"Yes, you have already, others will as well. You will know them; you will know them by name. Many may perish, it has begun," said

310

Anzar. With that dire warning I continued my spirit walk. I did briefly contact my Native American spirit friend, Leon.

"Hey, Leon. I really like walking on this old medicine road," I said, referring to Valley Center Avenue.

"Two thousand years ago, heavily used. But they are still here, you can see them, if you believe," said Leon. It reminded me that we are never truly alone, those who inhabit the spirit world, the alien world, the quantum world, are always with us.

It was January 18, 2021, and time for another spirit walk. I have been taking spirit walks consistently since June 10, 2018 and have learned so much in such a short time. I had been having too many disquieting prison and military dreams lately. I have this feeling of dread that reminds me of the Phony War period of World War II, between the September 1939 attack on Poland and the April 1940 invasion of Denmark and Norway where not much happened.[231] You know something big is coming, but it has not hit yet. I asked my mom and dad if that is how they felt during the start of World War II. Mom told me to protect my family and friends and do the right thing. My spirit friend Maia told me to be careful at work and watch what you say. I often wonder if my time has come to retire as a professor because the prevailing mindset on campus seems alien to me. Could it be that I will no longer be welcome on my own campus? Maia advised me to hang in as long as I can and keep my head down and mouth shut. I was ready to contact Anzar.

"Lots of turmoil, a breakdown of civil society into factions until consolidation, a reconversion after that. Keep love in your heart, that is the key. More alien stuff revealed. Legal procedures will not provide healing, more infringement on free speech, be careful," said Anzar.

Many see foreign influences in our inner turmoil, but we must already have internal problems for them to exploit. Clearly, greed and corruption need to be rooted out in every level of government, not merely replace one corrupt regime with another like the Who song, "Won't Get Fooled Again." [232]

Meet the new boss
Same as the old boss

Inauguration Day has passed with 26,000 National Guard troops guarding the capitol and no perceived threat, according to the military.[233] It was quite remarkable to see such a show of force. I wondered if we are all caught up in a power game in Washington, DC, which would make us all pawns. It was January 21, 2021, and my worries continued. I received a message as I woke up this morning. In America today, there is an undercurrent, shiny hopeful veneer on top of a dark festering undercurrent. People think those in power now will bring about change and happiness, but the mood is dark beneath, a thin crust of ice they are skating on. It was time to try trance mediumship where I would let Anzar speak though me, using his voice which would then be recorded on my phone.

"Hello, Anzar, I said.

"Hello," said Anzar, in a voice distinct from my own.

"So, this message about dark undercurrent, what will happen?" I asked.

"It will break through, more calamities to come. Over reactions, under reactions. Be considerate, keep love in your heart," said Anzar.

"Thank you, Anzar. Hard to do though," I said.

"You do not have any other choice. What will be will require that you keep love in your heart," he said.

"My friend Terry suggested that I write a book about you and our integration. What do you think?" I asked.[234]

"Yes, if it is right, and if you do it well. If you stay true to the message and the meaning and the mission," said Anzar.

"Yes, I would," I said.

"And what would be your purpose?" asked Anzar.

"To have your voice heard by more people," I said.

"If riches and fame are what you seek from my words, other than normal compensation, then no. Profit should be a secondary thing, the primary thing is to help," he said.

"Thank you. You have mentioned that President Biden won't last long, is he ill?" I asked.

"He is ill, maybe last a few weeks, a few months, maybe a few years. But he will not finish his four-year term," said Anzar.

"You mentioned lots of ships are coming," I said.

"Yes, you will see what you need to see. And then you must do what you must do," he said.

"To help people?" I asked.

"A leap of consciousness, a reconversion, to the old wisdom," said Anzar. I played a recording of this trance mediumship session with Anzar and one of my friends said: "he sounded like he's straight off the rez," meaning that he sounded like a wise, old Native American medicine man.

January 23, 2021, was a cold, rainy Saturday here in our neighborhood. I took my spirit walk as a big storm was approaching with clouds rolling over the mountain tops.

Hey, Anzar, thank you for always being with me, helping me. What do you have to say today?" I asked.

"All of this is an illusion," said Anzar.

"What do you mean?" I asked.

"Do you want to see reality?" he asked.

"Yeah. I catch glimpses, right?" I asked.

"Yes. Part of the change you are going through, the integration process. Truth and love are the reality. Everything emanates from that," said Anzar.

"Okay. Seems so simple," I said.

"Your book must be the truth. Seek all viewpoints, listen and learn, do what is right with love in your heart," he said. I then heard something whispered in Norwegian, but I could not make out what was whispered. The illusion Anzar spoke of is the material world we live in that we have constructed through our consciousness. The quantum world is the real reality he referred to in his simple message. As much as I appreciate his wisdom and guidance and that of my other spirit friends, we must take care of ourselves. We must be our own best advocate, and others can help, but you must initiate action and make it happen. "God helps those who help themselves" is a quote that many believe is directly from the Christian bible, but it was Benjamin Franklin.[235] Nonetheless, I believe it to be true.

A few days later, Anzar shared more.

"Hey, Anzar, what is going on?" I asked.

"Lots of activity in the heavens; preparations being made for the reconversion. Spiritual disclosure more than anything. You see what you must see to believe," said Anzar.

"I understand. Thank you. It's hard to keep love in my heart, but I know it's the most important thing."

"Military action coming, be prepared. Deception warfare," said Anzar. Just a moment after he said that a military helicopter flew low and directly over my head.

I had a frightening nightmare early in the morning of January 27, 2021. A giant mountain was crumbling and falling on top of us. My dreams were quite often unpleasant, whether war, prison, or natural disasters, probably not good omens. It was a cool Wednesday when I took my spirit walk.

"Hi, Gene, is passing on from this world and going to the next like a dream you don't wake up from? In other words, when we dream in this world, we come back to this world when we awaken. But when we die in this world, we stay in the dream. What do you think Gene?" I asked.

"Yes," he said.

"What about the mountain dream, crumbling and falling on us?" I asked.

"Symbolic of your world, old structures falling away and down on top of your heads," said Gene.

"What forms do ETs take, not just bipedal, right?" I asked.

"Gaseous, crystalline, cloud, just light, solid amorphous object, anything they want, by vibrating matter in and out of this reality," said Gene. Gene then disappeared. He was a great friend in this life and is a great friend beyond this life.

"Anzar, you said Biden is ill, maybe will last a few weeks, months, or years?" I asked.

"Yes, deteriorating," said Anzar.

"Is he being manipulated?" I asked.

"Yes, in exchange for becoming president and his dream coming true, he has given up some control," he said.

"Alien stuff?" I asked.

"Yes, more will come out soon. There will be lots of ships for all to see," said Anzar. The world falling apart and spaceships and aliens appearing, I guess that really is a Big Show.

My next spirit walk was on Saturday, January 30, 2021. It was a cool morning and we had heavy rains and some hail yesterday.

"I'm hearing race war…that is really sad and disturbing," I said.

315

"Yes, turmoil, President Biden may lose control as his illness progresses. Many interested parties look to take advantage, foreign and domestic. Not good. Be safe, be home, teach online, stay close to home, close to relatives and friends, keep them safe, do not take too many chances. Highly volatile situation. Variants are bad. It will be determined that release of virus from China was accidental. Be prepared," said Anzar. Boy, did he say a mouthful. I hope that President Biden is okay, but it makes sense that if he were suffering that power players in Washington, DC and elsewhere would seek more power. As far as a race war goes, that would be devastating. Extremists take advantage of folks that are in pain and suffering. They never gain a foothold where people are living in peace, have enough to eat, decent housing, and prosperity. I ended the month with yet another war nightmare. I was running to a bunker amid massive explosions all around. There was also a release of toxic gas. What more could go wrong? Also, on a sad note, the death toll in the United States reached 432,189 by the end of January 2021.

Monday, February 1, 2021, was cool with a few drops of rain coming down. Perfect weather as far as I am concerned being as that I am from Seattle. I have taught my students to be more cognizant of their own history, that is why I stress personal history and responsibility. That was also something my dad taught me, stick up for yourself, do not let anybody push you around, and take your responsibilities seriously. He was also a man of his word. Many of his agreements were done with a handshake. Old school. He came to me in a vision the other night and told me to watch out for people deceiving us. He was always incredibly careful and worried that someone would take away everything he had worked so hard to attain.

"Hey, Anzar, how am I doing?" I asked.

"Okay. Doing okay. Doing terrific," he said.

"Very funny," I said. He knew he was being funny.

"Lots of ships, people will see them, mini-civil war, continuing pocket revolution, big challenge from China, from strength comes peace, fall challenges. Disunity leads to despair. Discord leads to disaster," he said. I have learned to take Anzar's words and warnings to heart.

My next spirit walk was on a cool, sunny Wednesday, February 3, 2021. Every day I say to keep love in my heart and operate from a position of love. I have noticed that some folks feel that they must put themselves down to make others feel better. This is not love and does not make you or the other person feel better. Love must begin with yourself. As my favorite Seattle TV personality J.P. Patches said: "Be kind to each other and be kind to yourself. This translates to good deeds."[236] I was ready to connect with Anzar.

"China is a problem. They will need to be challenged, stopped, and held in check short of war. It will be tough love, not bellicose. Alien technology is to be used for peaceful purposes, not for war, maybe for protection from military action, that is permitted. Be careful of those who claim to be your friend but actually are not and do not have your best interests at heart," said Anzar. I have been telling my students for the past five years that the 2020 presidential election would bring a paradigm shift in the American political system. This happens about every 40 years. The last one was in 1980.

"There will be a dramatic shift to the left, a political paradigm shift," said Anzar. I am not political, and I do not belong to any political party, but my hope is for national healthcare so I can retire, and Ginger has coverage. And not only for my family, but for millions of my fellow Americans who live in fear of losing their life savings if they get sick. As I was finishing up my spirit contact, I thought I heard someone say that velociraptors will make a comeback. That cannot be right, can it?[237]

The following is from my February 5, 2021, spirit walk. It was a sunny, Friday morning as I headed toward the San Gabriel Mountains.

317

"Hello everybody, can't really do the public spirit walks any more. Who is watching and listening? Anzar, I'm in the universe and the universe is in me. I pictured a sea cucumber in my mind as I said that. Then I heard the song "I am the Walrus," by John Lennon and the Beatles.

I am he
as you are he
as you are me
and we are all together[238]

"President Trump will be acquitted, will cause more division, headed towards maximum division, then finally reconversion. Existential calamities," said Anzar.

"Thank you, can you manifest some UFOs?" I asked. Instantly, I was able to see some UFOs manifest briefly over the San Gabriel Mountains.

"Share the message of love, share the knowledge, and share the wisdom. Extraterrestrial technology and wisdom are precious gifts for all, not a strategic advantage for the few," he said.[239] We will have to work together for joint survival as President Reagan, my old mentor Bernard Sternsher, and Norwegian explorer Thor Heyerdahl said.

February 7, 2021, was Super Bowl Sunday. The information I am getting is that conflict with China and Iran is looming. My daughter Caitlin had a nuclear war dream, and I had another military dream where I was preparing for a special forces operation. Two days later while on a spirit walk, I connected with Anzar.

"Hello Anzar, what is going to happen today," I asked.

"Acquittal for the former president, exposure, will be clear soon Biden is not totally in charge," said Anzar.

"China and Iran?" I asked.

"Economic, political threats, and the threat of open military conflict. Close, on the precipice. Intervention," he said.

"Leap of consciousness, reconversion?" I asked.

"Ongoing, true bravery only emerges during adversity, brave in heart, brave in action, putting others before one's self," said Anzar. I was able to reach my Native American spirit friend, Leon. He told me that we are connected and the reason I see UFO activity over the San Gabriel Mountains is because I am walking the sacred old medicine road to the sacred mountains.

"Prepare for the third wave variant, pocket revolution continues," said Anzar.

On Thursday, February 18, 2021, I took my spirit walk on a beautiful sunny day and was ready to contact Anzar and my spirit friends.

"Hey, Anzar, thank you for all your help. So, I think you sent me a download of information that extraterrestrials, non-human intelligences, and extra-human intelligences from the future, are all around us all the time?" I asked.

"Interdimensionally, they pop in and out all the time. You can articulate all this. If you can, come here at night, easier to see things," said Anzar. I would love to, but I do not trust the drivers around here, I could get run over.

On Saturday, February 20, 2021, I made another trek up Valley Center Avenue toward the San Gabriel Mountains for my spirit walk.

"Thank you all for being here. I'm trying to always keep love in my heart and operate from a position of love. The message is love. Anzar, what can you guys tell me? What do we need to prepare for?" I asked.

"Third wave, not as bad as the second, worse than the first. More natural disasters, lots of ships, popping in and out of our dimension. Recognition of other worlds, shocking, some will panic, stay calm," said Anzar.

"Thank you," I said.

"President Biden will go too far, actually those who maintain control will go too far, and there will be a lot of push back. Existential threat will unite us, probably China, as they get more aggressive," said Anzar. Although I hear encouraging things, a lot of what Anzar and my spirit guides tell me is upsetting. I support our president and hope everything works out, but do any of us really know what is going on in the corridors of power in Washington, DC?

On a sunny, warm Monday, February 22, 2021, I took my spirit walk with love in my heart, hoping that everything will be better, and we remain at peace.

"Hey, Anzar, I listened to some interviews with Jason Reza Jorjani conducted by my friend Jeffrey Mishlove, what do you think?" I asked.

"The singularity, technology apocalypse, Jason is on to something, yes. Part of what we are doing is trying to help mitigate that, with love. Non-political, non-binary, not binary politics, and unitary service to humanity, is what we need. All for one, one for all, as d'Artagnan said in *The Three Musketeers*," said Anzar.[240] It always amazes me when Anzar mentions literary and historical figures and even makes pop culture references, he is really cool. On a sad note, we have now lost more than 500,000 people during the COVID-19 pandemic.

February 24, 2021, was a sunny, warm day. I wanted Anzar to manifest some UFOs for me. Recently, he had shown me quite a few over the mountains.

"Here we go again. If you feel like manifesting, please go ahead. Anzar, what can you guys tell me?" I asked.

"Jason and the Argonauts," he said.

"I will refamiliarize myself with the story," I said.[241] I do know that it is an archetypal mythic story that is basically a call to adventure. Sometimes Anzar likes to really force me to think, I guess that is a good thing.

"Was American Airlines story true? Did the pilot see a UFO?" I asked.

"Yes," said Anzar.

"Will we get radar?" I asked.

"Yes, I think so, lots of ships," he said.[242] We certainly live in exciting times, or are they scary times? Maybe both.

On February 26, 2021, I took yet another spirit walk heading north to the San Gabriel Mountains. It is weird to go back and look at my journals one by one for the last three years. I have learned a lot and there is no substitute for experience, especially when it comes to this stuff.

"Hey, Anzar and all my spirit friends, thank you for being my advisors. What is coming up?" I asked.

"Variants will cause a problem. Get the Johnson & Johnson vaccine," said Anzar.

"American Airlines UFO incident, what do you think?" I asked.

"Yes, it was a UFO," he said.

"Who was it?" I asked.

"One of the alien races. They just happened to pop in and pop out. Lots of ships all around us, all the time. Just like those who have passed on, they are with us, same realm. The paradigm shift in the political system happened very quickly and there will be turmoil as a result," said Anzar. I have always favored progressive change, using the example of the progressive era in US history (1900-1920). The old saying is, two steps forward, one step back. It is good to remind ourselves of the classic definitions of conservative, liberal, and radical. Conservatives do not mind change, but it must be slow, and methodical, and they are in no hurry. Liberals want substantial change, and they want it sooner rather than later. Radicals want everything changed immediately. This was explained to me by my first academic mentor, Dr. Sidney T. Mathews. He was a US Army historian in World War II and later a professor of history and political science at Campbell University in North Carolina.[243]

My next spirit walk was on a sunny Monday, March 1, 2021. I was thinking this morning that it has almost been one full year in lock-down because of the COVID-19 pandemic. Bizarre time. A thought came to me as I started my walk, youthful exuberance is often mistaken for extremism. Young people need guidance and moral leadership.

"Hey, Anzar, what do you think of the *Anzar* book? How should I organize it?" I asked.

"How, why, who, where, when, what? Basic investigative questions," said Anzar.

"Good way to organize it. I will try. What more can you tell me?" I asked.

"All for one, and one for all, the Three Musketeers. Your friends Terry and Jim will be in the spotlight this year," said Anzar. Again, with the Alexandre Dumas reference, it must be incredibly significant.

"You will be needed to talk about alien stuff," added Anzar.

A few days later I had another military dream. I was in combat shooting at the enemy behind built-up berms. There were bullets flying everywhere and there was not much cover. I saw a Middle Eastern enemy on the other side. I was afraid but I kept going. I had no helmet and was in civilian clothes. I took refuge in a building, answered the phone that was ringing on the wall, and talked to a nurse at a hospital who spoke about children injured by war and the orphans of enemy soldiers. Tracers flew over my head as I woke up. Not long after, I had a prison dream. I was visiting the old Mannheim confinement facility where I worked from 1979 to 1981. It had been converted into a museum. Most of the old prison was in ruins, but some parts were preserved behind glass. As people wandered through, they seemed blissfully unaware of the terrible things that had happened in the prison.

I made my spirit connection at home on March 14, 2021. The message I was getting was to keep doing what is right and keep going where my soul drives me. I will know what to do.

Some ETs attempt to tamper with our genetics and our souls. They do not necessarily mean to harm us, but they are not overly concerned with our ultimate well-being either. They may not understand love and compassion. Is it possible that TTSA is a front to manage disclosure, compartmentalized like all clandestine agency dealings. TTSA briefed President Trump and the Biden/Harris campaign. I believe the Space Force is a partial response to both terrestrial threats and perceived extraterrestrial threats.

"Anzar?" I asked.

"We are related, connected, an aspect of you is an aspect of me," said Anzar.

"Holographic model?" I asked.

"Yes, that is part of it, right direction. You are in the universe and the universe is in you," he said.

"Geological event in summer?" I asked.

"Major tectonic plate shift, volcanism, earthquakes, worldwide," said Anzar. The calamities just keep coming, I guess.

"Beware of moral reductionism," said Anzar. I see that as a major problem in American society. It is easy to see things as black and white, but it is much more complicated.

On March 16, 2021, I dreamt I was in the military again and had mentioned something of importance to a general referring to herbs or berries or substances (class 2) that could enhance intelligence and telepathy. I told my captain that I had spoken to the general and he was mad. Then he showed me a memo that mentioned my name. Some of my colleagues at my college were in the dream working in the same group, Then I saw someone wearing a mask with eyes and mouthpiece that looked like concentric circles, layered. It was surrounded by text in a strange incomprehensible language, that looked somewhat like Sanskrit.[244]

My next spirit walk was on Monday, March 22, 2021. We are all immunized now, and I feel much more secure, although it is still wise to be cautious because the COVID-19 virus is on the rise again.

"Hello Anzar, is there a Persian connection?" I asked.

"That is an influence, that is why there is a town called Anzar in northern Iran," said Anzar.

"Uhura Mazda? The name for a god in ancient Iran. Are you Uhura Mazda?" I asked.[245]

"That is who I work for," he said.

"I will look more into ancient Persian history. So, they're connected to you and you're connected to me," I said.

On March 28, 2021, I had a strange lucid dream. I met someone who was part of a paramilitary group of some sort and asked if I would like to come along to see their training site. He showed me a hologram map of the route to some mountain range, but I cannot remember the name. I got into a very highly modified Blackhawk helicopter. It was whisper quiet with no vibration, and it flew itself, no pilot. I thought back to the noisy old UH-1 Huey I flew in the US Army and was amazed. We flew extremely fast (I would say greater than 300 kts which exceeds the max speed of any terrestrial helicopter) and low between trees, power lines, bushes, with instant control and maneuver impossible in a regular helicopter. I think now that it was a spacecraft made to look like a helicopter. We landed and other members were buried and hiding but my host spotted them. I then went into a very sophisticated training facility where young people of all races and ethnicities were training hand to hand, and with special weapons. I asked myself, "why am I here," and then I woke up. This makes me wonder if some of the helicopters and other aircraft that have plagued some experiencers like my friend Terry, may be only disguised as such. Later, I remembered the name of the mountain, Copper Mountain.[246]

My next spirit walk was on a warm Monday, March 29, 2021. As I started my walk on what was a beautiful day, I saw a sad sight. There was a homeless lady, crumpled up on the sidewalk, in front of the high school. At first, I thought was a bag of garbage, then I saw feet. I could not tell if she was breathing. I flagged down a police officer who told me that someone had called it in. I hope she will be okay, she did respond to the officer, so that was a good sign. As I continued on my spirit walk, I started to cry.

The Derek Chauvin murder trial continued. It is hard to watch, and I do not know how it will turn out. I figured he would at least get manslaughter. I felt ashamed that I would worry about such petty things when there are people killed every day and some who die alone on sidewalks. I must keep love in my heart and always operate from a position of love and not let the weight of the world get me down.

"Hey, Anzar, I think God put that woman in front of me today to remind me of how lucky I am and to keep love in my heart," I said.

"Perhaps. Disclosure is ongoing, we are here, helping, but you must help yourselves too. Everything will be okay, be alert, be strong, be smart," said Anzar.

"Thank you for always helping me. What can you tell me about what is coming up?" I asked.

"Government agencies will resist release of information on UFOs that is due in June. They look at UFOs as a threat from other nations.

The people must have a grassroots revelation, and not rely on government disclosure. More calamities to come, more riots, border crisis, push back to new laws, and it could be that President Biden is not well," said Anzar. President Biden being sick would be a crisis in and of itself, so I hope he is okay.

Early in the morning on April 5, 2021, I had a vivid dream. We were visiting someone in a house made of old, salvaged, industrial materials and it was fascinating. I entered the laundry room area, and a huge praying mantis was on the wall, maybe six to seven inches long. He jumped on me and began to communicate. He said he would not hurt me. The night before, I had watched a video with Jeffrey Mishlove talking about precognition versus prophecy. Precognition is when you have an unexplainable knowledge of what will happen in the future, and prophecy is having a deep understanding of the past and the present to see where things are going.

Later, on my spirit walk, I checked in with all my spirit friends and my ancient alien mystic advisor.

"Anzar, what was this dream vision with the praying mantis? Was it Dr. Xotran?" I asked.[247]

"No," said Anzar.

"Was it an alien?" I asked.

"Yes," he said.

"Was it a helper and is it possible to talk to that entity?" I asked. Anzar nodded his head yes and smiled.

"Praying mantis entity, can you tell me your name? Please, tell me, what did we talk about?" I asked.

"I am nearby," said the praying mantis entity.

"What is your name?" I asked again.

"Hard to pronounce: B'Sansur," said B'Sansur, who I assumed was female.

"Thank you. I know you were talking to me, but I can't remember much. Did it have to do with precognition and prophecy?" I asked.

"Yes, I can give you information. About the likelihood of events like Anzar and help you prepare," she said.

"Like what?" I asked.

"Revealing from the government about contact. Revelation continues as people become more open, accepting, and able to understand. There are factions among the ETs at odds with each other over contact with humans," she said.

"So, you're helping Anzar?" I asked.

"Yes, and I can anticipate your next question, I am the same race and species as Dr. Xotran, but not a doctor, more of a historian/philosopher, your counterpart," said B'Sansur.

"Are we related?" I asked.

"From the distant future, yes," she said.

"So, is Bob Lazar telling the truth?" I asked.

"Yes, some of it, as Anzar said. He worked at S4 and saw alien spacecraft, and the propulsion units," said B'Sansur.

"Thank you, B'Sansur, same initials as mine, Bruce Solheim, BS," I said. I could not help but be reminded of the two space intelligences Ted Owens communicated with as documented in Jeffrey Mishlove's book, *PK Man*. They were little praying mantis or grasshopper beings he called Twitter and Tweeter.[248] Life is a wild ride, for sure.

My Thursday, April 7, 2021, spirit walk was dedicated to finding out more about B'Sansur.

"Hey, Anzar, can you tell me more about B'Sansur? I want to make sure that she's real before I tell my friends," I said.

"Yes, she is real," said Anzar, smiling.

"Hello, B'Sansur," I said.

"Of course, I am real. You know, you saw me, and talked to me," said B'Sansur.

"Before I ask Anzar, let me ask you, what is going to happen?" I asked.

"The nature of this murder trial, and the possible negative ramifications, are such that the verdict has to be guilty," she said.[249]

"It has been horrible to watch, but I figured I had to as a historian," I said.

"China covering up, of course they are behind the virus, it will be exposed, totally, eventually, they will, however, take Taiwan, not much can be done about it," said B'Sansur.

"Thank you, can I just call you B?" I asked. B'Sansur nodded her head yes and waved.

"Hey, Anzar, do you agree with B'Sansur?" I asked.

"Yes," he said. Later, I heard the words "Conflate consciousness." Conflate meaning to meld. That sounds somewhat like the integration concept that I have gone through with Anzar. More insights and information are better than less. I guess I am lucky to have a couple of non-human intelligences helping me, along with my other spirit friends. All of us need as much help as we can get.

I had a bizarre dream on April 11, 2021. I was watching a spontaneous outdoor rock concert, AC/DC, along with some famous guest performers whom I cannot remember. They were playing at an intersection of two streets in a neighborhood that seemed unfamiliar to me at the time, but now that I think about it, the intersection looked a lot like the crossroads where George Floyd was killed (East 38th Street and Chicago Avenue). After the concert, I was walking home playing my guitar, and I saw the police stopped in front of a neighborhood house and were approaching the door. I kept walking and then I arrived at my old house where I grew up in Seattle. I proceeded to my old bedroom where I slept when I was a little kid. I decided to play "Blowin' in the Wind" by Bob Dylan and was crying. Ginger, my wife, walked in and asked me to play something cheerier, but I kept playing the song and she left. She came back a few minutes later to announce that I had a visitor. A man in a suit, who looked oddly familiar, walked into my room. He was profoundly serious. "Were you aware that there is a death contract out on you?" he said. I shook my head no and then I looked out the window in my bedroom to the darkness in my backyard. This was the backyard that frightened me so much as a child, where I saw Anzar the first time. Now that I think about it, I believe the serious man in the suit was Derek Chauvin.

I had an at-home spirit connection on April 15, 2021 and decided to confirm my understanding of Anzar to make sure the details were correct.

"Anzar, just to confirm, who are you and when did you make contact with us on Earth?" I asked.

"I am the Progenitor, early man, 500,000 years ago, I gave you nudges," said Anzar as he smiled.

"What is my role?" I asked.

"You are a seer, a seeker, a prophet, a sage, you must help others evolve," he said. I will not let any of that go to my head because the mission is more important than the man.

"Where were you born?" I asked.

"I was born in the Orion constellation, Rigel system, 1 million years ago," said Anzar.[250]

"When did you pass into spirit?" I asked.

"I passed into spirit shortly after I contacted early man," he said.

"Is a major world war coming with China, Russia, and Iran?" I asked.

"Yes, major war, armed conflict, naval warfare, possible nuclear warfare coming with China, Russia, and Iran, a new Axis," said Anzar.

"What can I or we do?" I asked.

"Promote peace, logic, cooperation, and common defense," he said.

"What is the Akashic field and record?" I asked.

"The Akashic field is life, where I am, where Gene is, all knowledge, same as the implicate order," said Anzar.

"Is my diagram of 'My Personal Quantum Reality' accurate?" I asked.[251]

"Your diagram is essentially correct and divinely inspired," he said.

"When is the Big Show and what is it?" I asked.

"The Big Show has begun, shock and awe to come, stand ready, the righteous will emerge," said Anzar.

"How can I prove your existence and our communication?" I asked.

"To prove to skeptics is folly, to reinforce the open-minded is easy. Follow the truth, speak the truth, then they will see if they are ready," he said. I was glad that Anzar helped clarify who he is and what is going on and what my role should be.

My Saturday, April 17, 2021, spirit walk was made even more enjoyable by the sunny weather. The topic of discussion, however, was not nearly as bright and cheery.

"Welcome to everybody. Thank you all for being here. Very serious time, I know what you told me Anzar, we have to be prepared for another great war, at least the chances are," I said.

"Lots of variables, may not happen, but be prepared," said Anzar. I have been thinking quite a bit about my parents who lived through the Nazi occupation of Norway. This reflection has come because of my watching and enjoying the TV series, *Atlantic Crossing* on PBS Masterpiece.[252] The Norwegians created the series that deals with a little-known relationship between the Norwegian Crown Princess Martha, and US President Franklin D. Roosevelt. I was brought to tears many times during the series thinking about how my parents suffered during World War II. I have also thought about how much I miss my friend Gene. I could not have written this book, or my *Timeless* trilogy, if not for him.

"Hey, Anzar, another Great War?" I asked.

"Taiwan Straits, Ukraine, Arctic. Stop the threat and prevent it, UAPs are the key. Learn the technology to make nuclear weapons obsolete," he said.

"I'm assuming you will still let us use conventional weapons," I said.

"Unfortunately, yes, if you must, but we cannot allow you to annihilate all life on the planet with nuclear weapons," said Anzar. Then it dawned on me, the recent UFO reports came after the use of the atomic bombs in World War II. The ET intervention began after the atomic bombing of Japan. There is a sacred spiritual nature to ET contact.

"What can you tell me about revelation?" I asked.

"Spiritual, psychological, deep within you, a leap of consciousness, the evolution of humankind, be on the leading edge of that. There are irresponsible leaders with no insight or long view on history, or a universal view, consumed by maintaining a greedy grip on power. They seek to divide the people and take advantage of them. Be outspoken but operate from a position of love. Do not let ego get in the way of responsibility, obligation, and mission," said Anzar.

Anzar has been saying more lately, that must mean that things are heating up. I know there will be more and more UAPs, everywhere, and I will have to help people to understand the higher purpose. The goal is to render nuclear weapons obsolete, so we cannot destroy ourselves and our home. I suppose President Reagan was right in that respect with the Strategic Defense Initiative (also called SDI or Star Wars).[253] I believe he was inspired by the movie, *The Day the Earth Stood Still* that came out in 1951, and a movie he was in called *Murder in the Air* that premiered in 1940.[254]

My spirit walk on Tuesday morning, April 20, 2021, was noisy with more than the usual number of cars and trucks and motorcycles. The weather was pleasant with a low overcast condition.

"Hey, Anzar, I'm writing the book, and I have some ecstatic truth in there, hope it is okay," I said.[255]

"Yes, intention is primary. Lot of information on UFOs coming out, news media coverage," said Anzar.

"What can you tell me about déjà vu?" I asked.

"Just as Dr. Neppe laid out, your emphasis will be the psi version," said Anzar.

"What more can you guys tell me?" I asked.

"Lots of ships, messengers are here, more coming, possible riots, worst yet ever, perhaps a purging of the most extreme elements, then redemption," said Anzar. I suppose Anzar was referring to what might happen if the police officer, Derek Chauvin, is acquitted in the killing of George Floyd. I am sure he will be convicted at least of manslaughter. I hope we find a peaceful outcome in the end. As of April 24, we have lost 568,237 people in the United States to COVID-19.

I did not take a spirit walk on April 21, 2021. I felt the fear, frustration, anger, hope, and anguish of the American people during the Derek Chauvin murder trial. Collectively, there was a lot of focused attention and energy on the day of the verdict. My wife Ginger, my mother-in-law Mary, and I were watching the announcement of the verdict on TV. The announcement was delayed, so I stepped away to check my email and the number three appeared before my eyes, prominently. Wherever I looked, I saw the number three. A few moments later, I went back into the kitchen where Ginger and Mary were sitting and watching TV and the judge in the trial made his announcement. Guilty on all three (3) charges. I thought for sure that the jury would find him guilty of manslaughter and was surprised that they also found him guilty of the two murder charges. My fear was that a manslaughter verdict or acquittal would lead to rioting.

A *Forbes* magazine poll found that 90% of Democrats thought the verdict was right, whereas 54% of Republicans agreed with the jury's verdict.[256] In a *USA Today* poll taken in March 2021, 64% of black Americans felt that Floyd's death was a murder, whereas 28% of white Americans believed it was murder. White Americans believed Floyd's death was due to police negligence (33%), while only 16% of black Americans thought it was negligence.[257] Interestingly, according to a CBS News/YouGov poll after the guilty on three counts verdict, 70% of white people thought it was the correct verdict and 93% of black people agreed. The trial had shifted the polling numbers.[258]

I did not tell Ginger and Mary about seeing the number three just moments before the announcement. As the judge revoked Chauvin's bail and the deputy put the handcuffs on the former police officer and led him away, I had a profound feeling of having already seen that scene. This is an example of subjective psi experience déjà vu because it combines the profound experience of having seen the event before along with the knowledge of the outcome of the verdict before it happened (a distortion in time).[259] After I wrote all this down and articulated my feelings, I calmed down and could relax. I wish for peace and harmony for us all. We are all brothers and sisters and we must all be the light.

CONCLUSION

We have reached the conclusion of the book, dear readers. In the introduction I mentioned how unbelievable it is to have a connection to an ancient alien. Some of you might have agreed and questioned my veracity. I do not blame you. But now, I hope you are at least curious if not mildly convinced that I do indeed communicate with an ancient alien mystic named Anzar the Progenitor. Let us clear up a few points before we all go about our normal lives. Maybe we can start with the question of reality itself.

The Essence of Reality

The founder of existentialism, the German philosopher Martin Heidegger, sought to clarify the question of being. In his book, *Being and Time*, Heidegger asks what it means "to be." His view was that being and thinking are the same based on the Greek philosopher and father of metaphysics Parmenides.[260] Heidegger looked to poetic language as an escape from the overly technological world. His poetic language would free him from dehumanization allowing his poetic being to be revealed through what he called *aletheia*, the Greek word for disclosure. This ties into my childhood notion that machines were not becoming more human, humans were becoming more like machines. It also relates to the process of disclosure vis-à-vis UFOs and aliens which requires what Anzar called a leap of consciousness.[261]

Having already discussed physicist David Bohm and his explicate, implicate, and super implicate order of reality earlier, I can now note that American author Michael Talbot goes further in his book, *The Holographic Universe*.

"Our brains mathematically construct objective reality by interpreting frequencies that are ultimately projections from another dimension, a deeper order of existence that is beyond both space and time: The brain is a hologram enfolded in a holographic universe."[262]

335

Talbot was referencing the work of both David Bohm and neurophysiologist Karl Pribram.

"For Pribram, this synthesis made him realize that the objective world does not exist, at least not in the way we are accustomed to believing. What is 'out there' is a vast ocean of waves and frequencies, and reality looks concrete to us only because our brains are able to take this holographic blur and convert it into the sticks and stones and other familiar objects that make up our world. How is the brain (which is itself composed of frequencies of matter) able to take something as insubstantial as a blur of frequencies and make it seem solid to the touch? ...In other words, the smoothness of a piece of fine china and the feel of beach sand beneath our feet are really just elaborate versions of the phantom limb syndrome."[263]

Two realities, the particle-based reality and the wave-based, but which is real? They both are or neither is. We are, according to Bohm, a blur of interference patterns enfolded throughout a cosmic hologram of which we are part and maybe even created.[264]

Evidence of Contact

My first contact with Anzar in 1964, although he ultimately saved me from a child abuser, was traumatic enough to cause a serious speech impediment. I was taken out of my regular class each day for speech therapy for nearly two years. My stuttering was so bad, that I was afraid to speak for fear of being teased. To this day, there is a remnant of that stuttering that I must quickly compensate for as I speak. According to research, speech difficulties can emerge after an emotional trauma, known as psychogenic stuttering. It is much less common and not the same as developmental stuttering. A psychogenic speech disorder is related to anxiety, depression, conversion disorders, or an emotional response to a traumatic event. "These psychological changes interfere with the person's voluntary control over any component of speech production and can most commonly be perceived as disturbances in fluency, such as stuttering, or changes to voice. Childhood traumatic experiences play a key role not only in the physical causes of stuttering but also in complicating the problem further by generating social anxiety and related personality problems."[265] The shock of seeing Anzar at age six was enough to cause me to begin to stutter when I had not stuttered before. I am not angry or upset, the experience has made me who I am, and I am grateful to my friend the Progenitor. It was a small price to pay for saving me from a sexual predator.

Free Will

In an interview with Jeffrey Mishlove on *Thinking Allowed*, the inventor of the Bell-47 helicopter, Arthur M. Young described the free will sandwich.

1. Determinism
2. Free will
3. Fate

The hand controls the fingers, the arm controls the hand, the shoulder controls the arm, and the brain controls the shoulder. Determinism is that you control what you can comprehend below it not what is above it. For example, the hand controls the fingers, but not the arm. We exercise free will in deciding when to move our shoulder, which moves the arm, which moves the hand, and ultimately moves the fingers. Fate is what is above us and not within our control. Let us say that you would like to move your fingers, but they are frozen due to you not having gloves in below-zero weather. There could be many reasons for you not having gloves, some which may have been within your control at one point, but you do not have control of the weather. "I think we are all, to the extent that things happen on a larger scale, parts of a plan larger than ourselves. And that would be fate," according to Arthur M. Young.[266]

Catching Waves and Running Takeoffs

So how do you use physics to catch a wave? When you are lying on a surfboard, waiting to catch a wave, you are at rest. But when you see a wave approaching, you begin to paddle your arms so that you can move towards the shore. You accelerate until your velocity is the same as the velocity of the wave and then you feel a brief shudder as the board catches the wave. At this point, gravity, buoyancy, thrust, and drag are in perfect balance.

In a running takeoff in rotary wing flight, when you start moving forward while in a ground hover and reach a speed of approximately 16 to 24 knots, you experience effective translational lift (ETL), which is achieved a split second after you feel a brief shudder in the helicopter. You have then increased your lift as your main rotor moves out of the disrupted air caused by downwash. I have experienced both catching a wave and ETL and have related them to my paranormal experiences. I do so through what I call my focused calm during meditative spirit walks that provides me with the opportunity to catch a wave into the spirit world and achieve effective translational lift to a higher consciousness.

The Science Behind "Be the Light!"

Arthur M. Young, who was not only an inventor, but also a cosmologist, astrologer, philosopher, and author, believed the photon was outside of time, formless, and timeless. He also noted that Deoxyribonucleic acid (DNA)[267] emits light and is a super conductor (materials that transport electricity with no energy lost) at ambient temperature.[268] So, in other words, we have an internal light source that transports energy within our bodies.[269] You regularly hear psychics and mediums say that they are light workers, but what is the connection to science? Maybe it is best to describe and define what a photon is to aid in our inquiry.

A photon is a particle of light defined as a quantum of electromagnetic energy. Photons are always in motion and, to all observers, maintain a constant speed of light in a vacuum (2.998 x 10^8 m/s). According to the photon theory of light, photons behave like a particle and a wave, simultaneously.[270] Since pure energy has no mass, then a photon theoretically could be considered timeless. Because photons are not subject to the laws of entropy and decay, photons do not experience time. Only matter is subject to the laws of entropy and decay. From the perspective of a photon, there is no such thing as time or distance.

Russian scientist Pjotr Garjajev reportedly intercepted communication in the form of ultraviolet photons from a DNA molecule in one organism (a frog embryo) with a laser beam and then transmitted it to the DNA (a salamander embryo). The result was that the salamander embryo developed into a frog. Dr. Garjajev claimed that this communication was not something that happened only inside of individual cells or between one cell and another. He claimed organisms use light to communicate with other organisms and suggested that this could help explain telepathy and extra sensory perception (ESP).[271]

So, to summarize, photons are light, photons are timeless, and our DNA emits light, therefore, we are timeless, as my spirit friend Gene told me in October 2016 when he convinced me to tell my paranormal stories that became my *Timeless* trilogy of books. On December 4, 2018, Anzar first told me to be the light. Gene also said it and now my comic book character Snarc says it too. I just thought it was a genuinely nice thing to say and assumed it was external light that we acknowledge in a symbolic way. There are so many ways to interpret what Anzar meant and so many ways that light has been referred to in religious texts and elsewhere, but it never occurred to me that Anzar and Gene meant exactly what they said, we are creatures of light, we are light, down to our DNA, and we are timeless and have incredible, largely untapped paranormal capabilities.

The Era of Reconversion

Anzar said that we are entering an Era of Reconversion. We have lost our way in modern society. The twelve core values in the Native American Lakota way of life are bravery, fortitude, generosity, wisdom, respect, honor, perseverance, love, humility, sacrifice, truth, and compassion. These should not be new to any of us since that is what our own elders have also taught us. I believe we are more alike than different. We must return to our true selves to put things back in balance on Earth. By making the invisible world visible through expanding our consciousness, hopefully, it will allow us to see the light within ourselves and others.

Our Response to Disclosure

The US intelligence agencies and Department of Defense are required to report back to the US Congress in June 2021 about what they know related to UAPs. I assume this will be delayed or incomplete, and that is to be expected. They probably mostly assume that the Chinese or the Russians are behind this UAP technology and that this is a defense issue rather than a spiritual and evolutionary one. And even if they fear that aliens are behind it, they will likely respond negatively and inappropriately. We have seen this replayed in countless alien movies where our first response is to roll in the tanks and missile launchers and mindlessly blast away. I look at the example of the isolated people on North Sentinel Island in the Indian Ocean and how they respond to outsiders, even attacking and killing them.[272] Corporations, the media, and governments have their own agendas that seek to profit from and control the technology presented by ETs. Purity of our consciousness and love must drive the revelation, not greed for power. People who have had alien contact are needed now more than ever to help calm fears and provide guidance.

Who Do My Friends Think Anzar Is?

I asked some of my friends in the CERO group who have seen my reports for the past three years about Anzar. Two of my CERO friends said that they believe Anzar is exactly who he says he is. They do admit that they were not sure at first, thinking maybe Anzar was just me, but now they are sure that Anzar is indeed an ancient alien mystic. Another one of my CERO friends wrote:

"Since you began telling us about Anzar, I always had the impression that he is an alien/sentient being who is guiding you. In my three decades of working with abductees/experiencers, I found that each person has a special being 'assigned' to them from early childhood who follows them throughout their lives. This being is always a 'familiar' figure when taken aboard a spacecraft and when the person sees or senses the being, they experience a sense of 'calm.' Many have stated this being feels like a family member."

My Paranormal Life

I believe everything I do has a paranormal connection, which means all my books, comic books, plays, and my life in general. We write what we know. Most of my theatrical plays have paranormal elements that are based on experiences I have had. I have been described as a paranormal lightning rod. In 1997, I had a vision where the Progenitor (Anzar) spoke to me, and as astonishing as that was, I felt I already knew him. Based on a hypnotic regression session with Yvonne Smith that dealt with my conscious memories of strange events when I was six years old, I discovered that I had met a large alien before, and that alien, turned out to be Anzar.

As for my comic book character Snarc, the idea came to me when I was working in a prison guard tower at the US Army Confinement Facility in Mannheim, West Germany. The basic concept is that an alien hybrid comes to Earth to save humanity. I felt like I already knew who Snarc was and had dreamt of him before. While in engineering school, I wrote and drew a comic strip featuring Snarc. It was popular with students and staff. Then I dropped out of engineering school and rejoined the US Army, this time as a helicopter pilot. I had a series of nightmares about combat in the helicopter and eventually got out of the military. Snarc was still in my thinking but I had little time to develop the story. Then, in January 2019, my second oldest son Byron, who is an engineer, created a bust of Snarc and I was inspired to create the comic book. *Snarc*, although technically fiction, is based on my life experiences, and not just in this lifetime. Interestingly, my wife Ginger believes that I am Snarc. My artist friend, Gary Dumm, and I work hand in glove in an intuitive way on the comic book. If I am Snarc, then he is the Cosmic Staff (Snarc's wise-cracking companion and advisor in the series).

Déjà vu has been with me my whole life. I believe that we manifest our own realities through consciousness. Déjà vu provides us with brief glimpses of other realities and possibilities. It is like we are testing out future paths. As a young child, I remember thinking that I had already died and had come back not necessarily as a different person, but the same person on a different trajectory. What I believe ties all this together is my theory that the spirit world, the alien world, and the quantum world are the same thing. In the quantum subatomic world time is not linear, that is our artificial construction of reality, it is all happening at once. I believe that is the mechanism of déjà vu and, in my case, ties into my connection to Anzar and my creation of Snarc.

Prophecies, Predictions, and Precognition

Anzar always reminds me that predictions are often wrong, but preparations never are. He adds a caveat to most of his prophecies (i.e., there are many variables so it may or may not happen). Anzar has said some interesting things that could be looked at as both predictions and prophecies, so it is important to understand the difference between precognition or prediction and prophecy. Prophecy is based on having a deep understanding of the past and the present to see where things are going. Predictions based on precognition are based on being aware of events before they happen. Some have asked me: "Are you claiming to be a prophet based on your connection to Anzar?" My answer is no, I am not claiming anything except that I have the connection. Now, Anzar has called me a prophet, among other things: "You are a seer, a seeker, a prophet, a sage, you must help others evolve," as he said on April 15, 2021. And when he came to me in 1997, he said: "You are one in a long line of seers…you must be the connector, the bridge-builder." I have resisted the label of prophet, but I do wholeheartedly accept my mission. The view I have on being a prophet is like how I deal with my students in the classroom when it comes to how they should address me. I hold a Ph.D. in history but I let my students know that they can call me Dr. Solheim, teacher, professor, or Bruce—whatever they feel comfortable with. I always add that I get paid the same no matter what they call me which puts them at ease and makes them laugh.

Anzar appeared to me in 1997 (later I found out that I have known him since I was a child), calling himself the Progenitor. He told me his name was Anzar on November 24, 2018, and we have been in regular contact since. Here are some of his predictions, prophecies, and precognitive statements, some of which were in the spirit walk transcripts earlier in the book.

On March 1, 2019, Anzar told me that a catastrophe was imminent. "Be prepared, have resources, timeline could be off, store resources, one month's worth. Stick close to friends and family," he said. And when I asked for more specific information about the catastrophe two days later, he said: "Multiple, not just one, catastrophe. Multiple things happening. Worldwide." He included alien contact, natural disasters, political and economic turmoil, internal to the United States.

On March 7, 2019, Anzar told me that preparations would be needed and "people will need calm, reassuring voices and their

343

spirituality." After my UFO sighting on March 14, Anzar told me that the aliens were here to try to help with the calamities he had warned me about.

At the beginning of the pandemic, on January 31, 2020, Anzar said that COVID-19 was one of the calamities he had predicted and that it came from a weapons lab in Wuhan, China. He also mentioned that it was likely an accident. On March 4, 2020, he said that COVID-19 was just one of seven calamities that would befall us. Among the others he mentioned, earthquakes, and the escalation of conflict. A few days later he added weather-related anomalies, ET semi-disclosure, tornadoes, waves and water, more haunted houses as spirits merged through, and financial collapse.

On March 14, after shortages and hoarding, Anzar said that the government had plans for martial law.[273] He mentioned that ETs were involved with these calamities: "helping and provoking, both, depends on the group," he said. He again reminded me that people will need a calm voice of reason.

On April 17, 2020, he said that there would be a celestial anomaly, but it would be a sign of protection for humans. As it turned out, this may have been the comet Neowise, which appeared in July and will not be back for another 6,800 years.[274] At the end of April, Anzar again mentioned the celestial anomaly and added a warning about the second wave of the COVID-19 virus, and political instability.

On May 17, 2020, Anzar doubled down on his warning about political instability and upgraded it to a devastating rebellion and insurrection, a foreshadowing of the summer of protests and riots related to the killing of George Floyd in Minneapolis and the US Capitol insurrection on January 6, 2021, in Washington, DC.

On July 12, 2020, with ongoing protests and riots in American cities, Anzar warned about worsening civil unrest bordering on civil war, economic collapse, and a potential for international conflict. And on September 30, 2020, my ancient alien mystic friend warned of further calamities, and an election debacle.

On October 18, 2020, Anzar mentioned insurrection again, and added chaos, intervention, and finally, clarity. "Stand by, stand ready to help," he said.

We all know that the period from the US presidential election through January 20, 2021, was quite a turbulent time in America. We saw the election vote count challenges based on accusations of voter fraud, and of course the January 6, 2021, US Capitol insurrection, and subsequent second impeachment of Donald Trump, and his second acquittal by the US Senate.

In a free-form connection with Anzar on October 27, 2020, he said: "Convoluted, everything, expression, departure, insurrection, undecided, nobody will know, mini-revolution, pocket revolution. Movement, think of movement in your action and motivation," said Anzar. Although free-form is always challenging to decipher, the raw information can be quite jarring and therefore helpful. Anzar seemed to capture exactly what was about to happen.

December 16, 2020, Anzar anticipated the events of January 2021. "The pocket revolution, civil unrest, bordering on civil war, President Trump not going away, with powerful following." We ended the year in the United States with much uncertainty and almost completely divided.

After Joe Biden's inauguration, Anzar noted on January 26, 2021, that, "Military action is coming, be prepared. Deception warfare." Just a moment after he said that a military helicopter flew low and directly over my head. A sign of things to come? I hope not.

What Anzar Has Taught Me

As amazing as Anzar's precognition, prophecies, and predictions have been, I believe the most extraordinary part of our connection and integration has been his guidance and advice on life, both here in this dimension, and beyond. It has been a humbling journey as well as an enlightening one. Dear readers, these are some of the most significant bits of wisdom I have learned from my contact with Anzar. Some ideas and phrases are simple, almost deceptively so, and others are more complex and require deep contemplation, but all are priceless in my estimation and I hope yours.

1. "Youthful exuberance is often confused with extremism. Harnessing and directing that youthful energy is the job of elders."

2. "Be the light."

3. "Stay together, stay in the light, trust the light, even if darkness seems stronger, you must trust the light. The voice of calm reason and benevolent authority will prevail—a holy authority."

4. "The worlds will come together."

5. "Predictions can be wrong, but preparations are never wrong."

6. "Keep love in your heart and always operate from a position of love."

7. "Mythology becomes the history."

8. "What is good will be good. Good brings good."

9. "It is what it will be."

10. "I am in the universe and the universe is in me."

11. "You know what will happen in the future because you manifest it."

12. "You can catch a time wave."

13. "All of this is an illusion."

14. "Manage expectations. Be happy with who you are. If exceptions occur, be grateful."

15. "Do not expect to be rewarded for doing the right thing."

16. "Help alleviate the suffering of others."

17. "Becoming is the most important thing."

18. "Realize that you only have a piece of the puzzle and you need others."

19. "It is not about being right or wrong, it is about being helpful."

20. "Good is what you do, not what you are. All is good for all time."

21. "This may be as good as it gets. Own who you are, with all your flaws, happiness is hard work and shows up in unexpected ways."

22. "The journey is only beginning."

23. "The alien, spirit, and quantum worlds are all the same things."

24. "There is no need to fear death, it is just another beginning."

25. "We are all the aliens."

26. "You cannot use alien technology to harm others."

27. "Some abductions are reunions."

28. "Just like computer hackers use slave or zombie computers to do their dirty work, malevolent entities can do the same thing to humans and make them perform whatever function they want them to do."

29. "The concept of good aliens and bad aliens is subjective."

30. "The aliens will show you whatever you need to see."

31. "Experiencing is believing and believing is experiencing."

32. "You are entering an Era of Reconversion through a leap of consciousness."

33. "Depict me as you wish."

34. "Everything is the way it has been for thousands of years. Your space is limited in this life and then is eternal in the next."

35. "Remember, outer space and inner space are the same."

36. "Energy manifests in material constructs of our reality, and we can help and shape that reality. We cannot just be good; we must make good things happen. Unfortunately, those of evil intent can make bad things happen. In a way, it is a contest, so stay on the side of the light and be the light."

37. "Some people are agents of change. Someone can be such an agent, either wittingly or unwittingly, and often that change can ultimately lead to good results, or it can lead to bad results. As such, good people can do good things, bad people can do bad things, good people can do bad things, and bad people can do good things."

38. "There is no light without the dark."

39. "The old ways of thought are no longer sufficient. You must all evolve to your higher consciousness."

40. "There is a spiritual drought, and when the rains of truth come, they will be powerful, and people must be ready to accept the flood of enlightenment and the paradigm shift that follows."

41. "Let them into your heart: the strong, the foolish, the weak, and the wise—all of them. And do not let your heart harden."

42. "A leap of consciousness and bridled versus unbridled reality. Hard to accept, but it is reality, nonetheless. Comfortable reality is not true reality, to see the world and universe as it really is through enlightenment does not come easy."

43. "Cool and calm, rational, liberal in thinking and conservative in action. Idealistic in thinking and realistic in action. Good combination. As for the alien stuff, it is always there, and always has been, and always will be."

44. "The spirit is the most essential thing, that is what touches you when you are not physically together with others; it is the most essential part."

45. "Extraterrestrial technology and wisdom are precious gifts for all, not a strategic advantage for the few."

I wanted to separate out a few quotes from my friend Gene. His advice and wisdom and help in this paranormal journey has been both essential and appreciated.

1. "It is all true!"

2. "Where I am there is no future and no past, just an eternal now."

3. "Is it so hard to believe in one more miraculous thing when you already believe in so many extraordinary things?"

4. "Do everything to your fullest, put everything into your role in life because it echoes in all of eternity."

Summary

In this book, I have included my dreams in addition to the spirit communication, and analysis of paranormal events and theoretical concepts. I believe dreams play a much larger role in our lives than just a way in which our everyday life's troubles manifest upward and play out in the dreamworld. Our dreams provide us with clues from what David Bohm called the implicate order where the spirit world, alien world, and quantum world reside. Dr. Montague Ullman, the founder of the Dream Laboratory in Brooklyn, New York believed that dreams are not just for the individual, they are for all of humanity. "He also agrees with Bohm on the importance of wholeness and feels that dreams are nature's way of trying to counteract our seemingly unending compulsion to fragment the world."[275] Ullman believed that dreams represent a "natural transformation of the implicate in the explicate."[276] Mystics for thousands of years have noted a feeling of oneness with the universe. "[Bohm and Pribram] suggest that perhaps mystics are somehow able to peer beyond ordinary explicate reality and glimpse its deeper, more holographic qualities." Philosopher Jason Reza Jorjani, in his book *Prometheus and Atlas*, wrote: "What is demanded of us is a perseverance of Atlas and a daring of Prometheus. Mankind is about to be gifted with a new world, but only if we can bear it, and only if we can steal it."[277] This corresponds with what retired US Army Colonel Philip J. Corso, who wrote the book, *The Day After Roswell,* was told by an ET on the White Sands Missile Range in 1957.

"What do you have to offer?" asked Colonel Corso.

"A new world, if you can take it," said the ET.[278]

I was listening to an interview with Donald Hoffman, a cognitive psychologist, and he described our perception of everyday reality as a user interface for the true objective reality, quantum reality, or the implicate order that David Bohm described. The user interface is necessary for us to live our lives and survive. If we were to see only true objective reality it would be like me trying to type these words by dealing directly with the toggling voltages, underlying programming, and electronics of my computer. Instead, I have an easy-to-use interface that maximizes efficiency.[279]

This brings me to my last point: With this leap of consciousness, we will be able to see and comprehend objective reality more easily. It is no surprise that UFO or UAV videos are being released by the US government. They know that we are at the brink of this paradigm shift and they can no longer control the interface. Sources inform me that Mr. Z, a former government official, said that evidence points to more than one alien species competing here on Earth for control and for resources. He, along with a scientist, had briefed President Trump about understanding UAVs and the possible ongoing threat that aliens and their craft pose. Mr. Z believes that this battle between groups of aliens has begun and we are caught in the middle of a global and intergalactic conflict. The spiritual component is key as these government insiders have described it as a "struggle between good and evil." There are dozens of ET races, some hostile against one another, some hostile against humanity. As disconcerting as this may be, we will be able to handle the truth, and we will prevail, of that I am certain. Anzar has helped me see the oneness of all and through his simple phrase, "Keep love in your heart and always operate from a position of love," has planted the seeds of wisdom for us to cultivate an understanding of our place in the universe as we take the leap of consciousness into a new Era of Reconversion and ultimately save not only our planet but perhaps others as well.

"I happen to have been privileged enough to be in on the fact that we've been visited on this planet, and the UFO phenomenon is real."

"White Sands was a testing ground for atomic weapons — and that's what the extraterrestrials were interested in. They wanted to know about our military capabilities. My own experience talking to people has made it clear the ETs had been attempting to keep us from going to war and help create peace on Earth ..."

–Dr. Edgar Mitchell
Apollo 14 astronaut, 6th man on the moon[280]

Figure 7: Cover of Snarc #1 comic book.

Figure 8: Cover of Snarc #2 comic book.

ABOUT THE AUTHOR

Bruce Olav Solheim was born in Seattle, Washington, to Norwegian immigrant parents. Bruce was the first person in his family to go to college. He served for six years in the US Army as a jail guard and later as a warrant officer helicopter pilot and is a disabled veteran. Bruce earned his Ph.D. in history from Bowling Green State University in 1993. Bruce is a distinguished professor of history at Citrus College in Glendora, California. He was a Fulbright Professor and Scholar in 2003 at the University of Tromsø in Northern Norway.

Bruce has published 10 books and has written 10 plays, five of which have been produced. *The Bronze Star* won two awards from the Kennedy Center American College Theatre Festival. *The Epiphany* was commissioned by the Kingdom of Norway and funded for a full production run with the original American cast. Bruce founded the veterans program at Citrus College and co-founded Boots to Books, the nation's first college-credit transition course for veterans. Bruce is also a co-founder of Lockdown Theatre, which has produced three streamplays (online, live, remote actors) during the COVID-19 pandemic. He has published a trilogy of paranormal books about his personal paranormal experiences: *Timeless, Timeless Deja Vu*, and *Timeless Trinity*. Bruce has also published a comic book and a graphic novel featuring an alien hybrid character named Snarc.

He has been on many radio shows and podcasts including *Coast to Coast AM* four times and will be a featured speaker at Contact in the Desert 2021. Bruce is married to Ginger, the girl of his dreams, and has four children and two grandsons.

ABOUT THE ARTIST

Gary Dumm is a life-long Cleveland resident and artist who worked with Harvey Pekar on *American Splendor* since Pekar began self-publishing that comic 42 years ago. He has shown artwork in exhibitions nationally from Cleveland to San Francisco and internationally from Canada to Germany. His cartoons have been shown in *Entertainment Weekly*, the *New York Times*, the *Village Voice* and France's *le Monde* and in *Cleveland Scene, Free Times,* and *Plain Dealer*. Currently, Gary writes and draws pieces for *Music Makers Rag* (biographies of blues musicians helped by that organization out of North Carolina) and juggles several graphic novel projects. His talented wife, Laura, adds color to his work as required, allowing him to do that much more in black and white. You can learn more about Gary and Laura's art at www.dummart.com.

ENDNOTES

1. Anzar in Arabic means vision, eyesight, intelligence, and insight. There is an Anzar High School and Anzar Lake in San Juan Batista, California. Anzar is also the name of a small town in Northern Iran, and the name of the god of rain in ancient Berber mythology in Morocco.

2. Philemon was an entity that appeared to Jung in a dream in 1913. In *Memories, Dreams, Reflections*, Jung wrote about the dream where Philemon first appeared. After the dream, Jung painted the image, because he did not understand it. Philemon played an important role in Jung's fantasies and represented superior insight and functioned like a guru to him. See https://philemonfoundation.org/about-philemon/who-is-philemon/.

3. Radin, Dean. Parapsychological Association Presidential Address 2018. See https://www.parapsych.org/media/player.ashx?id=xP6t-rRSBzw.

4. Ibid.

5. Google Ngram is a search engine that charts word frequencies from a large corpus of books that were printed between 1500 and 2008. The tool generates charts by dividing the number of a word's yearly appearances by the total number of words in the corpus in that year. Thereby a book's content is split into case-sensitive text blocks–so called *n-grams*. See https://journals.plos.org/plosone/article?id=10.1371/journal.pone.0213554.

6. Although I use the word disclosure throughout this book because it is in common usage in the ufology community, I believe the better word would be revelation with all that implies.

7. MUFON website: https://www.mufon.com/ufology.html.

8. Ibid.

9. From the NSA website: https://www.nsa.gov/Resources/Everyone/foia/freq-req-info/ufo-topics/number a.

10. Elizondo, Luis. "What We Think of as 'Paranormal' May Be Something Else Entirely." In *Forbes* https://www.forbes.com/sites/quora/2019/03/13/what-we-think-of-as-paranormal-may-be-something-else-entirely/number 38095963543d.

11. Ibid.

12. Ibid.

13. Ibid.

14. Gordon, Stuart. *The Paranormal: An Illustrated Encyclopedia*. North Pomfret, VT: Trafalgar Square, 1993.

15. Solheim, Bruce Olav. *Timeless Deja Vu*. Glendora, CA: Boots to Books, 2019, p. 184.

16. The Parapsychological Association. https://www.parapsych.org/articles/53/344/psi.aspx; also see Philip Ball. "The Strange Link Between the Human Mind and Quantum Physics." BBC (16 February 2017). http://www.bbc.com/earth/story/20170215-the-strange-link-between-the-human-mind-and-quantum-physics.

17. For more information, please see The Parapsychological Association. https://www.parapsych.org/base/about.aspx.

18. Pigliucci, Massimo; Boudry, Maarten. *Philosophy of Pseudoscience: Reconsidering the Demarcation Problem*. Chicago: University of Chicago Press, 2013; Smith, Jonathan. *Pseudoscience and Extraordinary Claims of the Paranormal: A Critical Thinker's Toolkit*. Hoboken, NJ: Wiley-Blackwell, 2009; Park, Robert. *Voodoo Science: The Road from Foolishness to Fraud*. Oxford, England: Oxford University Press, 2000, pp. 196-200; Radin, Dean. *Entangled Minds*, New York: Paraview Pocket Books, 2006.

19. Boyle, Alan. "How to Spot Quantum Quackery." https://www.nbcnews.com/sciencemain/how-spot-quantum-quackery-6C10403763.

20. Ibid.

21. Ibid.

22. Ornes, Stephen. "The quantum world is mind-bogglingly weird." (14 September 2017). https://www.sciencenewsforstudents.org/article/quantum-world-mind-bogglingly-weird.

23. Planck, Max. *The New Science*. Meridian Books, 1959.

24. Planck, Max. *The Observer* (25 January 1931).

25. Matthieu, Ricard, Trinh Xuan Thuan. *The Quantum and the Lotus: A Journey to the Frontiers Where Science and Buddhism Meet*. New York: Broadway Books, 2004.

26. Wheeler, John A. "Information, physics, quantum: The search for links," in W. Zurek, *Complexity, Entropy, and the Physics of Information*. Redwood City, CA: Addison-Wesley, 1990.

27. Schrodinger, Erwin. *The Observer* (11 January 1931); *Psychic Research* (1931), Vol. 25, p. 91.

28. Proietti, Massimiliano, et al. "Experimental test of local observer independence." *Science Advances* (20 Sep 2019), Vol. 5, no. 9. https://advances.sciencemag.org/content/5/9/eaaw9832.

29. Radin, Dean. Real Magic: Ancient Wisdom, Modern Science, and a Guide to the Secret Power of the Universe. New York: Harmony Books, 2018.

30. McKie, Robin. "Royal Mail's Nobel guru in telepathy row." *The Guardian* (29 Sep 2001). https://www.theguardian.com/uk/2001/sep/30/robinmckie.theobserver.

31. Glorfeld, Jeff. "Science history: The man attempting to merge physics and the paranormal." *Cosmos* (18 March 2019). https://cosmosmagazine.com/physics/science-history-the-man-attempting-to-merge-physics-and-the-paranormal.

32. Popkin, Gabriel. "Einstein's 'spooky action at a distance' spotted in objects almost big enough to see," (25 April 2018). https://www.sciencemag.org/news/2018/04/einstein-s-spooky-action-distance-spotted-objects-almost-big-enough-see.

33. Ibid.; see also, Sophia Chen. "Even Huge Molecules Follow the Quantum World's Bizarre Rules." Science (23 September 2019). https://www.wired.com/story/even-huge-molecules-follow-the-quantum-worlds-bizarre-rules/.

34. Horgan, John. "Brilliant Scientists Are Open-Minded about Paranormal Stuff, So Why Not You?" *Scientific American* (20 July 2012). https://blogs.scientificamerican.com/cross-check/brilliant-scientists-are-open-minded-about-paranormal-stuff-so-why-not-you/.

35. Burns, Charlene. "Wolfgang Pauli, Carl Jung, and the Acausal Connecting Principle: A Case Study in Transdisciplinarity," (1 September 2011). https://www.metanexus.net/wolfgang-pauli-carl-jung-and-acausal-connecting-principle-case-study-transdisciplinarity/.

36. Fike, Matthew. Monroe Institute. Book review of *Entangled Minds* by Dean Radin. Winter/Spring 2007. https://www.monroeinstitute.org/book_review/ Entangled%20Minds%3A%20Extrasensory%20Experiences%20in%20a%20Quantum%20Reality.

37. Solheim, Bruce Olav. *Timeless Deja Vu: A Paranormal Personal History*. Glendora, CA: Boots to Books, 2019.

38. Ibid.

39. Swedenborg Foundation. https://swedenborg.com/recap-the-spirituality-of-extraterrestrials/.

40. Ambrosino, Brandon. BBC Future (16 December 2016). https://www.bbc.com/future/article/20161215-if-we-made-contact-with-aliens-how-would-religions-react.

41. NASA grant to study theology. https://whyevolutionistrue.wordpress.com/ 2016/08/17/whats-up-with-the-nasa-grant-to-study-theology/.

42. Sagan, Carl. *The Cosmic Connection: An Extraterrestrial Perspective*. Garden City, N.Y., Anchor Press, 1973.

43. Ibid.; Ambrosino, Brandon. BBC Future (16 December 2016). https://www.bbc.com/future/article/20161215-if-we-made-contact-with-aliens-how-would-religions-react.

44. Pew Research Center. https://www.pewforum.org/2017/04/05/the-changing-global-religious-landscape/.

45. *Cosmos: A Personal Voyage*. PBS, 1980; Mathew, Santhosh. *The Guardian* (26 April 2017). https://www.theguardian.com/commentisfree/2017/ apr/26/discovery-of-alien-life-religion-will-survive.

46 . McNally, Richard J., and Susan A. Clancy. "Sleep Paralysis, Sexual Abuse, and Space Alien Abduction." *Transcultural Psychiatry* (March 2005), vol. 42 (1), pp. 113-122.

47. Ibid.

48. Ibid; Other debunker articles that I reviewed are: Neimark, Jill. "Are Recovered Memories Real?" *Discover Magazine* (August 2004). http://www.discovermagazine.com/2004/aug/are-recovered-memories-real; McCracken, Samuel. "Close Encounters of the Harvard Kind." *Commentary* (March 200), pp. 48-52; Perina, Kaja. "Cracking the Harvard X-Files." *Psychology Today* (March/April 2003), pp. 66-76, 95.

49. McLeod, Caroline C., Barbara Corbisier, and John E. Mack. "A More Parsimonious Explanation for UFO Abduction." *Psychological Inquiry*, vol. 7, no. 2 (1996), pp. 156-168.

50. I consulted the East Los Angeles Veterans Center (part of the Veteran's Administration or VA) director, Manuel Martinez. He is a combat veteran and has been providing PTSD therapy for combat veterans for more than 35 years. He told me that PTSD cannot be faked. "If someone is capable of changing their reality, they could possibly have a more severe psychological disorder." Also, my own research released in 2020 based on surveying CERO (Close Encounter Research Organization) members in the United States and France shows that 56 percent of those experiencers who were surveyed reached the standard threshold score for PTSD as established by the VA. The survey was a slightly modified version of the standard PCL-5 (PTSD checklist) used by the VA which is based on the DSM-5.

51. Hopkins, Bud, David Jacobs, and Ron Westrum. *Unusual Personal Experiences: An Analysis of the Data from Three Major Surveys*. Las Vegas: Bigelow Holding Corporation, 1992; and here a few more works by advocates of the experiencers or those who are neutral researchers: Jacobs, David. *Secret Life: The Structure of Meaning of UFO Abductions*. New York: Simon & Schuster, 1992; Jacobs, David. "A Brief History of Abduction Research." *Journal of Scientific Exploration*, vol. 23, no. 1, (2009), pp. 69-77; Hopkins, Bud. *Missing Time: A Documented Study of UFO Abductions*. New York: Richard Marek Publishers, 1981; Vallee, Jacques. *Passport to Magonia: From Folklore to Flying Saucers*. Washington, DC: Henry Regnery Company, 1969; Vallee, Jacques. *Dimensions: A Casebook of Alien Contact*. Chicago: Contemporary Books, 1988; Mack, John E. *Abduction: Human Encounters with Aliens*. New York: Scribner, 1999; Appelle, Stuart. "The Abduction Experience: A Critical Evaluation of Theory and Evidence." *Journal of UFO Studies*, no. 6 (1995/96), pp. 29-78.

52. For details on "My Personal Quantum Reality" see Solheim, Bruce Olav. *Timeless Deja Vu*. Glendora, CA: Boots to Books, 2019, p. 158.

53. Norwegians, and all Scandinavians for that matter, tend to be rather modest. This regional cultural value stems from something called *"Janteloven,"* which translated into English means, "the Law of Jante." The premise of *Janteloven* is that you are not to think you are anything special or try to hold your head up above anyone else. *Jantelov* was created in 1933 by a Danish-Norwegian writer named Aksel Sandemose. It was featured in his book entitled: *En Flytning Krysser Sitt Spor* (A fugitive crosses his tracks). Sandemose wrote about working-class people in the fictional Danish town of Jante. All the people in Jante held the same social position. This cultural attribute of humility was already common in Scandinavia for centuries, but never expressed the way Sandemose described in his book. *Janteloven* could also be used to justify criticizing people who are trying to climb up the socio-economic ladder. Americans pride themselves on their rugged individualism. We are competitive with one another. Scandinavians feel little of that pressure to keep up with the Jones, as we say in the United States. *Janteloven* calls for people not to compare yourself to others, instead, you compare yourself to yourself. Since Scandinavians are always rated as the world's happiest people, maybe there is something essential for us to learn about *Janteloven*. See the story "At Least We are Not Zero," in Solheim, Bruce Olav. *Timeless Deja Vu*. Glendora, CA: Boots to Books, 2019.

54. Radin, Dean, et al. "Exceptional experiences reported by scientists and engineers." *Explore*, Volume 14, Issue 5, September 2018, pp. 329-341. https://www.sciencedirect.com/science/article/abs/pii/S1550830718300119.

55. Corso, Philip, and William J. Birnes. *The Day After Roswell*. New York: Simon & Schuster, 1997.

56. Chomsky, Noam. *New Horizons in the Study of Language and Mind*. Cambridge: Cambridge University Press, 2000.

57. YouGov poll on aliens. https://today.yougov.com/topics/lifestyle/articles-reports/2015/09/28/you-are-not-alone-most-people-believe-aliens-exist.

58. ICAR Blood Type Data. https://icar1.homestead.com/contactee-blood-types.html.

59. Khan, Razib. "The Basques may not be who we think they are." *Discover Magazine* (18 February 2010). https://www.discovermagazine.com/the-sciences/the-basques-may-not-be-who-we-think-they-are.

60. Edgar Cayce Readings. "Arcturus. A Compilation of Extracts from the Edgar Cayce Readings" (1971). https://www.edgarcayce.org/uploadedfiles/member_section/circulating_files/21858Arcturus.pdf.

366

61. For more, go to: http://www.rasmussenreports.com/public_content/lifestyle/ general_lifestyle/june_2019/very_few_see_ufos_as_threat_to_u_s.

62. YouGov poll on the existence of aliens. https://today.yougov.com/topics/ lifestyle/articles-reports/2015/09/28/you-are-not-alone-most-people-believe-aliens-exist.

63. See details of these abduction/reunions in Solheim, Bruce Olav. *Timeless Trinity*. Glendora, CA: Boots to Books, 2020.

64. Some believe that aliens are future humans. See Masters, Michael P. *Identified Flying Objects: A Multidisciplinary Scientific Approach to the UFO Phenomenon*. Butte, MT: Masters Creative, 2019.

65. See "The Devil in Me" in Solheim, Bruce Olav. *Timeless Trinity*, Glendora, CA: Boots to Books, 2020.

66. Interview with Dr. Edwin M. Young on April 22, 2019. *Timeless Esoterica Radio Program*. http://artistfirst.com/drbruce.htm.

67. Randall, Lisa. "Ghosts, Aliens, Quantum Gravity, Extra Dimensions, Sci Fi and the Rules of Science." *Scientific American* (22 September 2011). https://www.scientificamerican.com/article/ghosts-aliens-quantum-gravity/.

68. Marden, Kathleen. *Extraterrestrial Contact: What to Do When You've Been Abducted*, Kathleen Marden, Newbury Port, MA: Red Wheel/Weiser, 2019, p. 131.

69. Sarfatti, Jack, interview with Jeffrey Mishlove, *Thinking Allowed*. https://www.youtube.com/watch? v=rGR3SOiTTLc. It is interesting to note that the implicate order is also the Akashic Field. See https://www.academia.edu/ 28379390/Ervin_L%C3%A1szl%C3%B3s_Holofield_The_Akasha_and_David_Bohms_Implicate_Order, p. 3.

70. Galarneau, Lisa. "Introduction to the Modalities of Contact." https://medium.com/the-foundation-for-research-into-extraterrestrial/introduction-to-the-modalities-of-contact-2583604d04fe.

71. Consciousness and Contact Conference. https://www.unknowncountry.com/ new-observations/consciousness-and-contact-2020-an-amazing-conference-an-amazing-discussion/.

72. Pew Research Center. https://www.pewforum.org/2009/12/09/many-ameri-cans-mix-multiple-faiths/number ghosts-fortunetellers-and-communicating-with-the-dead; https://news.gallup.com/poll/266441/americans-skeptical-ufos-say-gov-ernment-knows.aspx.

73. Daniels, Craig. "David Bohm All Moments Are Really One." (19 December 2016). https://www.whatisdialogue.com/david-bohm-all-moments-are-really-one/.

74. See the full story called "My Nazi Aunt," in Solheim, Bruce Olav. *Timeless: Deja Vu*. Glendora, CA: Boots to Books, 2019.

75. See "The Progenitor," in Solheim, Bruce Olav. *Timeless: Deja Vu*. Glendora, CA: Boots to Books, 2019.

76. My son Leif and I saw a UFO on March 14, 2019, as Anzar predicted. See my story "UFO," in Solheim, Bruce Olav. *Timeless Trinity*. Glendora, CA: Boots to Books, 2020.

77. Detected by radio astronomy, a fast radio burst (FRB) is a transient radio pulse of length ranging from a fraction of a millisecond to a few milliseconds, caused by some high-energy astrophysical process that is not really understood yet. An average FRB releases as much energy in a millisecond as the sun puts out in three days.

78. Oumuamua was the first confirmed interstellar object observed in our solar system. The name means messenger from afar or scout in Hawaiian. Oumuamua was estimated to be almost 1000 meters long and cigar-shaped and traveling at nearly 59,000 miles per hour. Some scientists speculated that it was a remnant of an alien civilization and the hyperbolic trajectory indicated that it came from Vega, the brightest star in the northern constellation of Lyra only 25 light-years from the Sun. Vega, along with Arcturus and Sirius, is one of the most lumi-nous stars in the night sky.

79. Arcturus is a red giant star in the Northern Hemisphere and the brightest star in the constellation Boötes (the Herdsman). Rigel is a blue supergiant that is the brightest star in the constellation Orion (the Hunter). According to some, the Siri-ans are a group of humanoids from the Sirius star system who originally came from Vega in the Lyra constellation.

80. My cousin Berit lives in the San Diego area. In 2000, I visited her and thought she was suffering a nervous breakdown, but actually she was being harassed by military and/or intelligence personnel and alien entities. I wish I could have done more to help her then, but I was not ready to face my own experiences much less deal with hers.

81. To the Stars Academy (TTSA) is an organization founded in 2017, by Tom Delonge of the band Blink-182.

82. MUFON is the Mutual UFO Network, founded in 1969.

83. *Snarc* number 1 came out in November 2019, and *Snarc* number 2 came out in March 2021. The original concept came from a vision I had while I was in the US Army stationed in West Germany in 1980. I wrote and illustrated a comic strip called Snark when I was an engineering student at Montana Tech in Butte, Montana in 1982.

84. The Ides of March. Julius Caesar was assassinated on March 15 in 44 BC.

85. The origin of human language is a topic without clear answers. Some say that it began only 100,000 years ago, others say that a proto language was used much earlier including noises and gestures used by modern primates.

86. In Greek mythology, Prometheus is a god of fire and a trickster. Prometheus is credited with the creation of humans from clay and stole fire from the gods to give to humans.

87. On November 14, 2004, 100 miles southwest of San Diego, the USS Nimitz and the USS Princeton were among the ships conducting training prior to be deployed to the Persian Gulf. At 2 pm, two F/A-18 F Super Hornet fighter jets from the Nimitz received unusual orders to break off their training. The Princeton had been picking up mysterious objects on their sophisticated radar system and the jets were sent to investigate. US Navy pilot Commander David Fravor reported that he saw a white object that looked like a forty-foot-long Tic Tac. Lieutenant Commander Chad Underwood was able to take video footage through his gunsight. These videos were released in 2017.

88. Mishlove, Jeffrey. *The PK Man: A True Story of Mind Over Matter.* Newport News, VA: Hampton Roads, 2000. Jeffrey Mishlove is a parapsychologist and host of *New Thinking Allowed.* The subject was Ted Owens, a man who possessed superhuman telekinetic abilities that were well documented.

89. I have taken a keen interest in the King assassination. From 1963 to 1968 there were four major political assassinations in America: JFK in 1963, Malcolm X in 1965, MLK in 1968, and Bobby Kennedy (RFK) in 1968. I have always been suspicious of these horrible, violent events in our history. In my view, we have not been told the truth. MLK was killed a year after he came out against the Vietnam War and announced his Poor People's Campaign. I believe that was not a coincidence. He challenged the power structure of American society and was eliminated.

90. For details on the 1977 incident please see the story "Mel's Hole," in Solheim, Bruce Olav. *Timeless Trinity*. Glendora, CA: Boots to Books, 2020.

91. Simeon Hein has a Ph. D. in sociology with an emphasis on how humans interact with technology. He founded his own research and teaching company, the Mount Baldy Institute, in 1996, to give people the opportunity to learn resonant viewing, a type of intuitive training that taps into human creative unconscious intelligence. For more see: https://simeonhein.com/about/.

92. See my story "Rescue Operation," in Solheim, Bruce Olav. *Timeless Trinity*. Glendora, CA: Boots to Books, 2020.

93. See my story "Special Processing," in Solheim, Bruce Olav. *Timeless Trinity*. Glendora, CA: Boots to Books, 2020.

94. See my story "Poliomyelitis and the Angel," in Solheim, Bruce Olav. *Timeless: A Paranormal Personal History*, 2nd ed. Glendora, CA: Boots to Books, 2020.

95. See Masters, Michael P. *Identified Flying Objects. A Multidisciplinary Scientific Approach to the UFO Phenomenon*. Butte, MT: Masters Creative, LLC, 2019.

96. Stanton Friedman, who died on May 13, 2019, was a nuclear physicist and professional ufologist who was the original civilian investigator of the Roswell UFO incident.

97. Contact in the Desert (CITD) is one of the biggest UFO conferences in the world. For more information go to: https://contactinthedesert.com/.

98. See my story, "Big Bad John," in Solheim, Bruce Olav. *Timeless Trinity*. Glendora, CA: Boots to Books, 2020.

99. Ibid.

100. My dad's youngest sister, Walborg, was a member of the Gestapo in Norway during the Nazi occupation in World War 2. She was sentenced to death for war crimes, but the sentence was later commuted to life. See my story, "My Nazi Aunt," in Solheim, Bruce Olav. *Timeless Deja Vu*. Glendora, CA: Boots to Books, 2019.

101. Navarre Scott Momaday, who was born February 27, 1934, is a Kiowa novelist, short story writer, essayist, and poet. His novel *House Made of Dawn* won the Pulitzer Prize for Fiction in 1969, and he is considered the leader of the Native American Renaissance in literature.

102. The US Space Force was established on December 20, 2019, with the 2020 National Defense Authorization Act. Its responsibilities include developing military space professionals known as guardians, building military space systems, and growing a military doctrine for space power. Here is the doctrine that was released in June 2019: https://www.spaceforce.mil/Portals/1/Space%20 Capstone%20Publication_10%20Aug%202020.pdf.

103. Corona virus timeline. https://coronavirus.jhu.edu/vaccines/timeline.

104. Indonesian earthquake information. https://www.thejakartapost.com/news/ 2019/07/14/powerful-7-3-magnitude-quake-jolts-halmahera-people-rush-out-homes-in-panic.html.

105. Bob Lazar is a scientist who worked at S-4 at Area 51 in the Nevada desert. He claimed to have worked on alien technology and seen flying saucers stored at the facility. https://www.mysterywire.com/area-51/bigelow-lazar/.

106. See my story, "Big Bad John," in Solheim, Bruce Olav. *Timeless Trinity*. Glendora, CA: Boots to Books, 2020.

107. Information on hydrocelectomy. https://my.clevelandclinic.org/health/ treatments/16232-hydrocelectomy.

108. Jacques Vallee is a French astronomer, computer scientist, and ufologist. He also believes that the alien world, spirit world, and quantum world are connected. For more see: https://www.jacquesvallee.net/.

109. The full details can be found in my story, "Via De Anzar," in Solheim, Bruce Olav. *Timeless Trinity*. Glendora, CA: Boots to Books, 2020.

110. For full details, see my story, "A September to Remember," in Solheim, Bruce Olav. *Timeless Trinity*. Glendora, CA: Boots to Books, 2020. Also, check out the cover, it depicts the female reptilian. Hypno-therapist Yvonne Smith has provided hypnotic regressions for hundreds and hundreds of people in her 28 years of work and said that rarely does she hear about contact with reptilians.

111. Heimdall, in Norse mythology, protects Bifrost the Rainbow Bridge between Asgard and Earth. During Ragnarök, the final battle, he sounds his horn warning the gods of the invading giants. Loki, the trickster god, will battle Heimdall and when they slay each other, the world burns and sinks into the sea.

112. Edward Snowden interview. https://www.cnn.com/2019/10/23/us/edward-snowden-joe-rogan-conspiracies-trnd/index.html

113. In his book *The Day After Roswell*, Corso claims he saw and dealt with extra-terrestrial artifacts recovered from a crash near Roswell, New Mexico in 1947. He oversaw distributing the alien technology to defense contractors who developed particle beam devices, fiber optics, lasers, integrated circuits, and Kevlar, among other things. Simultaneously he was responsible for spreading misinformation about the reality of alien contact and technology.

114. For more on Zoroastrianism see https://www.hinduwebsite.com/zoroastrianism/ahirman.asp or https://www.ancient.eu/zoroaster/. For an interview with Jason Reza Jorjani and Jeffrey Mishlove on *New Thinking Allowed*, see https://www.newthinkingallowed.org/understanding-zarathustra-with-jason-reza-jorjani/.

115. For a definition of thought form see https://www.lexico.com/definition/thought_form.

116. Members of the Theosophical Society, Besant, A., and Leadbeater, C.W., wrote *Thought-Forms*, originally published in 1901 in London.

117. Oswald allegedly tried to kill Major General Edwin Walker seven months before he allegedly shot President Kennedy. Walker was an extreme anti-communist and strident critic of JFK and his brother Robert F. Kennedy (RFK). It seems strange that Oswald would try to kill Walker who hated Kennedy and then try to kill Kennedy himself. This author does not accept the Warren Commission findings that Oswald was the lone assassin. Some of the most compelling evidence against a single shooter is the story of Dr. Charles Crenshaw who treated JFK in trauma room one at Parkland Memorial Hospital on November 22, 1963. The following is a video interview with Dr. Crenshaw. https://www.youtube.com/watch?v=BzCHYH260t4.

118. Lovelace, Terry. *Incident at Devils Den*, 2018.

119. Strieber, Whitley. *A New World*. Walker & Collier, 2019.

120. First Case of 2019 Novel Coronavirus in the United States. *New England Journal of Medicine*, March 5, 2020. https://www.nejm.org/doi/10.1056/NEJMoa2001191.

121. Centers for Disease Control and Prevention (CDC). Jernigan, DB. Update: Public Health Response to the Coronavirus Disease 2019 Outbreak — United States, February 24, 2020. MMWR Morb Mortal Wkly Rep 2020;69:216–219. DOI: http://dx.doi.org/10.15585/mmwr.mm6908e1external icon; and https://www.cdc.gov/mmwr/volumes/69/wr/mm6908e1.htm?s_cid=mm6908e1_w.

122. First Coronavirus Death. https://www.nbcnews.com/news/us-news/1st-coronavirus-death-u-s-officials-say-n1145931.

123. Governor Gavin Newsom Declares State of Emergency. https://www.gov.ca.gov/2020/03/04/governor-newsom-declares-state-of-emergency-to-help-state-prepare-for-broader-spread-of-covid-19/.

124. Health and Human Services Orders Respirators. https://www.hhs.gov/about/news/2020/03/04/hhs-to-procure-n95-respirators-to-support-healthcare-workers-in-covid-19-outbreaks.html.

125. Pandemic Shortages. https://komonews.com/news/nation-world/government-report-anticipates-18-month-pandemic-significant-shortages; and President Declares State of Emergency. https://trumpwhitehouse.archives.gov/presidential-actions/proclamation-declaring-national-emergency-concerning-novel-coronavirus-disease-covid-19-outbreak/.

126. Update on US Death Toll. https://www.usatoday.com/story/news/health/2020/03/16/coronavirus-live-updates-us-death-toll-rises-cases-testing/5053816002/.

127. Bay Area Shelter-in-Place Order. https://www.sfchronicle.com/local-politics/article/Bay-Area-must-shelter-in-place-Only-15135014.php; and https://www.sccgov.org/sites/covid19/Pages/public-health-orders.aspx.

128. See my story, "Big Bad John," in Solheim, Bruce Olav. *Timeless Trinity*. Glendora, CA: Boots to Books, 2020.

129. According to CNN, 2.8 million people have died worldwide from COVID-19 as of March 27, 2021. See https://www.cnn.com/interactive/2020/health/coronavirus-maps-and-cases/.

130. Governor Newsom Issues Stay-at-Home Orders. https://thehill.com/homenews/state-watch/488575-california-gov-newsom-orders-all-californians-to-stay-in-homes.

131. See the movie *Rescue Dawn* (2006) by Werner Herzog. Also see the documentary *Little Dieter Needs to Fly* (1997) by Werner Herzog. Ginger and I interviewed Werner in Hollywood when the film *Rescue Dawn* was released.

132. For more on President Theodore Roosevelt and Big Stick Diplomacy see: https://www.nationalgeographic.org/thisday/sep2/big-stick-diplomacy/.

133. Timeline of President Donald Trump and World Health Organization comments on coronavirus. https://www.npr.org/sections/goatsandsoda/2020/04/15/835011346/a-timeline-of-coronavirus-comments-from-president-trump-and-who.

134. See my story, "The Progenitor," in Solheim, Bruce Olav. *Timeless Deja Vu.* Glendora, CA: Boots to Books, 2019.

135. Hospital ships ordered to New York. https://www.armytimes.com/news/your-army/2020/03/24/three-army-field-hospitals-ordered-to-new-york-washington-states/; and Emergency hospital built in New York. https://www.businessinsider.com/photos-emergency-coronavirus-hospital-built-in-nyc-javits-center-2020-3; and https://www.usatoday.com/story/news/factcheck/2020/04/01/fact-check-does-new-york-have-stockpile-unneeded-ventilators/5097170002/.

136. Coronavirus Outbreak. https://www.cnn.com/world/live-news/coronavirus-outbreak-03-24-20-intl-hnk/index.html.

137. DBT is a cognitive-behavioral treatment developed by Marsha Linehan, Ph.D. in the 1980s to treat people with borderline personality disorder, but is now used to treat depression, and PTSD (post-traumatic stress disorder). "Dialectical behavior therapy (DBT) provides clients with new skills to manage painful emotions and decrease conflict in relationships. DBT specifically focuses on providing therapeutic skills in four key areas. First, *mindfulness* focuses on improving an individual's ability to accept and be present in the current moment. Second, *distress tolerance* is geared toward increasing a person's tolerance of negative emotion, rather than trying to escape from it. Third, *emotion regulation* covers strategies to manage and change intense emotions that are causing problems in a person's life. Fourth, *interpersonal effectiveness* consists of techniques that allow a person to communicate with others in a way that is assertive, maintains self-respect, and strengthens relationships." See https://www.psychologytoday.com/us/therapy-types/dialectical-behavior-therapy.

138. Hemingway, Ernest. *A Farewell to Arms* (1929).

139. Hugh Thompson story. https://www.latimes.com/opinion/op-ed/la-oe-wiener-my-lai-hugh-thompson-20180316-story.html.

140. David Allen Willson was born in Seattle, Washington, on June 30, 1942, on what his mother remembered as the hottest day of the summer. During World War II, while his father served as a US Marine on Iwo Jima, he lived with his mother in a series of tourist cabins in California, in his maternal grandmother's Seattle basement, and in a boxcar in Montana. He learned to write in first grade in Missoula, Montana, and realized then that he wanted to grow up to write books—probably about war, as there was so much of it to write about. As fate would have it, he had the chance to experience war first-hand—appropriately, behind a typewriter: he was drafted into the US Army in the 1960s and was sent to Viet Nam. He received the Army Commendation Medal for his service in the Inspector General's Office. For war writing, he has published three semi-autobiographical novels: *REMF Diary*, *The REMF Returns*, and *In the Army Now*. David has been the editor of *Viet Nam Generation Journal*, and a contributor to *Vietnam War Literature: An Annotated Bibliography*. He has been a regular reviewer of war literature for both print and online editions of VVA (Vietnam Veterans of America) *Veteran*, and has authored many other articles for the magazine, including an account of his VA treatment for multiple myeloma, related to the Agent Orange he was exposed to in the water at Long Binh, where he served in Viet Nam.

141. *Foot Soldier: The World War I Soldier*. History Channel Documentary. Please see: https://www.youtube.com/watch?v=bEHmEQXhqtE.

142. The Kon Tiki Expedition. See https://www.kon-tiki.no/expeditions/kon-tiki-expedition/.

143. The Tigris Expedition. See https://www.nytimes.com/1981/08/16/books/the-floating-haystack.html.

144. March 29, 2020 is when I started Lockdown Theatre, an online, live streaming theatre production company. Since March 29, 2020, we have produced four streamplays. See https://www.facebook.com/LockdownTheatre/.

145. Aliens. See https://mysteriousuniverse.org/2018/12/aliens-believe-in-us-but-not-too-much/.

146. COVID-19 Updates. See https://www.vox.com/2020/4/15/21222375/coronavirus-covid-19-test-update-end-social-distancing; and https://ourworldindata.org/coronavirus.

147. For more on the philosopher Georg Wilhelm Friedrich Hegel, please see https://plato.stanford.edu/entries/hegel/.

148. Malcolm X assassination. See https://swap.stanford.edu/20141218232251/ and http://mlk-kpp01.stanford.edu/kingweb/publications/papers/unpub/ 650224-000_Malcolm_X_assassination.htm.

149. Extraterrestrial research. See https://medium.com/the-foundation-for-research-into-extraterrestrial.

150. See *Snarc*, https://www.bruceolavsolheim.com/snarc.html. Snarc was a comic strip (then spelled Snark) I did while in engineering school at Montana Tech in Butte, Montana, in 1982. Thirty-seven years later, I came out with the *Snarc* number 1 comic book.

151. For more on the famous Martin Niemöller's quotation see: http://marcuse.faculty.history.ucsb.edu/projects/niem/articles/Marcuse2014Niemoeller-Quote147gWeb.pdf.

152. For Red Elk stories, see https://www.amazon.com/Short-Stories-Tellings-Medicine-Wakhan/dp/0615445993/ref=sr_1_2?dchild=1&qid=1617153979& refinements=p_27%3ARed+Elk&s=books&sr=1-2&text=Red+Elk.

153. Here is an article about Jason Hargrove: https://www.cnn.com/2020/04/03/ us/detroit-bus-driver-dies-coronavirus-trnd/index.html; and here is an article about Areema Nasreen: https://www.bbc.com/news/uk-england-birmingham-51952607.

154. Mason, Robert. *Chickenhawk: Back in the World*. New York: Penguin Books, 1994. I met both Robert and Patience Mason when my friend David Willson and I organized a Vietnam War Writers Conference in 1998 at Green River Community College.

155. Dulce Base was reportedly a jointly operated human and alien underground facility under Archuleta Mesa on the Colorado-New Mexico border near the town of Dulce, New Mexico. See https://www.discovery.com/exploration/Secret-Underground-Alien-Base-Dulce-New-Mexico.

156. Jim Marrs was a Vietnam veteran, a journalist, and a consultant on the Oliver Stone *JFK* movie, which was partly based on his book, *Crossfire: The Plot that Killed Kennedy*.

157. For more on philosopher Arthur Schopenhauer see https://plato.stanford.edu/ entries/schopenhauer/.

158. Here is an article about Leilani Jordan: https://www.cbsnews.com/news/grocery-store-worker-leilani-jordan-died-coroanvirus-kept-working-wanted-to-help-people/.

159. For more on war correspondent Peter Arnett, see https://www.pbs.org/weta/reportingamericaatwar/reporters/arnett/.

160. See my story "Hawkeye," in Solheim, Bruce Olav. *Timeless Trinity*. Glendora, CA: Boots to Books, 2020.

161. For Dr. Martin Luther King's speech on starvation wages and advocating democratic socialism, see https://www.democracynow.org/2018/4/2/starvation_wages_are_a_crime_lessons.

162. Abraham Lincoln team of rivals, see https://www.smithsonianmag.com/history/abraham-lincoln-team-of-rivals-180954850/.

163. See my story "Fly Me to the Moon," in Solheim, Bruce Olav. *Timeless*, 2nd ed. Glendora, CA: Boots to Books, 2020.

164. One of my favorite songs (my mom too) was "These Boots Are Made for Walkin'," by Nancy Sinatra, released in 1965.

165. From the poem "O Me! O Life!" in *Leaves of Grass*, Walt Whitman, 1892. Whitman, one of my favorite poets, was inspired by the American frontier and greatly admired Ralph Waldo Emerson and the transcendentalist movement. See https://www.poetryfoundation.org/poems/51568/o-me-o-life.

166. See Stanislavski at https://www.biography.com/actor/constantin-stanislavski; and a monologue from William Shakespeare's comedy *As You Like It*.

167. See the Los Angeles-based rock group X at https://www.songfacts.com/facts/x/los-angeles.

168. For the Epiphany/Apenbaringen theatre play, see https://www.youtube.com/watch?v=jn-wpb_8xbI; and https://www.youtube.com/watch?v=OCVcgbpDrIs.

169. For more on Carl Jung, see http://www.drpaulwong.com/the-depth-positive-psychology-of-carl-jung/.

170. For more on bilocation, quantum superposition, and teleportation, see https://mysteriousuniverse.org/2017/01/seeing-double-strange-cases-of-bilocation/; and https://jqi.umd.edu/glossary/quantum-superposition; and https://phys.org/news/2020-06-teleportation-quantum-world.html.

171. For more on the classic double-slit experiment, please see https://www.discovery.com/science/Double-Slit-Experiment.

172. For more on weather anomalies, see https://weathersource.com/blog/tis-the-season-for-weather-anomalies/.

173. For more on Holocaust survivor Viktor Emil Frankl, please see https://www.univie.ac.at/logotherapy/lifeandwork.html.

174. For more on Carl Jung, see https://www.psychologistworld.com/cognitive/carl-jung-analytical-psychology.

175. For the real story of Ty Cobb, see https://imprimis.hillsdale.edu/who-was-ty-cobb-the-history-we-know-thats-wrong/.

176. For more on memories, see https://link.springer.com/article/10.3758/BF03196318; https://webfiles.uci.edu/eloftus/Morgan_Misinfo_IJLP2013.pdf?uniq=-5q3yfp; and https://www.sciencedaily.com/releases/2015/08/150817132325.htm.

177. Coronavirus data, see https://ourworldindata.org/coronavirus.

178. Letter from Thomas Jefferson to Lafayette, see https://sites.lafayette.edu/slavery/a-lifetime-passion/jefferson-letters/.

179. For more on *Gun Fighter Nation*, see https://www.nationalbook.org/books/gunfighter-nation-the-myth-of-the-frontier-in-twentieth-century-america/; and https://www.kirkusreviews.com/book-reviews/richard-slotkin/gunfighter-nation/.

180. My youngest son Leif and I love *Jaws* and have watched the movie dozens of times. See https://www.theguardian.com/film/2015/may/31/jaws-40-years-on-truly-great-lasting-classics-of-america-cinema.

181. For more on the Kent State Shooting, see https://www.history.com/topics/vietnam-war/kent-state-shooting#section_8; and https://www.kent.edu/may-4-historical-accuracy.

182. For more on the Scranton Commission and the song "Ohio," see https://www.library.kent.edu/special-collections-and-archives/mission-betrayed-richard-nixon-and-scranton-commission-inquiry-kent; and to watch a performance of the song "Ohio" by Crosby, Stills, Nash, and Young, please go to: https://www.youtube.com/watch?v=gajEmrJR03c.

183. "We Can Work It Out" by the Beatles was released in 1965. Here is an official video: https://www.youtube.com/watch?v=2Q_ZzBGPdqE.

184. For an in-depth video interview of John Keegan, see https://www.c-span.org/video/?178919-1/depth-john-keegan.

185. For more on Bertolt Brecht, see https://www.bbc.co.uk/bitesize/guides/zwmvd2p/revision/1.

186. For more information on the classic Beatles song "Let It Be," see https://rockpasta.com/paul-mccartney-explains-how-let-it-be-was-written-to-james-corden/.

187. Here is a video of Peter Gabriel performing "Family Snapshot." https://www.youtube.com/watch?v=EYnk8a—fXQ.

188. Here is Disturbed performing Paul Simon's "The Sound of Silence." https://www.youtube.com/watch?v=Bk7RVw3I8eg.

189. Strieber, Whitley. *A New World*, San Antonio, TX: Walker & Collier, 2019.

190. For more information on Franklin D. Roosevelt, go to the FDR Library at: https://www.fdrlibrary.org/fdr-biography.

191. For more information on the non-profit organization Oceti Wakan, please see http://www.ocetiwakan.org/.

192. For more information on Ernest Hemingway, please see the Ken Burns documentary on PBS: https://www.pbs.org/kenburns/hemingway/.

193. Find out more about Dante here: https://digitaldante.columbia.edu/dante/divine-comedy/.

194. You can find out more about my theatrical plays at: https://www.bruceolavsolheim.com/dr.-bruce-olav-solheim-s-theatrical-plays.html.

195. For more on the Lakota Way, see https://www.penguinrandomhouse.com/books/289750/the-lakota-way-by-joseph-m-marshall/.

196. For more on Edwin Rolfe, see https://www.poetryfoundation.org/poets/edwin-rolfe; and https://www.jstor.org/stable/4612937?seq=1.

197. The play takes place in 1867 in Virginia City, Montana, a rough and tumble mining town. David's great-great grandfather had lived there after the Civil War. For more on Virginia City, see https://virginiacitymt.com/.

198. Time is an illusion. See https://www.scientificamerican.com/article/time-s-passage-is-probably-an-illusion/.

199. For the entire MLK speech, see https://www.afscme.org/about/history/mlk/mountaintop.

200. For your viewing pleasure, here is the official video for this classic Rolling Stones song: https://www.youtube.com/watch?v=Ef9QnZVpVd8.

201. *Little Big Man* was one of the first Hollywood films to portray Native Americans in a positive light. For more information on *Little Big Man*, see https://www.loc.gov/item/prn-14-210/new-films-added-to-national-registry/2014-12-17/.

202. For more on Joseph Campbell, go to https://www.jcf.org/about-joseph-campbell/.

203. White House Lockdown. https://nypost.com/2020/05/29/white-house-placed-on-lockdown-due-to-george-floyd-protest/.

204. Coronavirus data, see https://ourworldindata.org/coronavirus.

205. For more on Samuel P. Huntington, see https://www.huffpost.com/entry/samuel-p-huntington-a-gre_b_190373.

206. For more on *The Four Agreements* and author Don Miguel Ruiz please go to: https://www.thefouragreements.com/.

207. For more on Rumi, please see https://arquivo.pt/wayback/20090629034959/http://portal.unesco.org/culture/en/ev.php-URL_ID=34694&URL_DO=DO_TOPIC&URL_SECTION=201.html.

208. See more on US Grant here: https://www.pbs.org/wgbh/americanexperience/features/grant-biography/.

209. For more on author Viet Thanh Nguyen see https://vietnguyen.info/home.

210. You can listen to General Dwight D. Eisenhower's D-Day speech here: https://www.washingtonpost.com/video/national/listen-to-eisenhowers-d-day-speech/2017/06/06/d170db5e-4ae1-11e7-987c-42ab5745db2e_video.html ?fbclid=IwAR2FqOPBJlCq485Z5hiQeC7LLdUaObZ5qP74-IiyIbhvZe5XGYID-WjQfhKc.

211. The quote is usually attributed to P.T. Barnum, but there is little evidence to support that attribution. Here is a link to the archive of P.T. Barnum: http://dl.tufts.edu/catalog/ead/tufts:UA069.001.DO.MS002.

212. June Gloom is an actual meteorological phenomenon in Southern California where the skies tend to be grey and the temperatures cooler in late spring and early summer. See https://weather.com/science/weather-explainers/news/june-gloom-southern-california-west-coast.

213. More on the Neowise comet here: https://www.space.com/comet-neowise-visible-evening-sky-july-2020.html.

214. TTSA is To the Stars Academy founded by musician Tom Delonge. See https://home.tothestarsacademy.com.

215. For details, please see my first book, Solheim, Bruce O. *The Nordic Nexus: A Lesson in Peaceful Security*. Westport, CT: Praeger, 1994.

216. It reminded me of my interdimensional vortex that I use in my *Snarc* comic books. That is how Snarc and his Cosmic Staff can travel through time and space. See Snarc at www.snarccomic.com.

217. For coronavirus statistics see https://www.nytimes.com/2020/07/24/health/cdc-schools-coronavirus.html; and https://thehill.com/policy/healthcare/510103-us-posts-more-than-25000-covid-19-deaths-in-july.

218. This is one of my favorite episodes. For more detailed information on this episode, see https://memory-alpha.fandom.com/wiki/Errand_of_Mercy_(episode).

219. For more on *The Fantastic Four*, see https://www.looper.com/300036/the-untold-truth-of-the-fantastic-four/; and https://www.cbr.com/fantastic-four-joe-sinnott-jack-kirby-partnership/.

220. See https://memory-alpha.fandom.com/wiki/The_Way_to_Eden_(episode); and https://memory-alpha.fandom.com/wiki/Garden_of_Eden.

221. For more on the Harlem Renaissance please see https://www.history.com/topics/roaring-twenties/harlem-renaissance.

222. As I am writing this in April 2021, it startled me when I read the word insurrection. Anzar was foreshadowing the events of January 6, 2021. Whether it should be classified as an insurrection or not is perhaps debatable, but the key is that insurrection is the word that most people use to describe the event.

223. For coronavirus data see https://covidtracking.com/data/national.

224. See my story "Treetop Warriors," in Solheim, Bruce Olav. *Timeless.* Glendora, CA: Boots to Books, 2020.

225. Bob Lazar called it element 115. Lazar, Bob. *Dreamland.* Interstellar, 2019; and his appearance on the Joe Rogan podcast that started the storm Area 51 movement. https://www.youtube.com/watch?v=BEWz4SXfyCQ.

226. For more on Bernard Sternsher and his Great Depression and New Deal scholarship, see https://witzler-shank-perrysburg.tributes.com/dignitymemorial/obituary/Bernard-Sternsher-91973586.

227. *The Marriage of Heaven and Hell* is a book by the English poet William Blake. Written like biblical prophecy, the work expressed his revolutionary beliefs. For more on William Blake, see https://www.gutenberg.org/ebooks/45315.

228. For more information on Haim Eshed, see https://www.jpost.com/omg/former-israeli-space-security-chief-says-aliens-exist-humanity-not-ready-651405.

229. For more information on the Transcontinental Railway and Operation Warp Speed, see https://www.history.com/news/transcontinental-railroad-chinese-immigrants; and https://www.defense.gov/Explore/Spotlight/Coronavirus/Operation-Warp-Speed/.

230. This quote is usually attributed to US Senator Hiram Johnson from California in 1918, but there are other possible sources as well. See https://www.theguardian.com/notesandqueries/query/0,5753,-21510,00.html.

231. For more on The Phony War, see https://www.warhistoryonline.com/world-war-ii/the-phony-war.html.

232. The song "Won't Get Fooled Again," is on the 1971 *Who's Next* album by the British rock band the Who. To see a performance of the song go to: https://www.youtube.com/watch?v=UDfAdHBtK_Q.

233. For more on the National Guard at the US Capitol, see https://www.military.com/daily-news/2021/01/21/26k-guard-troops-dc-did-not-face-single-inauguration-security-threat-top-general.html.

234. By the way, that is the book you are reading now.

235. Although this quote is not directly from the Bible, there are other passages in the Bible that allude to this concept. See https://www.openbible.info/topics/helps_those_who_help_themselves. As for Ben Franklin's quote source, see https://www.bartleby.com/essay/Analysis-Of-Benjamin-Franklin-s-God-Helps-P3SQNPKVU5ZW.

236. For more on J.P. Patches go to: https://jppatches.com/pages/the-amazing-history-of-j-p-patches.

237. Find out more on velociraptors here: https://www.livescience.com/23922-velociraptor-facts.html.

238. For more on the Beatles song, "I am the Walrus," please go to: https://www.thebeatles.com/song/i-am-walrus. To hear the song, please go to: https://www.youtube.com/watch?v=Dn4SCyBmAOo.

239. When Reagan and Gorbachev met in Geneva in 1985, they discussed an alien invasion. See https://www.smithsonianmag.com/smart-news/reagan-and-gorbachev-agreed-pause-cold-war-case-alien-invasion-180957402/.

240. For more on *The Three Musketeers* by Alexandre Dumas, see https://www.gutenberg.org/files/1257/1257-h/1257-h.htm.

241. For more on Jason and The Argonauts, see https://theargonauts.com/about/the-story-of-jason-and-the-argonauts/.

242. For more on the American Airlines pilot UFO story, please got to: https://www.cbsnews.com/news/ufo-american-airlines-pilot-new-mexico-long-cylindrical-object/.

243. Here is one of Dr. Mathews' books: https://history.army.mil/html/books/011/11-7-1/index.html.

244. Sanskrit is regarded as the ancient language in Hinduism. Sanskrit is also widely used in Jainism, Buddhism, and Sikhism. Perhaps it is coincidental, but India is currently the hotspot for COVID-19 infections and deaths. As of May 4, 2021, the Asian nation, which is the second-most populous in the world with 1.4 billion, has surged to 215,542 deaths, which is fourth place in the world behind the United States with 577,045 as of Sunday, Brazil with 407,639 and Mexico with 217,233. See https://www.upi.com/Top_News/World-News/2021/05/02/india-coronavirus-surges-50-world-total-400000/5031619961755/.

245. Ahura Mazda is the creator deity and highest deity of Zoroastrianism. See https://www.ancient-origins.net/human-origins-religions/ahura-mazda-0014964.

246. UFOs near Copper Mountain. https://www.ufocasebook.com/2017/photographs-of-ufos-idaho-and-colorado.html.

247. See my story "Special Processing," in Solheim, Bruce Olav. *Timeless Trinity*. Glendora, CA: Boots to Books, 2020.

248. More on the Ted Owens, PK Man, story here: https://mysteriousuniverse.org/2020/04/the-bizarre-case-of-ted-owens-the-contactee-given-super-powers-by-aliens/; and https://www.williamjames.com/pkman.htm.

249. The national agony of the Derek Chauvin murder trial hopefully will lead to a peaceful outcome and provide healing. See https://www.bbc.com/news/world-us-canada-56802198.

250. The Rigel star system is trinary and is said to have no known planets, although no one is certain. Rigel is classified as a blue giant and is expected to eventually end its stellar life as a type II supernova. It is one of the closest known potential supernova *progenitors* to Earth. See https://arxiv.org/abs/1201.0843.

251. My Personal Quantum Reality diagram can be found in Solheim, Bruce Olav, *Timeless Deja Vu*. Glendora, CA: Boots to Books, 2019, p. 158.

252. For more on *Atlantic Crossing*, see https://www.pbs.org/wgbh/masterpiece/shows/atlantic-crossing/; and https://www.pbs.org/wgbh/masterpiece/specialfeatures/atlantic-crossing-what-you-need-to-know-before-you-watch/.

253. More on SDI at: https://2001-2009.state.gov/r/pa/ho/time/rd/104253.htm.

254. For more on *The Day the Earth Stood Still*, see https://www.imdb.com/
title/tt0043456/; and http://www.sentientdevelopments.com/2007/01/revisiting-
day-earth-stood-still.html; and for more on *Murder in the Air* see
https://www.youtube.com/watch?v=zkOy2Dhp2OA.

255. Ecstatic truth as described by German film director Werner Herzog whom I
interviewed in 2007: "There are deeper strata of truth in cinema, and there is such
a thing as poetic, ecstatic truth. It is mysterious and elusive and can be reached
only through fabrication and imagination and stylization...Cinema Verité is de-
void of verité. It reaches a merely superficial truth, the truth of accountants." For
more information see: https://www.rogerebert.com/roger-ebert/herzogs-minne-
sota-declaration-defining-ecstatic-truth.

256. Derek Chauvin trial polling at https://www.forbes.com/sites/jemimamcevoy/
2021/04/25/nearly-half-of-republicans-think-derek-chauvin-verdict-was-wrong-
poll-shows/?sh=5cb0272f66e8.

257. Black Lives Matter polling at https://www.usatoday.com/story/news/
politics/2021/03/05/americans-trust-black-lives-matter-declines-usa-today-ipsos-
poll/6903470002/.

258. Chauvin verdict opinion poll at https://www.cbsnews.com/news/chauvin-ver-
dict-opinion-poll/.

259. See the research of Dr. Vernon Neppe, the world's leading authority on déjà
vu, at http://www.pni.org/key-articles/deja-vu.html.

260. For more on Parmenides, go to https://iep.utm.edu/parmenid/.

261. It should be noted that Heidegger did belong to the Nazi party, but according
to Hannah Arendt, it was an error in judgement that did not impact the brilliance
of his philosophy. See https://www.ontology.co/heidegger-aletheia.htm.

262. Talbot, Michael. *The Holographic Universe*. New York: HarperCollins,
1991, p. 54.

263. Ibid.

264. Ibid.

265. For more on stuttering and trauma, please go to: https://movementdisorders. ufhealth.org/2015/08/10/psychogenic-speech-disorders-is-it-all-in-your-head/; and "Traumatic Childhood Experiences and Stuttering: A Case Study" by Rakesh Maurya and Dr Sheela Singh. This article can be found at: https://www.re-searchgate.net/publication/288668346_traumatic _ childhood_experi-ences_and_stuttering_a_case_study.

266. *Thinking Allowed* transcript of an interview with Arthur M. Young and Jef-frey Mishlove: https://www.williamjames.com/transcripts/young4.htm.

267. Description of DNA. Deoxyribonucleic acid is a molecule composed of two polynucleotide chains that coil around each other to form a double helix carrying genetic instructions for the development, functioning, growth and reproduction of all known organisms and many viruses.

268. For information on room temperature superconductors, see: https://www.msn.com/en-us/news/technology/physicists-made-a-superconductor-that-works-at-room-temperature-it-could-one-day-give-rise-to-high-speed-float-ing-trains/ar-BB1am00A.

269. National Institute of Health (NIH). Biophoton emission. New evidence for coherence and DNA as source https://pubmed.ncbi.nlm.nih.gov/6204761/.

270. Photon definition and properties. https://www.thoughtco.com/what-is-a-pho-ton-definition-and-properties-2699039.

271. "Is DNA the next internet?" See http://viewzone.com/dnax.html.

272. Sentinel Island indigenous people. See https://www.news.com.au/lifestyle/ real-life/american-tourist-killed-by-bow-and-arrow-after-he-landed-on-a-remote-island-in-the-indian-ocean/news-story/7157ade6b6b9a1f69f140f74f9ab8b24.

273. For more on California governor Newsom's plans for martial law, see https://thehill.com/opinion/judiciary/489748-californias-newsom-is-wrong-mar-tial-law-is-always-a-last-resort; and https://www.military.com/daily-news/2021/04/23/california-guard-members-feared-fighter-jet-would-be-ordered-frighten-protesters.html.

274. Here is more information on comet Neowise: https://blogs.nasa.gov/ Watch_the_Skies/2020/07/17/see-comet-neowise-a-once-in-a-lifetime-event/.

275. Talbot, Michael. *The Holographic Universe*. New York: HarperCollins, 1991, p. 63.

276. Ullman, Montague. "Wholeness and Dreaming," in *Quantum Implications: Essays in honour of David Bohm.* Edited by B.J. Hiley, Birkbeck College, University of London and F. David Peat, Ottawa, Canada. Routledge & Kegan Paul, London and New York 1987, pp. 386-95.

277. Jason Reza Jorjani, *Prometheus and Atlas.* Arktos Media Ltd. 2016. See more on Jason Reza Jorjani at: https://jasonrezajorjani.com/.

278. For more information on Colonel Philip Corso see http://www.openminds.tv/corso-notes/3514.

279. Donald Hoffman interview: https://www.youtube.com/watch?v=iAfjsktMXu8; and Donald Hoffman's TED talk: https://www.youtube.com/watch?v=oYp5XuGYqqY.

280. Edgar Mitchell interview, July 23, 2008, with Kerrang Radio by Nick Margerrison; and *Daily Mirror* interview, with Dr. Edgar Mitchell.

Made in the USA
Monee, IL
03 August 2021